CyberHorny

Navigating a Sexual Dystopia

Published by:
Cyberhorny LLC
73 White Bridge Rd
Suite 103 #318
Nashville, TN 37205

www.cyber-horny.com

publishing@cyber-horny.com

ISBN: 978-1-962521-02-4

Dedicated to all my lil peeps, and all the weird whores out there who feel invalidated. Let this Cyberhorny hitchwhore's guide support, cushion, and insulate you from the hazards of the cyber world.

Foreword by the Editor

"The world has become chaos, but the book remains the image of the world" - Deleuze/Guattari[1]

We are all perverts, this is nothing new. What is pinpointed in this sext is the imminent dynamic imposed by the cyber world. The *rapprochement* between individual and internet, interfered with by all the dynamics of the social and the unconscious. The echoes back and forth that impact, create, destroy, and mutate the subjectivity of all involved. The dynamics of profilicity that reverberate from projection to integration - as I send a pic and get one back - the gauze of subjective destitution that envelops all parties involved. Am I this Thing that I am looking at, is she or he this or that. The devil of subjectivity gives birth to the demonic horde of intersubjectivity.

This project is an attempt at a reconsolidation, a reintegration. A partnership forged between our most base and animalistic drives and our most suprahuman and quasi divine capabilities. Redemption. Profane made sacred. This project will take you on a ride, a rollercoaster of neurosis. Seven flags. Art out of banality, anality, cyber-corporeality. I saw the theory in the porn and jacked it until it was set free.

A footnote in *Beyond Sexuality* adroitly expands the classic rationalizations of unsafe sex: **"To the fact that perhaps the majority of unsafe sex occurs under the influence of alcohol and drugs should be added the qualification that it occurs also under the influence of the unconscious."** This doesn't even begin to cover the unconscious, sexual in the sense of Freud as well as collective in that of Jung, factors conflagrated by the imposition of the cyber world. Haunted by [symbolic] castration an inchoate collection of desires craves the illusion of synthesis. This is what we are working with, what plagues her and subscribers to her onlyfans.

Cyber horny dating apps and websites have become a crossroads where the influence of the unconscious on sexuality is exacerbated - reorienting, decimating the subjectivities of users. These technologies open up intersubjective

---

1 They called this idea trite, when in fact it was one of their most profound

fields in which trauma, repetition, and other forms of idiosyncratic neurotic/ obsessive patterns are encoded into the communication of users and further entrenched in their attachment dynamics and sexual performativity. Anonymity - even partial - fuels perversion. @cj1045038 is going to send messages that 'Caleb' would never think of. All who engage in these spheres are targets for this sexual mania but what transpires when you have to court it, balance it and negotiate with it for a living?

Having survived the cyber sexual psychic damage of the field up to this point, questions such as … 'why' … have begun to come up. Nastya Valentine grounds her new analysis of this sphere in that which most subsumes it yet is least included in its discourse - a collective and sexual unconscious. "Once the unconscious is taken into account, we can no longer really justify thinking about sex as interpersonal. Each person in a sexual encounter relates to an unconscious fantasy, to an imaginary image, or to a signifier before he or she relates to the other person(s) present" (Jacques Lacan). The textual linguistic[2] elements of signification in the messages sent, words spoken while camming - the frame of experiences provided to clients all demand analysis. Nastya is molded into a different fantasy image by each subscriber consciously and unconsciously.

Everyone is involved in a constant process of 'cat-fishing' or stitching together a shambling fantasy vision of themselves. Based on what we believe the other that we want wants. Once sex is introduced into this distillation it becomes more like the non-sexual elements in pornography - which, often ridiculed for their role in presenting an idealized version of sex, are the only realistic parts. We all come with a script, we all bring a film crew. We all cast characters and play a role. In the porn of the cyber world, we become only guilty of what we are unable to fantasize about fully. Precisely because the exchanges of fluids, body parts, and kinetic energy are precluded by the cyber realm - the interplay between images, signifiers, information, data, and etc become hyper eroticizied. Not to mention dynamics of fiscal eroticism: investment, profit, threats of divestment from subscribers.

Who is Nastya when she logs on? Who is she when she logs off? Does she log off? The existentialism already lurking in her mind, the fundamental questions of 'what do I want' and 'who am I' become tainted by commerce. And of course the question of 'who I am I' is embroiled in the deeper questions of: who am I *to you*, who do *you* want me to be, who do *you* want to pay me to be. These fiscal-erotic-existential pressures came to a head when she broke a cardinal rule of the field and dated a subscriber.... We hope things common from her experience can become points of insight for not only other digital sex-workers, but for all of us trapped in the libidinal digital. Dating and eroticism being among the most rapidly appified (gamified) facets of online life.

---

2 After all *eye roll* "the unconscious is structured like a language".

What is it that she wants? What do we want when we log on? Money. What else? Control? A forum to mediate intimacy. Validation. As the motivations of the simps are interrogated, Valentine's own attraction to this profession must too come under the knife. What is her relation to sex. Through the classic, trite post-structural lens, sex is formulated never only as sex but as constituted by dynamics of transgression, power, recognition, status and myriad other socially constructed forms. But on the level of the real (that which underlies the mediation of reality by image and language) there is never a sexual relation.[3] In the psychoanalytic tale this is because each party projects their fantasy onto the other, and love comes to account for this gap. Being a cyberwhore is risky business. And in the cyber realm the gap deepens and the fantasies must be intensified in order to sustain the entire precarious endeavor.

It must be difficult to manipulate the desires of others for a living if we accept the premise that our desires are inexorably unknowable. Concisely expressing key psychoanalytic tenets, James Baldwin wrote:

> *I do not remember, will never remember, how I howled and screamed the first time my mother was carried away from me. My mother was the only human being in the world. The only human being; everyone else existed by her permission. Yet what the memory repudiates controls the human being. What one does not remember dictates who one loves or fails to love.What one does not remember dictates, actually, whether one plays poker; pool, or chess. What one does not remember contains the key to one's tantrums or one's poise. What one does not remember is the serpent in the garden of one's dreams. What one does not remember is the key to one's performance in the toilet or in bed. What one does not remember contains the only hope, danger, trap, inexorability, of love—only love can help you recognize what you do not remember—it has something to do with the fact that no one wishes to be plunged, head down, into the torrent of what he does not remember and does not wish to remember.*

Indeed. Valentine is (obviously) not exactly a *person* to these subscribers; she is perhaps more of a site of experimentation for their own desires. Dehumanization this, objectification[4] that - these simple ideas have to be dispensed with. There is a transformative quality in the exchanges between cyber whore and cyber simp. An entire dynamic and intersubjective world exists beyond facile condemnation.

It is not an original idea that the internet is a scrying mirror. How easy it is to cast a little spell with my keyboard and see some naked people. But this is what separates Valentine from most OF/porn creators, what makes this project

3 We relate to each other only in fantasy, on metonymic signifier. This is why everyone cries out 'oh daddy' during sex. Two human beings are never having sex with only the literal being of 'each other'.

4 PLEASE stop sexualizing my tight wet pussy - dasha

a retaliation against the bland monolithic porn infrastructure. The libidinal capture of the subject by the blank slate of say 'big titty milf' is not as applicable to her work which, as will become apparent, can be quite eroto-philosophical. And in other instances can be quite banal: running the gamut from sexy shrek to seductive Simone de Beauvoir.

Psychoanalysis, much like porn, is deeply invested in the sexual. Throughout the book the editor (me)- a self appointed psychoanalyst[5] brings to the fore these connections: in footnotes on psychoanalytic theory, regular theory, little jokes, quotes, and so on. We must forge connections between what happens in the *conscious* minds of porn consumer and porn creator vs. what might be at play in their *unconscious* minds. This dialectic is the site where authenticity is formed.

What Valentine puts forward here is an attempt to shatter the fraudulent authenticity and artifice of this cyber horny hell-scape and graft a cartography of the real alien networks and pathways that constitute it. Her life is the medium. A retort to fantasy projection. The field, by its nature, is rife with unconscious drivers, fraudulence, manipulation, and darkness. *Cyberhorny* is an illumination. Sex work is neither valorized or demonized in this project. It is only through an objective gaze that its dynamics can be fully apprehended. But this is not just a stark and drab academic analysis. As she does online, Nastya Valentine incorporates her own self - her history, traumas, and emotions, - into the examination. After all, how can a field replete with idiosyncratic libidinal impulses be analyzed without the incorporation and utilization of the self.

---

5 Following the dictum of Lacan: The analyst's authorization derives from her— or himself alone

Weaving a Cyberhorny Narrative:

The introduction provides an overview of this text.

Chapter 1 is a review of the sexual reality online;

Chapter 2 dissects desire and how sex drives manifest online;

Chapter 3 is about presenting the online persona;

Chapters 4A and 4B talk about how I started in sex work, and my motivations.

Chapter 5 is about handling the distress that comes from fragmentation and sexual economics, the negotiations of transactional sex.

Chapters 6A and 6B explores how I navigate relationships, both in the cyber parasocial realm, and my personal life.

Chapter 7 is about unpacking the XXX trauma oasis: how my work borders on therapy when men want to be seen and heard in an intimate way.

Chapter 8 delves into the dark agony of internet marketing.

Chapter 9 discusses the cycles of success and failure in the creator economy.

Chapter 10, intellectualizing the feminine - sex workers have capacity for intellectuality, and the ability to create critiquable art - yet they also can fall into a category of somewhat redpilled pornstar tradwives. Discourse on the roles of women within society, and within the profession of sex. An appreciation for the word "whore".

Chapter 11 deals with sexual and emotional pathologies; discourse on validation; body image.

Chapters 12A and 12B consider the psychic consequences of being nude online, and the psychology of knowing your nude image is circulated and fantasized about on the internet; a special focus on body image discontents.

Chapter 13, e-trauma coping and beginnings of healing, and real-life implications of sexual trauma. Maintaining well-being within trauma; how creativity and spirituality mitigate inner turmoil.

Chapter 14, real life and its nonlinearity. Bringing it back to 1, where it goes from irl to online; now going back from online to irl with what we've learned.

The afterword offers concluding statements and seamlessly reiterates the main thesis statements.

Where do I even start?
Everybody sells something.

Cyberhorny: exactly what it sounds like, the state of being horny online. This book is the culmination of my Cyberhorny research project that began in 2021. I had a lot to say about sex, cyber sex in particular. **As every end is also a beginning - this culmination will also be a vehicle to embark on new projects, and examine continuously unfolding paths in the constantly evolving sphere of the horny internet. The book is a vehicle.**

The cyberhorny world is essentially uncharted terrain. It's easy to get lost in the myriad of OnlyFans advertising posts, cyber thots, horny dudes, disembodied dick pics, e-girls, scammers, spammers, and various other depraved denizens of the nsfw web, both great and terrible.

*** DISCLAIMER: some of the events, characters, and places in this book have been changed for discretion and anonymity ***

It is also easy for me to get lost in that miasmatic swarm of characters. To avoid confronting them. Porn has a lot of haters. People have strong feelings about sex work. Strong enough to act on them, and to limit the sex workers' online existence.

Many viewers don't practice discernment and lump all OF girls into the same category. We seem to be punchline fodder, or memed in "made a OF when covid started" type image macros. In online forums, sex work is the butt of every joke and morally considered a disgrace – "I'd sooner disown my daughter than have her be a stripper or do porn", etc. Those same men later frequent the titty bar and google search "pregnant lactating teen latinas". People really do be pointing fingers with one hand and jerking off with the other.[6]

---

6 The impulse to split is inherent to pornography. You see both breasts as good or bad in a consolidated image. This is easier integrating the split nature of the porn star. Like a baby, the viewer can see the breast as only good or bad - feeding me or not feeding me.

This will serve as a deep dive into experiences not just limited to the sexual, but the psychological, metaphysical, emotional, spiritual, existential – and a platform to share these experiences with you.

If you're going to be crazy, you might as well get paid for it.

Porn is free and abundant online. Why then, subscribe to someone's OF? For most people, the appeal is in the parasocial contact with their digital beloved. It ranges from being a type of artistic patronage, to Girl Friend Experience interaction, or a simple good old lurk and jerk.

However, on the darker side of the parasocial coin is this: Many people send me hateful messages saying I have nothing to offer to this world. I am worthless, I am useless. This contributes to any defeatist thoughts I've already internalized via depression.

Having online haters is taxing. There are times when I want to quit because people who don't know me claim to despise me and what I represent. This is why the project matters and is about more than just my own struggle. I am the vessel whose experiences the topics speak through. It's important to have a social commentary on digital transactional sex.

You may already know these buzzwords: simulation, dopamine, metaverse, Pornhub, looksmaxxing, onlyfans, bimbofication, ego death, liminal space, gen z, zoomers, millennials…[7]

Moral decay is a click away.

FANTASY IS HOW DESIRE SUSTAINS ITSELF
-BIG L

Sex and technology have become so inseparable. There is no shortage of infographics, write ups, other online ephemera discussing the intersection of S + T in a constant meta analysis. Porn ads. Hentai collages. Cultural critics. Meme admins. OF models. Pushy instagram ads. Incels. Femcels. Subtweets. Subreddits. AI programs. Text notifications from spammy political campaigns. Echo chambers. The internet is a reality, a new dimensional plane that interacts with, and deeply affects, our daily lives. In most parts of the world, humans must contend with the cyber zone for ordinary tasks: communicating with others over text or email, getting an uber, contactless payment, social media, working from home, ordering supplies or groceries, googling instantly available information at our fingertips, online gaming, etc.

---

7 .I would think how words go straight up in a thin line, quick and harmless, and how terribly doing goes along the earth, clinging to it, so that after a while the two lines are too far apart for the same person to straddle from one to the other; and that sin and love and fear are just sounds that people who never sinned nor loved nor feared have for what they never had and cannot have until they forget the words."

The overwhelm of the cyber zone is such that the brain short circuits, freezes, glitches, shuts down in feeble attempts to process it all. Analysis paralysis. I find that in the sea of chaos [Tim Leary footnote] it's best to not process or intellectualize at all — rather, but be in it, become part of it, live in it to navigate it.

In investigating the deeper psychological elements of digital sex work, it's obvious that many civilians already operate under the belief that sex work is dark and dangerous. Yet they are also fascinated by it. Well okay yeah I operate under the belief of sucking d...

The anonymity of the internet presents possibilities for masked predators. It also presents an openness which would not be as raw without that mask of anonymity. Within a screen absent of identity, there are channels of desire, longing, yearning unleashed - almost more primally than with the knowledge of who the desirer is. See: Eyes Wide Shut, sniffy's, anonymous OF-generated usernames.

Eyes Wide Shut illuminati masked sex orgies. Kubrick was a horny legend. Died 1999, Onlyfans founded 2016, welcome back father of cinema.

Anyone can be anything. "On the internet, no one knows you're a dog".

Adult content on the internet through the years has been ringfenced - evident in the ways that Tumblr in 2014, OnlyFans' attempt to curtail porn in 2021, and Reddit going public in 2024 have limited access to NSFW media, the right wing proposals of Project 2025, and the way that many shadow bans across Twitter/X, Instagram, and TikTok have been enforced. *I write more about this in a later chapter's **Planet Bimbo** segment, how adult creators' visibilities and livelihoods are mercilessly treated by administrative systems. Profit driven platforms will never prioritize xx creators, even if their accounts generate a major chunk of profit. Given that porn is 2nd to only animal videos in the general use of the internet, restriction and erasure of adult workers seems like a staggering denial of an inconvenient truth. Viewing this from all perspectives, the necessity of these restrictions is obvious - keep 18+ content in 18+ spaces - though with the excessive policing by moderators, this organizational content restriction furthers sex worker erasure, stigmatizing and demonizing. The nuisance of these restrictions also makes it more difficult to reach a target audience when advertising.

There is no targeted audience for Cyberhorny, it is for everyone. For the players in this line of work, newcomers and veterans, for curious perverts, for grumpy academics, for die hard Nastya fans, for livid Nastya haters. I am used to people being obsessed with me, and I am used to people hating me. This book may in fact not be simply a singular volume, but one of multiple if things still require being written. **A woman on the internet? In this economy?**

A woman on the internet curating a fantasy. I joined for money and validation, but I operate on the currency of desire.

It's common to deride platforms like OnlyFans as hubs of sin, but I find a myriad of positives within the sin. First of all, I am very glad to not have to go to an office or a salon or be on a societal timetable. With my physical levels of tiredness, fatigue, and chronic pain.. OF's work structure is a relief. A surprising element emerged within my day to day work structure that tickled my metaphysical curiosity: the drive to ask, 'what does everyone want from a sexual experience?'

I have taken care not to write in a way that is overly intellectualized or pretentious — I write for the layman. The text ranges from research based to anecdotal. Inevitably there will be some parts of the text that are more pedantic. Others still will be fluffy, nonsensical, or just straight up stupid. Stupidity is the new intellect. There are likely more questions in this book than there are answers. Keep in mind that I have been writing this book for a year.

What does everyone want, EXPERIENTIALLY? Something so rare and raw and extraordinary that it cannot be easily forgotten. Once you fuck me you can't unfuck me.

1: The Sexual/Digital Reality

Perhaps pornography is only an allegory, with a dimension added to the space of sex, a baroque enterprise of over-signification touching on the "grotesque" (literally, "grotesque") garden art added to rocky nature as pornography adds the vividness of anatomical detail. ~Jean Baudrillard, Seduction

THE METAPHYSICS OF BEING CYBERHORNY IN A POSTMODERN WORLD TOLD THRU THE PRISM OF A FEMALE INUNDATED WITH CONSTANT SEXUAL PROJECTION

The internet is reality's mirror.[8]

Much like this reality is the mirror of the ethereal domain. The unknowable. In our information age, we have a drive to know, to learn, to discern reality from deception. It is a daunting task to take on epistemology today with the "fake news" surrounding every second we spend online. This fake news is not limited to the political or conversational: it is photoshopped pictures, facetuned features, catfishing, incels using avatars of anime girls, the fraudulent presentation of one thing as another. At best an illusion, at worst a lie. How do we know which information to trust? How do we know what is real? Are you real, am I real, how do we know? Behind a screen, who am I? More importantly, away from the screen: who am I *really*? Moral decay is only a click away. Subscribe to my page to lift the veil of decency, and wait for a reveal that may never come. Illumination may never come, but you will. https://onlyfans.com/nastyavalentine

On March 27, 2020, I published my first OnlyFans post. Four years later I'm in my office pacing pensively - lingerie scattered on the carpet and ring lights with iPhones surrounding me like a mirrored funhouse - reflecting on having been naked online through a pandemic, contemplating the psychoanalysis of baring it all. Boudoirs have always been a center of fascination. The

---

8 In psychoanalysis the 'mirror stage' occurs when a baby sees itself in the mirror as a whole unitary image. This is obviously not the truth of the self - we are all fragmentary. Collection of drives and impulses seeking the *illusion* of synthesis.

boudoir is a visual echo chamber - traditionally the very term 'boudoir' means 'sulking-place'. To pout, sulk. The bedroom is one of my offices, a research center from which I interface with online clients who too engage in their own kind of cerebral, psychosexual activity within my chamber of reflection. For whom is my bedroom not a place to think, to sulk, to goon, to perv, to discourse, to ruminate? Ah yes, pull up a chair. Start gooning. What is the thinking man jerking it to today?

Dear reader, I propose here a few unanswerable questions:

What do we not know about the life and journey of a sex worker? What do we choose to not want to know? What do we willingly ignore? Do we even care to mix in the philosophical, the personal, with the pornographic? Dare we meld the thinking mind with the fleshy body? And to add another layer to this unholy copulation - the astral digital body?

Long live the new flesh
-Videodrome

Tikok, Insta, Reddit, Twitter are oversaturated with babes like me advertising sex appeal to lure the attention of men into our paid platforms, to get clicks on linktree or beacons from a bikini post or a titty bouncing video or a juicy thigh in a short skirt. Some will be enticed and click, others will completely ignore, others still will make the grandstanding statement of "I don't pay for porn", expressing derogatory views on women who successfully monetize their bodies in a patriarchal system. How dare a woman take agency of her body, commodify it into transactional sex and god forbid enjoy it. The nerve of a woman to be horny on the internet, to dehumanize and display herself as a sexualized object before any man can.

What is at the core of our devious presences online? It has to mirror a real-life desire, or reveal a deeper part of us to ourselves. Can we ever find dignity and authenticity in porn? Amongst deep fakes, AIs, bots, assistants, can we find something spellbindingly real? Is this even a question worth asking, because we want the fake to stay fake? Some of these questions arise in me as I rewatch Westworld, with its circuitous plots and mind-bending puzzles of consciousness and humanity within artificial intelligence programs.

Cut to me in my Dolores Abernathy cosplay: "these horny delights have horny ends."
All the internet's a stage and we are merely gooners.

The actors may be counterfeit but the roles and experiences they provide are very real. The celerity and transience of these transactions has an effect on the psyche. We want no interference in our intimate encounters. Private. Discreet. Encrypted. There is a certain solipsism in posting for digital connection – so saturated with others, we can't help feeling alone. So connected we are to our friends, our lovers, our coworkers, our parasocial objects of admiration while we sit in a room by ourselves with our phones and computers. We keep seeking, digging, doomscrolling, lurking, participating, projecting. Is it possible to find intimacy within structures of disconnect? Further, is it possible to market it? To sell it? To perform it?

Intimacy?? Love is an untapped market.

It's a body biography. Girl meat market. Brain meat grinder. Hustler cover of the girl in a meat grinder. I have to be all the girls. I change my hair color often, so every week it's like my subscribers are getting a different girl. Being in the same personality for too long can become monotonous – if not for me, then for my audience. On my page, I create narrative, drama. Serialize the porn from elements in my real life, like a mystery writer in a whocummedit. Storylines for the next month of Nastya Valentine. To create each new self, I must shed an old one.

Every once in a while life requires me to rewire my DNA and self-audit every element of my existence. These constant reinventions and shedding of old selves, transfigurations into newness, helped make my OF as dimensional, dynamic, and lasting as it can be. Iconic but unpretentious - that's what I intend my porn to be.

"Extreme seductiveness is at the boundary of horror" -George Bataille

Schroedinger's Sex: We have it, and yet we don't

Porn online is sex through a funhouse mirror, tilted upside down, warped through a quadratic equation of mental gymnastics. I have sex with myself (or sometimes another model in the girlie collabs), and the viewer has sex with himself, watching me as I contort, moan, and watch back. There is a projection of a fantasy. Their inner feelings become absorbed by me, a blank slate for endless permutations of closeness. The shorthand that I quickly learn and mime back. The character I become and re-become and un-become when I enter their dream. The screen to screen eye contact of intimacy. If digital eyefucking is an art, I'm Leonardo Da Vinci. A 3 dimensional orgasm flattened in 2D.

As a creator of porn, what is my goal: for the viewer to masturbate successfully? If the answer is "yes", I must curate a porn so lifelike, so personal (yet depersonalized), that he is right there with me. The only man in the room. The only man in the zoom meeting. This might sound so droll, so utterly clinical that you ask, "what is even the point?" – but the point is even underneath the layers of clinicality there really is a core of deep connection, insight, and pleasure. A heart that beats off with humanity's greatest value: the mistake, the error, the rawness. Imperfection becomes our gift as the uncanny valley deepens. Men no longer want the artifice of sex dolls, they want the real girl who plays the part of sex doll playing the part of the real girl. Pleasure is coded with just the right amount of predictability and surprise.

Making porn involves some degree of sensuality and pleasure, it's not just mechanical. Sure, it's performative in its obviousness, but for example in a collab, it's critical to have a sense of touching another person, even if it's just eye candy.

Sexual space is like a dream state; logic and reality do not matter. It's horniness and arousal that dictate reality, not the other way around.

Fantasy is a screen that separates us from the harshness of reality. -Lacan

There is a niche on the xx internet for every reality, every kink, every perverse thought from the collective to the specific - if it exists there is porn of it (Rule34).

We live in a reality that is often so bleak that an escape into fantasy can be a salve for pains of the heart. Fulfillment of an inner longing through kink expression can mitigate what constrains us in our quotidian drama. Of course we all want recreational sex and cyber sex to be fun, but when we stop to think about what is beneath the base layer of pleasure, we'll find some subconscious surprises. Can kinks be an encounter with the soul? Power dynamics a key to our innermost code? Strange things we're into, a personal blueprint of consciousness? Or maybe it's not that complicated and we just like the things we like because we simply do. We do the things we do, because we can.

I lean into an alternative niche with my content and online persona. Only a specific set of people will find my appeal attractive. Mass appeal vs. specificity: the discourse. Specific niches tend to attract men who go all in on a very specific fetish, and mass appeal attracts a wider audience which isn't as hyper fixated. Not all men will spend money on parasocial porn, specialized kinks, or girl friend experiences, but those who do tend to appreciate the value of these services and develop a loyalty to that type of intimacy.

"Of particular interest to an archetypal consideration of BDSM, Carl Jung's Red Book draws repeatedly upon images of suffering, torture, domination,

submission, and enslavement. In his Liber Primus, he wrote:
'I recognize that I am only the expression and symbol of the soul… completely subjugated, utterly obedient.'

As an archetypal theme with roots that extended into the collective psyche, Jung found that the dynamic of domination and submission has psychological value for the process of his own growth. … The Jungian concepts of individuation, differentiation, shadow, and syzygy contribute to a soul-based understanding of BDSM. Alternative sexualities are by their nature countercultural and subversive. At some point, a kinky person acknowledges that he or she cannot feel authentic or whole without allowing deeper truths to become part of life."
-Douglas Thomas, The Deep Psychology of BDSM and Kink

The Sexual Diary

I see my OF as an artistic experience and an intimate diary. Every post, every picture, is an acknowledgement of the sexual collective unconscious via the prism of my subjectivity.
Ppl fuck w me heavy; it's tangible.

In 2020 was live steaming everything. Everything. From the doctors, in my car, in the shower, bored, depressed, manic, opening gifts, crying, writing, masturbating, meta analysis of my online life, everything and anything that can be packed into a 24hr day and broadcast to thousands of viewers. That's how I gained my following: posting all the goddamn time. There was no strategy or formula, it was just chaotic mass posting. I had no idea what I was doing. I still don't.

In 2023 I slowed down to work part-time for a variety of reasons. This has consequences. My career seems to be in stasis. Neither here nor there. A sexy suspended animation. I've reached a point of doom singularity where thoughts and feelings blend, intertwine, cancel each other out. *I don't really care about what happens to my online self. I really care tho, actually.* These divisive thought processes confuse me.

How do I navigate this deep digital dysphoria? Especially when I want to keep many parts of my life quiet and private now. Thankfully people don't care and people forget - anonymity and transience is a blessing as much as it may be a curse. Eventually everything will be replaced, and the thing that replaces it will be replaced, and that thing too will be replaced by another. The entropic heat death of the universe. The last day of my Onlyfans. The ego death of the simulation.

What is the ego death of the simulation? Existence is a temporal art. In psychedelic literature, ego death is a terminology where the self's boundary is completely dissolved and one is left with a profoundly life changing existential experience. Simulation theory involves us as a collective being part of a human simulator not unlike a video game, our reality not being real.

Today the 'simulation' in memes and internet culture seems to be a buzzword that personifies the simulated reality as an ever-permeating entity; like the way sleep paralysis is manifested as a sleep paralysis demon at the foot of the bed, or the corner of the room. Can the simulation then dissolve its boundaries, and leave us in a collective transcendental intersubjective state where we fully can grasp and understand each other? Can this be the congratulations scene from Neon Genesis Evangelion? Through the ego death of our reality, can we understand each other?

SIMPulation and SIMPulacra

An early master at dissecting the genesis of hyperreality was Jean Baudrillard. In his philosophical treatise *Simulacra and Simulation*, he posits that within hyperreality (or the tendency for the artificial to be perceived as 'realer than real') people lose the distinction between reality and fantasy, and begin to engage in fantasy without realizing what it really is. We interact with fantasy every day, such that it is even chronically memed in "delulu" culture. It's for the girlies!! We make delusion *cute*!!

The simulacra that Baudrillard refers to are the significations and symbolism of culture and media that construct perceived reality, the acquired understanding by which human life and shared existence are rendered legible. They are copies, copies of copies, that have no origin or are so divorced from their origin that they are no longer connected. Simulacrum conceals no significant truth; rather, it reveals absence of it. The simulation is a real-time imitation of a process or system that would exist in "a real world". It's a play pretend world, a hypothetical plane that operates on its own rules. A video game is a simulation – hello, The Sims. Dare I bring up the theory that our very own corporeal world is but a simulated one.

OnlyFans in its own way is a simulation. What I post to this seductive dreamworld, pictures so divorced from who I am in waking life, screenshots of those pictures and edits to those formats, pictures revealing my naked body and posts of unfiltered personal thoughts, eventually reveal what is most empty and hollow about myself. I am not really there, am I? Wherever I go, I am somewhere. There is a Nastya somewhere, countless prototypes of this program, existing in 2D solipsism.

And yet, there is pleasure in dissecting, dismembering, mutilating fragments of these Nastyas' existence. Intellectual gooning. It's a dystopian pleasure, it reeks of pathology, and yet it's fascinated me enough to undertake the overwhelming process of writing a book. In another Baudrillard book, the dense and ornate *Seduction*, he takes one step further inside the simulation into the realm of the feminine: discourses on pornography, illusion, economy, fragility, reality, deception. A proto-*Cyberhorny*. I love his writing, I really do, but I can't help feeling a certain unease when men write about the female experience. This is a huge reason why I choose to make this book. This prism is for the girlies, by the girlies, about the girlies.

"Through her desire, a woman alters the unalterability within which a man cannot help but enclose her… Feminine sexual pleasure can always be rendered divine and thus controlled, reduced… When her desire is channeled into the demand for enjoyment, the world turns upside down. This is doubtless why our culture has taught women to demand nothing in order to induce them to desire nothing." Baudrillard, Seduction[9]

"I shall always acknowledge that a young girl is a born teacher, from whom one can always learn, if nothing else, how to deceive her." Baudrillard, Seduction

eGirl with eBook[10]: You Can't Spell Curriculum Without Cum

As I write this, as I revise and edit, I want to cry. I can't help my subservience to the female emotional state. I cannot live without interrogating my hysteria. The existence of a smokeshow in academia will seem to some people *so wrong, so out of place*, but we are gliding into a new age where the academics of our time will no longer look like Judith Butler. Philosophers won't wear outdated glasses and frumpy, homely robes. They'll wear thongs and hair

9 Pussy loose pussy obtuse

10 Pussy tight pussy write

extensions. I went to Boop College and majored in sksksksksksk with a minor in boob. Real knowledge will be luscious and formless, for information of the erudite feminine is beautiful – it won't need to be draped in the aesthetics of the old archetype. I'm just a girl.

WHY does mainstream academia need to be looking like harry potter and disguise their perversions for the sake of academic clout. -editor

I am not a haggard Zizek wannabe. I became a woman in my stripper heels.

Despite all that I say about being attached to projection and deception, ultimately my intention is to create a space of true authenticity, not manufactured authenticity, in the online x-rated world. In my own ideology, the most despicable thing is inauthenticity and arbitrary clout-chasing. The intersection of greed and social media, making us ever so accustomed to carnivorous marketing, does something harsh to our brains.

While we need money to survive, and it is a realistic goal to strive for, the mental problems and egoic illnesses caused by an obsession with accumulating money/status are horrifying. Being commodified as an object of value is surreal, but it is a sex worker's reality. (Arguably it is a civilian's reality as well). We all deal with this problem in different ways.

When your image - your naked image - is leaked and circulated online, passed around like a virtual cum dump, you need new coping mechanisms. Modern problems require modern solutions which create post-modern problems which require post-everything solutions.

I choose to write it out, acknowledging the burnout and depression I face along the way, and take breaks when I face those physical and mental challenges. Burnout is fucking real and it is heinous. Rest is not as valued in our society as it needs to be. It cannot be underscored enough that the hustle culture needs to die. The star needs to implode.

To be a star, you have to really take yourself apart and say "the rules don't apply to me." Objectively I, and people like me, shouldn't be able to succeed in an industry that harshly prioritizes self-promotion and self-objectification, but I want to show that there are creators out there who dissect this platform on a deeper level and can still fucking crush it.

My tenure in the school of Onlyfans has been life altering because it showed me my depths, my hells, my heavens. It showed me I could fulfill my dreams, if only for a moment – survive failure, survive success, and heal my trauma in the most unexpected of places: the omnipotence of the horny, gazing internet. The society of the spectacle, the circus, the drama. Remind me: how many wars were started over lusting for a woman? The pussy that launched 1000 loads. I must proceed with examining the thing that makes us make choices above all things wilful and logical: our sex drive.

✍

"What we call reality is but a linguistically sanctioned hallucination"
-Timothy Leary

"In societies where modern conditions of production prevail, all of life presents itself as an immense accumulation of spectacles. Everything that was directly lived has moved away into a representation."
— Guy Debord

2: The Sex Drive (Horny)

There is no other drive in this world, aside from the drive of survival, that influences humanity as much as sex.
-- Larry Flynt

Why do we have sex?

- A one and done frustration salve or power relation?
- Is it to get closer to someone, to be intimate?
- Is it instinctual, animal satisfaction?
- Soaking in the juices of our collective unconscious, a merger to destroy or expand subjectivity?
- A compulsion coded in our DNA, perverted by our minds, and propagated through cyberspace?

But also what even is sex today?

world with sex on the brain.
Constant loads to be release or accept.
What **is** arousal?
Longing?
Love? Does it really exist?

Sex becomes even more perverted through its presence on the internet.
This girl doesn't want a boyfriend, she wants 50 simps.
Gay guy don't want boyfriend;
He wants to rent out the motel six on wilcox room 212 and collect 50 loads

Behavioral Economics of the Cyber Sex Drive

A semi new sphere of behavioral economics is forming based on: functions of "man brain" when they are horny (according to poets and psychologists men are most vulnerable to arousal-influenced behavior between the hours of 2 and 6 AM) and the women who make careers cir**cum**navigating that. OF isn't about selling nudes, it's about selling intimacy. The fantasy instigates the behavior.

A man sees a photo of a busty, provocatively dressed girl on social media. It arouses him. She's speaking through the screen and into his mind: "you want to see more of me". The horny image is our Bene Gesserit *voice*. Do the thing. Click my profile. From the photo, he clicks her profile link. A plethora of raunchy pictures awaits: she shows almost everything. A breast is just barely covered by a crop top; her pose suggests she's about to take it off, her caption suggests there is a place it can be seen. Link in bio.

Men are visual creatures. He wants to see more, perhaps confess to her how turned on she makes him, communicate with her directly. Does vshe do sexting? He clicks that profile link; a titillating OnlyFans entices him that the model is friendly. Warm, welcoming, naked. She's offering a sale: 7.99$[11] for a month of access to her explicit archive and one on one private chats. A split second decision – he clicks "subscribe".

OnlyFans is like a virtual strip club: the monthly subscription fee is an access pass to get in the door. If the client wants a lap dance or naughty conversation, the model is paid for her time and service, and any extra content she may sell. From there, it's a 'choose your own adventure' led by the sex drive.

Upon subscription, the man receives an instant message in his inbox. The model sends an automated welcome message, a PPV (pay to view). "Hey baby, welcome to my page ;) Can I get you off? Unlock this message for $10 to see me take my panties off!" And damn, does he want to see those panties off. Instantly he unlocks the message, and a video of her removing her thong appears. He's fully hard and ready to go. Already in the horny state but not yet finished, he wants more. He replies, "damn baby that was hot, can I see you play with yourself?"

He sees a '…'
________ is typing,

"I'm glad you liked that ;) Wanna see more?"

Yes
Please

Another video to unlock. He ravenously clicks. Through the screen she shows him what two fingers can do once the panties are off in the following 20 second $10 video.

Oh my god
That's so fucking hot
Tell me to cum now baby

Yeah, that's the stuff

Another $10 later, he unlocks a **JOI** where she tells him how to cum for her, giving a countdown of 10, 9, 8… until he releases his load.

11 Only fans creators seem to always be offering sales…

***JOI** - jerk off instructions - are a very popular search in porn. Some men love when the girl tells him what to do to get off. A soft domination that's not as heavy as full-on dominatrix content, but accomplishes the goal of similar power dynamics.*[12]

Thank you,
He replies, and logs off. Mission accomplished. From the timeline of first seeing her pic, to getting piqued enough to join her spicy page, to the interaction which he finishes, his neurocircuitry was firing on all cylinders. The cocktail of serotonin, dopamine, vasopressin, and oxytocin has played its role. Cum and go. The majority of subscribers to most OF models are transitory – the male sex drive is transitory. They join, they browse, they cum, rarely staying the full month of their subscription before a hot new model captures their attention next week.[13]

The big creators understand these mechanics and structure their business models to be highly promo-based - more so than content-based. An influx of new subscribers every month, with an aggressive upsale in sexting and PPV, rather than relying on an existing pool of clients. Client retention is highly variable – only 10%-50% of subscribers generally retain, so getting new subs in the door with effective promo is the predominant strategy. To implement an effective strategy, OF creators must intuit and understand the behavioral economics of their target demographic's sex drive, which for *most* models is the "average male".

THE MORE IMPORTANT QUESTION IS WHAT IS *MY* SEX DRIVE LIKE
MY SEX DRIVE A TESLA

The female sex drive is much more subtle. What turns women on? Our libidos are so variant, and our bodies can be nonconcordant with our minds. Emily Nagoski delves deep into this in her book *Come As You Are*. Where men are visual creatures as far as libido is concerned, women are not usually turned on by the instant sight of someone attractive. We require care, safety, a delicate but determined longing. Often, the drive to be desired *is* our sex drive.[14]

Why are we so obsessed with sex?

A quick google search will pull up this and that, biological imperative this, intimate connection that, a thousand ways to intellectualize sex. My goodness, how hard we try to rationalize the intangible, the emotional, the metaphysical, the unknowable. But one look at the person we desire most, when our body reacts before our mind, when our heart rate is triggered, will tell us this:
sex defies logic, and the erotic exchange is driven by mystery more than analysis

---

12 But what is paid for more, and why do some men want the dominnatrix; some want the submissive? It is well known that submissive people in bed are often high-functioning in life and seek to release control; the opposite is true of dominant behavior in bed: these doms may lack a control in their daily life so they take it out in the bedroom.

13 Zizek voice: 'desire is based lack lack and so on...'

14 this distinction seems apparent in how men watch more porn generally than women - and women read more erotica than men. 'Fifty shades of Grey' vs. 'deepthroat.'

or extrapolation. We don't choose who we're attracted to[15], though we can spend countless hours theorizing on why. What we can choose is to engage in our fantasy - we can choose to connect, to deepen, to investigate.

Do I get horny being nude online, knowing so many people can see my body in states of undress? I get a sense of power and vulnerability all at once, a vindication for all the men who have rejected me on the premise of not being attractive enough, or too weird, or too out there.[16] Knowing that now guys pay to see my naked body, pay to talk to me, to have access to my time and my sexuality, is almost more valuable than the money itself. Let me get this straight: I love when men goon to me. It turns me on to receive their tips, their compliments, their support, their submission, their domination, and to have my image be at the center of their desire.

Desire in a sexual capacity is libidinal energy. Phenomenologically, the libido is what we encounter beyond sex: our rage, joy anxiety, dread, and frustration are all part of it. Sex is not really about sex; underneath our sexual urges, our horning and gooning and perving, we have a network of feelings that fuel our libido. Where do kinks come from? The unconscious made sexual, fixated on an object or action that turns us on at the deepest level.

"The psyche creates reality every day. The only expression I can use for this reality is fantasy." -Carl Jung

It is important to consider sexuality in this digital age not singularly from the Onlyfans perspective but from a whore's eye view of the entire system. Every one of us has a fantasy, a deep and impenetrable core desire. Those desires, especially when of a sexual nature, cannot be acted on within daily social spheres; this is why people subscribe and visit sex workers, to deviate from mundane daily life - to visit a world where fantasy is a reality and desires can be freely explored.

It is why the characters in Westworld went to the park; a human drive to encounter the beyond-human, the almost-human, the lifelike simulation. Deeper selves can reveal themselves to us by virtue of direct contact with the uncanny valley. There is a reason why I've often cosplayed characters like Rachael from Blade Runner, Leeloo from Fifth Element, Dolores from Westworld.

It's not enough to be a hot babe online losing a little piece of my soul to objectification. Merging with a character who isn't really real, who is already an object, takes my version of fantasy full circle, plays with the simulacra, dissociates me from my own cognition and reassociates me into a disparate sexistential cyber domain. I take great pleasure in that escape, in those levels of turning into

15 Or choose who is attracted to us

16 A repetition compulsion: the subject once wounded seeks out those same damaging circumstances over and over in attempt to conquer them.

an object who is a human who is an object who is a…

Self-Objectification

Night falls and the day has been slow.
Societal indoctrination blah blah…

Turning the self into an object huh? Well, I'm literally on a pillow. No one knows me like she knows me. You, too, can have the Nastya pillow in your home from cyber-horny.com/shop for the awesome price of 37.00 USD ★ Why do I feel so compelled to trap myself within inanimate objects? A genie in a lamp that can grant you three loads. When faced with the burden of subjectivity, objectification goes to its extreme. I am anything but myself. I am a pillow, a sticker, an image.

Comfortable, transient, disposable. That is how men see me. To play this game, I make an attempt to outwit them, to out-objectify myself. As a physical item that can be purchased, the game is rigged in my favor. You may objectify me in your mind, but I objectify myself in e-commerce. It's like a video game to me; a video game that I always win. It's one of my fragmentations.

When my bf said at the beach as I mentioned I wore "modest swimsuits" in public… "modest? You have a onlyfans" – I, a wordsmith, perhaps had poor choice of words. But yet, the central concept persists. There is a different layer of perception when it comes to the real-life world. One of modesty. A modesty that comes from insecurity, or fear of unwanted attention – whereas in the digital world, I find security in looking for attention. I find, I look, I excavate. Like a paleontogist digging for rare bismuth beneath the topographical layers of brimstone, I too spelunk into the layers of modesty and sex appeal that so wrap my inner world, that ensconce the cyber ether.

What can be, unburdened by what has been

Article Talk

From Wikipedia, the free encyclopedia

"What can be, unburdened by what has been" is a quote popularized and primarily used by Kamala Harris, the current vice president of the United States and 2024 Democratic presidential candidate.[1] A supercut of Harris repeating the quote was first shared by the Republican National Committee on social media platform X, on April 30, 2023, after which it became viral.[2]

The quote has been oft-cited as a meme also attributable to the KHive, Harris' Internet following, and used as a pejorative and subject of mockery by her opponents.[3]

See also [edit]

- We did it, Joe!
- You think you just fell out of a coconut tree?

Cogito Ergo Cum

How good does it feel to be inside me?
How good does it feel for me to be inside my mind every day?

Tall skinny pale feminine people that's who I'm into.

Emo boys.
Shawty with them SSRIS.
But I know that life is unkind so I've bent my desires into grosser richer ppl to survive.
When u ask for a pussy pic and shorty sends a pic of u[17]

The recursive dynamics of attraction back and forth between ourselves and others structure our identities. Culture/society (obviously) does this too. Melissa Grant points out that the words 'prostitute' and 'homosexual'[18] *only appeared when they are categories of individual jettisoned/stigmatized by mainstream society.*

The Love Map

The love map is how we develop our sexual preferences. Core memories from youth imprint on us certain fetishes. Fantasies. These pathways branch out into our behavior as adults.

Fantasy, close the pussy, put the cock in the cage, open the relationship. At our core there is that one person that fucked and raped and violated our love map; is this just a projection of who we are. It's a cognitive dissonance that I have a gentle energy but there are inner parts of me that give way to so much violence.

Cyberhorny Dream Diaries - the dreams of taking down Elon Musk are really a veiled symbolism for my grievances towards the father. The dreams too raise more questions than they answer. As I write in Chapter 4, core memories are a cemetery for me, the graves of which are *not* to be dug up. But occasionally, against my will and at the most inopportune of times, zombies rise, threatening to devour my flesh, my brain, my dignity. Only when I'm playing hide and seek with my dignity can I interface with those personal graves. I sublimate my questioning from the field of memory to the field of porn.
Can porn help us answer these questions?
The best pornos start with erotic
piano music,
lustful tomb explorers,
horny therapists,
angry step-dads.
Sexy pizza guy
Bubba the plumber

Introjection: we pick up the porn ethos we see. It's a social grace. Is it hard to brand yourself as a sex object here because, in traditional porn like above stated themes, sex explodes out of nowhere from the ordinary and mundane -

---

17 It may not escape the reader that nastya frequently employes comedic turns of phrase in instances where her own desire begins to break through, perhaps as a shield or as a vehicle

18 The very people writing this book

from precisely where it is not supposed to be.[19]

Do we even know what we want? Like the cheesecake factory menu, porn has infinite options. Turn-ons are varied; the biggest sex organ is the brain.

Why do people subscribe if porn is so available?

Pornhub, free and abundant as it is, can only go so far when the viewer wants to connect with the porn star. We live in an age where the models are more accessible, at least for the proper fee. The best things in life are free – the second best things in life have the type of paywall where it *feels* free, natural, organic, oasic, authentic.

A date with a porn star over Zoom. By the time you get there, the fun you're having is so lovely you forget the economics. How Lusty Lucy, 5'2 105lbs with 34DD breasts and a 40" natural ass, indulges her companion's 5.5" cock.

Stats instead of people: dehumanizing.

The specular image is being eclipsed by the regime of numbers; even on dating apps, men herald a height of over 6' to declare to a mate their value, and women all over the nsfw internet list letters and numerical values of their body like a barcode of aesthetics. No, this is beyond objectification – the numeralization of flesh is an entry in the menu, the endless buffet of digital nutrition.

Rule 34: if it exists, there is porn of it. If you wanna see a hentai Teddy Roosevelt carrying a big stick, it's out there somewhere…

These numbers and images, the signifiers of everyday life, are a boon to the lonely prostitute at night. As advertising and media become more and more sexual, the harder it is to stop being horny, and the more money she can make.[20]

Does the pervert have object permanence?

Between the hours of 2 and 6AM, the times I am offline, all bets are off. All jacks are off. The illusion, of course, is that I am online 24/7. A master class in fleeting penicianship. It is a minor miracle that I have done well, not maximizing my potential as an earner during the times that I sleep. I am the medium and the modicum of these men's random emotional releases, the blank slate on which they can unload. Physio-digitally they unload and release. They are physically doing an act on themselves but it's digital.

How they be typing these long ass messages with one hand? The horniness of men has become unrestrained and socially acceptable.

---

19 **[…] desire crawls, slips, escapes, like the ferret." - Jacques Lacan**

20 The harder you look the harder you look.

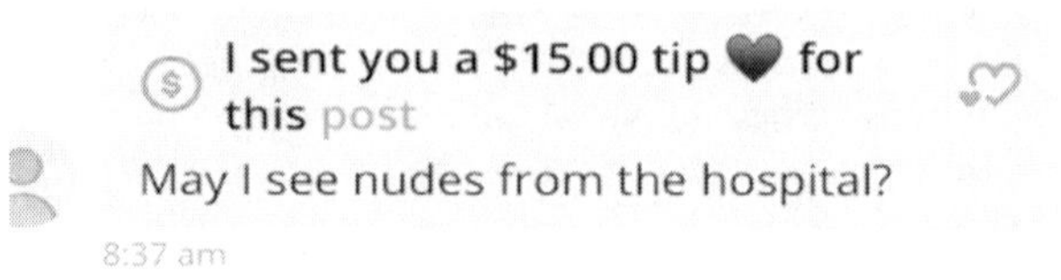

Inauthentimacy, Love Education, and Dissociation

We can then see there are so many things not covered by traditional sex education that need to be pondered (like an orb).

Obviously the onset of the social media regime has created a realm not covered in the traditional sex ed powerpoint. The teacher points to the white-board: 'penis.' 'vagina.' What is our contemporary epistemology of sexual information? Of the sex drive even. The scroller of the social media apps, porn sites, and general internet learns in a completely different way. It is depraved that sex educators are getting shadow banned and deleted from online spaces. The young people learning about sex do not learn anything from traditional channels.

Dis**ass**ociation of the online persona, egoic illnesses, sexual healing, inclusivity, accessibility, dark desires, e-capitalism, the desire for intimacy, the desire for a nice life, the desire for depravity, the compatibility of their dreams with reality, and so much more. Contemporary sexual education must add a semester on integrating desire into reality.

Sex education!?!?!?!? How about some **love** education to mitigate the effects of our new cyber horny paradigm.[21]

How do we gather information and how do we know it is real? Do we trust things online? Without sounding too much like a pretentious fuck, how do we reconcile the epistemology of fake news (fake porn / real porn / fake intimacy) and inauthenticity (**inauthintimacy)** online without going completely insane and disassociating?
Asking questions is sometimes more important than actually answering them. The secrets shouldn't be entirely revealed; a little mystery never hurt anyone. What is reality? I have no idea.

There's a reciprocal nature to these two realities - the digital and the physical. Adding sex to this mirror of infinite regress is disjointing since we can't actually fuck the person on the screen, but the human brain will process activities like masturbation as a reality.[22]

21 Love education is when you go to psychoanalysis 3x a week for 5 years.

22 Suppose someone is in love but doesn't get anywhere; being frustrated, one gets into a depression, saying that it is not possible to get away from the loved one. [...] Then one would say, well at the bottom there is the drive, the dependence, something which constantly occurs in a transference. Many analysands resent the transference because of the dependence it entails, but nothing can be done about it for they *are* dependent; they are driven... - ML Franz Alchemy

For every moment of triumph, for every instance of beauty, many souls must be trampled. Millions must die. When the going gets weird, the weird get horny. Weird times call for weird porn. Weird porn creates weird men. Weird men have weird fetishes. Weird fetishes create weird porn. Weird times call for weird porn.

Why do we even want sex? Why do we crave it, why do we risk it all for it? **Why do we make it so difficult?** As a human desire that's been there since the beginning of creation, we already have many answers to this that are primal. **Sex is of course reproductive, but as it has been compounded with the cyber world - the image reigns. Instead of producing children we now produce images, videos, and affective states. Always be content.**

The sex drive has become convoluted , though it was never pure in any sense, by the cyberworld.

My cat, objectifying herself before anyone else can.

My tenure in the school of self-objectification and reckoning with the sex drives of others has been illuminating because it showed me my desire. It showed me that when I embody this falsified persona, dovetail the cyber Nastya with the corporeal Nastya into cyber-corporeality, it is as real as I get. The line between fantasy/authenticity as it pertains to our libidos is paper thin. When I expose myself to the perverts,[23] I am fragile, delicate. I feel equal parts springtime flower and nuclear bomb. Believe not everything or anything you read, for even *I* massage, distend, and violate the truth.

---

23 In love - in life - in therapy - in sex work: there is the **transference**. The unconscious dynamics that the client projects on to the worker. People transfer onto others the ways they have learned to navigate people and the world since birth, molded by their pasts, parents, their drives.

“D.H. Lawrence had the impression – that psychoanalysis was shutting sexuality up in a bizarre sort of box painted with bourgeois motifs, in a kind of rather repugnant artificial triangle, thereby stifling the whole of sexuality as a production of desire so as to recast it along entirely different lines, making of it a ‘dirty little secret’, a dirty little family secret, a private theater rather than the fantastic factory of nature and production.”

— Gilles Deleuze

3: Presentation of the Online Persona: Everything is Cosplay

"The irony of life is that those who wear masks often tell us more truths than those with open faces."
— Marie Lu, The Rose Society

Tuxedo Mask
-Sailor Moon

"Every human wears a mask. There comes a time when we cannot remove the mask without removing our own skin." — Japanese proverb

Asuka and Misato from Evangelion. Rachael from Blade Runner. Snow White. Sailor Moon. Sexy Pikachu. Sexy nurse, maid, schoolgirl, elf maiden. Shrek, even. I have been them all. What else is left to be after all this time? Just me, whatever that means? At what point does the cosplay mask come off and the Nastya mask come on? When I put on my face, my best cyber self, there is no grand revelation behind the mask. The great discovery is what happens when the masks come off and the walls come down; even in the mundane-ness, the emptiness, the routine, there seems to be a far more interesting core than the layers it's conveniently wrapped up in. Isn't that the most interesting part though – the unmasking? The stripping. By the very act of stripping, we engage in a removal of all kinds of walls, physical and psychological, that unlock the grandiosity of vulnerability – if we dare to show others that part of us underneath the most exterior face. The true intimate act is letting somebody *see* us.

Do you really know what's behind the mask? A nursing student who's been turning 18 for five years. A malcontent masquerading as a MILF. A branded exhibitionist who's secretly shy. Anyone can be anyone.[24]

The problem with wearing masks: they can be ripped off any moment. We wear masks in the form of cyber avatars to conceal and reveal. To inhibit and uninhibit and exhibit. Behind our avatars we hide and protect parts of ourselves,

---

24 The exhibitionist is in fact, **plagued** by shame. He reveals himself to produce shame in his target. A desperate attempt to escape the shame he feels about himself.

as much as we reflect and expose parts of us. Carefully curated social presences. **Attempting to extract money from the simps, to manipulate their sex drives, keep them subscribed, we must experiment with a multitude of masks.**

A mask of horniness. A mask of innocence. We all know about the basics, that we all craft our masks to precision, that we strategically post to create a certain vibe, aesthetic, reputation. What do we want to show the world? What do we want to show ourselves? Who do we really let *see* us? We look good online. A world dominated by visuals. We know about the basics; but what about the psychological effects beneath all that drama? Is there pressure to be some type of way, not just for SWers but for civilians? Online, our real selves become our business representatives.

"Don't you know that a midnight hour comes when everyone has to take off his mask? Do you think life always lets itself be trifled with? Do you think you can sneak off a little before midnight to escape this?"
— Søren Kierkegaard

We create facades,
brands,
marketing campaigns.

No tree can grow to heaven until its roots reach down into hell. ~Carl Jung

Digital charlatans grasping at straws to remain relevant in a scheming, superficial, fast-past world where everyone else is doing some version of what we're doing: existing, and making money off our existence.

In existential commerce, the timeline never stops: 24/7 of treachery and authenticity in real time. Can we bend time to our will via premeditated scheduled posts and impeccable timing? Or is it only effective when we are actually present behind the screen? How far can we let go and let the game play out, rather than actively participating in the gameplay?[25]

I asked earlier if the pervert has object permanence. What about the model? Without her advertising, she doesn't exist. On a week off from posting, I kept having dreams that I was losing subscribers, that no one cared anymore, that by my absence online my real self was being deleted, even though my "real" self was thriving: sleeping, eating, watching tv, seeing my friends.

The balance can be hard to strike. Taking a week off from online sex work and digital marketing? You have nothing to lose but your simps. Seeing where your character ends can make you realize where you don't want to end up.

---

25 Psychoanalytic muttering about how everything we consciously put forward as 'identity' is a pathetic tarp over a boiling cauldron of unconscious drives

I be on my dishonest shit I be lying I be scheming playing tricks engaging in deception -editor[26]

Inauthintimacy and Anonymity

The anonymity of the subscriber is imperative. Behind a screen, they can choose to participate in the OF model's community, or stay silent, voyeuristic, "lurk and jerk" the day away. Only about 5-10% of fans will actively engage – as in, liking posts, sending messages, paying tips, voting in the model's polls.

[**Editor note:** Valentine reports that most of those who *interact* and don't simply lurk request to see butt/ass content. Images referencing the anal stage. In Freud's theories of psychosexual development he posited that those with disturbances in the anal stage become preoccupied with money - giving or not giving - retentive or unretentive. Money is shit.] "My kids think I got money coming out my ass"

Many subscribers are really just there to view the digital peep show. If they were to participate, the anonymity makes it easier. They could be whoever they want behind the screen. They could choose to be authentic. Subscribers present a version of themselves too - it is not only the model who is curating a personality.

Men who visit sex workers have historically preferred to remain anonymous; that kind of anonymity is easier than ever now. Choose your own character: Muscle.Daddy.69? Hemingway420? @cj08888267 ? PM_ME_BIG_TITS ? Random or intentional, your handle is how you make your way through these dark alleys. Do you want to be seen – by one particular person or by multitudes in an audience – and how do you want to be seen. Highbrow, lowbrow, confident, submissive. The choice is yours, and perception is ricocheted by everyone who witnesses you. Through those fragments of perception in real time, a character is built. Branding is a temporal art. World building, universe building, is shadow work. Presenting the online persona: men do it too. Anonymity is the handmaiden of depravity.

Subscribers can live vicariously through my expression of sexuality: for some the presence of being in a non-judgemental space - in relationship with a creator - IS the sex.

It's important to note that I hold no disdain for the men who frequent my page and interact with me + models like me: quite the opposite, I support and thank them. The obvious reason being I receive gifts and money, the less obvious reason being that it's a sensitive operation going into unorthodox places, even as a brief visitor. Every interaction is an energetic exchange. That information is very sensitive and needs to be protected.

---

26 No im not!!! (yes I am ;)

Why and *how* do people decide to post their naked bodies on the internet?

When people post nudes of their life/job influencing the nsfw content, (for example: a nurse stripping her scrubs to reveal titties, or a construction guy doing porn in his vest) that's marketing. When it's just partial object[27] posting (penis, vagina), that's exhibitionism and/or a call for validation. Attention is a powerful currency. The reward centers in our brains feel good.

What do we present as? And for who?

Presenting as a straight woman to the subscribers who are straight male (~90%)and the subscribers who are nonbinary, gender fluid, lesbian, trans, (non-straight male, ~10%).

Mild virtue signaling to appeal to non-male consumers. The cosplay of poverty - it's common. "Oh my I'm just a sweet college girl trying to pay my tuition" - meanwhile she's a mother of two with a six figure paying job.

Presenting as a certain desirable age online. We all lie about our age, don't we? At what point does it become unethical? Where do we draw the line when it comes to ethics in porn?

Presenting as neurotypical. I'm just a regular girl with many mental illnesses. Neurodivergent? Who, me?

Presenting a false personality to gain reward: when my cat meows like she's hungry right after I give her food, wanting another little treat.

Presenting as the girl next door. My dressed up aesthetic artistic content (which I like) never does as well as my girl next door throwaways (things I look like a potato in that the fans love cause it's "raw" and "authentic"). The false sense of realness. Manufactured authenticity.

* *hits cigar* *

Guys see us as objects; we see them as banks. The reductive villain vs villain storyline. In reality, there are no good guys or bad guys, just humans behind usernames trying to navigate this sphere of existence by any way they know. Sometimes those methods of navigation are dangerous, so keep your wits about you.

"How many of us want any of us to see us as we really are? Isn't the mirror hostile enough?"
— Jeanette Winterson

27 According to psychoanalysis the object cause of desire is comprised of these images imprinted on the baby as it is torn from the breast of its mother. Some aspect of her, the flaring of her nose, her movement of her eyes, the way she parts her hair, becomes an eroticized curse that forever chains desire to separation. This is part of the reason some simps want feet content, boob content, ass content and so on *zizek sniff*

Scammers online: hi baby :) I am sugar daddy I want to pay you $1400 a week for being my beautiful spoiled girl <3 I will send you a check give me your name and banking info. ☺

Scams work because they prey on the basic human traits we all possess: anxiety, greed, envy, desperation[28]. We've all been scammed in some form or another. The key is to learn from those mistakes and help others to avoid making those mistakes as well.

Never give anyone any sensitive information. People think sex work is easy: escorting, camming, stripping, being a sugar baby... but they fail to consider the dangers that come with living a type of double life. Feel it with your gut: if someone or something sounds too good to be true, it probably is. The protocol when you know you're dealing with a scammer is disengage immediately, calmly exit, block them, report them, and move on with your life. Quit while you're ahead. Being in this world can be nerve racking, especially for a beginner. Many people will try to bend you and break you. Have an iron will, tough skin, and superhuman resilience. Move on from mistakes quickly.

A good rule of thumb is to 'never jump higher than your ass' and not get yourself into any situations where you may be in over your head, especially if you're a risk-averse person who gets nervous at the concept of the unknown, unsafe, and uncontrollable.

We all carry: *Vestiges of Authenticity at odds with our Deceptions*

Ethos, Pathos, Logos. What are our methods of persuasion? Ethics and credibility. Essentially: how and why would you trust me? I have a reputation to protect. A reputation that in the years of doing this work has been honest, reliable, authentic. I am the genuine article. But yes, of course, sometimes I need to lie. So split the difference. You'll never guess where the line is. Because I have hidden it so deep within myself that even I do not know.

Violating the truth, engaging in deception and artifice to impress a mate. Flexing and fronting. Putting on a mask, lest it not slide off eventually. Cognitive dissonance. I lean authentic, but I also deceive. By the very nature of how dissociative the internet is, it's impossible not to deceive online. The fakest accounts of all seem the realest. If she uses *"I'm not like other girls" "I'm genuine" "I'm authentic*" "I'm real"* – what exactly does that say? Manufactured authenticity is very much a part of the game.

---

28 Scams work because we cannot see our own backs. We want to think we found the secret solution. That they really will do *that* for me. Scams work because human beings **refuse** to accept that they are born divided, thrown up against the bedrock of subjectivity that is castration. We all want to think we are special.

**Part of my Onlyfans bio was "I offer the very best authentic cyberhorny experience."*

So am I pulling your leg about that? I guess. I offer the very worst inauthentic experience the cyber world has to offer ✞

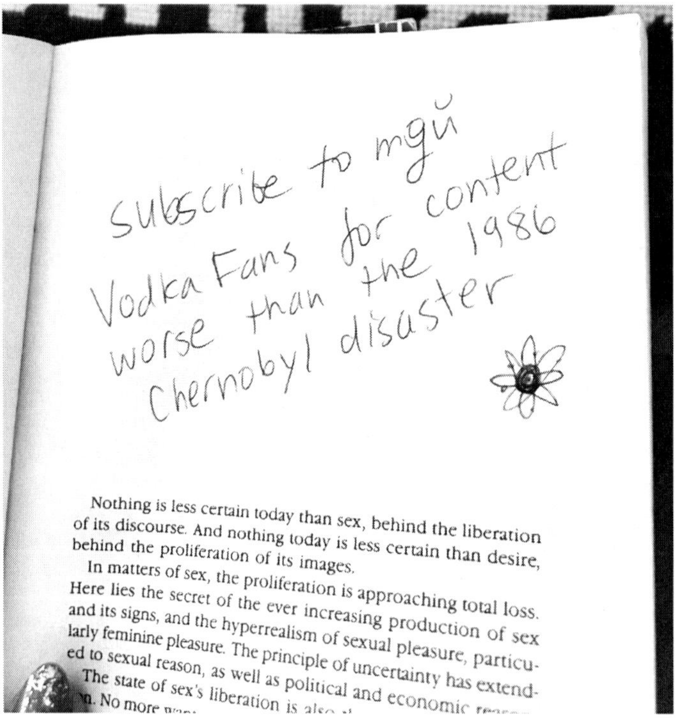
Subscribe to mgu Vodka Fans for content worse than the 1986 Chernobyl disaster

Nothing is less certain today than sex, behind the liberation of its discourse. And nothing today is less certain than desire, behind the proliferation of its images.

In matters of sex, the proliferation is approaching total loss. Here lies the secret of the ever increasing production of sex and its signs, and the hyperrealism of sexual pleasure, particularly feminine pleasure. The principle of uncertainty has extended to sexual reason, as well as political and economic reason.

The state of sex's liberation is also

Cognitive plateau. After extensive days on end of advertising, enduring 12+ hour screen time for weeks, of course my brain hits a plateau. A thousand plateaus. A thousand guys quoting Deleuze and Guattari in an infographic[29], folding decades of critical theory into clickbait.

These guys are voyeurs with no substance. Me, I am a pervert with substance abuse. "Ethnographers of looking at memes."

A MAN STREAMING??? That is fucking disgusting. Streaming is for the girlies. Broadcasting my life is my 9/11. Exposing myself is my Roman Empire. Fluff is the feminine domain. Cultural criticism is just gossip, and I have all the tea. XOXO.

The ("cultural critics") need to fuck; maybe they'll cancel each other

29 **"The self is only a threshold, a door, a becoming between two multiplicities"**
- Gilles Deleuze, A Thousand Plateaus: Capitalism and Schizophrenia

out. Internet researchers. What even is cultural critique? It is too hinged and curated; not unhinged enough. It's all about the curation, and not about having substance or message. It's all fluff in here, isn't it?

Who or what made you The Expert?? At 30 years old, a Master*? Preposterous. We're all nothing. Rage and shame at the audacity of my generation's egos. Rage and shame at mine not being big enough. For now…

*At 30 years old I am only a Master Baiter
I'm an expert at watch TV, take nudes, ice cream, petting cat. My secret talent is…….idk.

Before the internet, people held secret lives too.

It's wild to find someone's secret private life out there on the internet, especially if you weren't looking for it. Not all those who post nudes do it for work. Attention is a powerful currency. Rejection is a powerful currency. Validation is the most powerful stock exchange of them all. NASDIQ dropping on the Ball Street Market. Like Laura Palmer from Twin Peaks, some of the most bright and sunny people you know have demented secret lives.

You dig far enough, you'll wish you hadn't. Who I am online, is not who I am offline. Or is it? I'll never tell. My pussy lips are sealed. I used to literally never wear a bra. Now I have over 25,000$ of lingerie stuffed in my drawers like a bloated silk sausage in an overpriced LED casing.[30] Delusions of convenience. Sometimes we need to convince ourselves of one thing because we simply cannot believe the other.

Manufactured Authenticity

There are models who enjoy the sexual part of sex work, but most of the time it's a performance to attain capital. That doesn't mean it's all fake, however – when engrossed enough in the fantasy, it becomes real for both the performer and the audience. The client relations can often be more authentic than the marketing. When I'm talking dirty to CryptoLawyer05 I'm more present than when I'm doomscrolling through instagram wondering whether or not to post, to make a reel, or to delete my whole damn account.

While engaging in capitalist gameplay, models carefully curate and exude a receptiveness towards sex, embodying a "real" persona in which they love it, but not so overtly that they become over-the-top sex fiends. The balance here rests in nuance. A seeking man loves a secret slut. A girl next door. A fair amount of resistance and corruption. Empowerment? Confidence? Man repellant.

Generally the girl who is already confident in her body and herself does

30 Jesus fucking christ…

not need a random man to reassure her – the men love the act of reassurance and control. They subscribe to enact a fantasy and have a sense of influence over the model's sexuality. Since the interactions are all done in private, it feels like they're being a part of her life, which is fulfilling to both parties. The subscriber gets a parasocial connection with x-rated content, the model gets a stream of income. A win-win.

Are us girlies horny 24/7 and ready and eager to take loads 100% of the time? Midwest babes ecstatic at the sight of a dick? Luscious MILFs so eager to rate a cock because they crave the throb of it – or because the subscriber will pay them 50$? The thing is, you'll never know. That's part of the charm of gambling, isn't it? Figuring out which is real and which is illusory. Some babes really are lustful nymphos doing Onlyfans for the sexual release. Others are just trying to get by, performing a drama of horniness to pay their electric bills, child care, medical debts. Some may be in the middle, seeking validation and seeking financial stability. The girlies who do *really* well, let their assistants pretend to be them, giving their subscribers an exact replica of the original performance.

What do subscribers really seek? A fantasy, an escape – one that feels genuine. Lola Davina writes: "in the fantasy, they seek the real".

They don't know they're often speaking to bots and assistants online – not every model runs her own account. The most popular influencer accounts usually have a team to do their posting, scheduling, and sexting. Is this still ethical porn, as many advertise? What even is ethical porn? How ethical do I consider myself to be – when I expose my meta analysis and discuss the falsification of my character, while also breaking open the unbreakable safes of my psyche for an audience to read? What's my motive here? Do I want to be seen or concealed, or both? What does this unreliable narrator truly want? I can't seem to crack my own code. Perhaps by writing about the system at large, I can discover something about my microcosm. The great discovery is my small life. The artifice unveils the real.

The discourse of psychological splitting when one has multiple lives; the corporeal "real life" and the digital existence. How do you perform a role as a content creator, as a reality destroyer, without creating facades that destroy you?[31]

Business is good, I made many dudes cum this week. No loads refused. Loads of business, loads of compliments, loads of cash. Maybe I've gotten 3 hours of sleep if at all, and my brain is disarticulated, but the money I've made keeps me warm at night.

---

31 The analyst Melanie Klien believed that one must heal the split in oneself - integrate the shadow Jung might say - in order to view others as whole. To see someone else as more than just a needs-gratifying object.

Business was terrible this week, very few loads endured. Many loads refused, because my psyche could not endure these loads. Physical health returned while I slept; upon awakening, self-perception suffered as income fell. I am a failure as a pornographer.

We must ask if it is even possible to begin the deconstruction of the dichotomous pornographic perception. I have been like this my whole life, though. Any perception of failure leads me into the darkest corners of mania and depression. I started seeing a therapist because I could not take the failure of taking time off – even civilians have weekends. I had nothing. But I learned. It took time, but I learned not to equate numbers with good or bad – numbers on a scale, numbers on a bank statement. I stopped moving the goalposts. I stopped obsessively calculating and premeditating my states of emotion, my states of arousal, and let myself just be. Surrendering can be the hardest thing of all.

Even in states of arousal we become different: it changes our capacity to make decisions. It has been well documented that men are weakest between 2 and 5 am. (An idea so important we keep repeating it).

The pornopticon:
Foucault me all night long. **I open my computer and porn stares back.**[32]

[33]

TWERKers of the world unite.. Their chussys. ~Marx
Seize the means of reproduction.
Commodity fetishism at the techno-glory-hole.
Just me and my pornoptipussy against the world.

---

32 At the moment when the last prohibitions are being forgotten, there are still any number of intellectuals who continue to refer to them as if they were more and more crippling. Alternatively, they replace the myth of the prohibition with one that invokes an omnipresent and omniscient 'power' and can be seen as yet another mythic transposition of the strategies of mimesis. The greater part of Michel Foucault's work is **erected** on that false premise. - Rene Girard *Things Hidden Since the Foundation of the World.*

33 The split here: philosophical intellectual vs busty hooters girlie

Once you post something online, you have to deal with the consequences of it. Every step of the online footprint produces a chain reaction.

In our collective human perception, we move through multiple realities. The physical plane where we physically reside. The mental plane where we think. The backrooms of that mental plane that make up our unconscious. The spiritual plane with its subtle energy bodies. The digital astral plane where we interact in cyberspace. The temporal plane as we move through time. Our reality creates even more planes as humanity evolves.

What even is reality?   just stuff idk

Is it better to have lived and loved and lost your virginity, than never have lusted at all? Can the digital replace the flesh?

"Long live the new flesh" is a quote from Videodrome. It refers to the genesis of interaction between human reality, and technology. Now, the digital flesh we encounter is almost real. Is it beyond real?

Realer than real, beyond the Baudrillardian hyperrealism… he be purring: hyperreality is a state where we can no longer distinguish reality from mere representations of it. Loose copies of reality and the battleground of perception. What we know as the contemporary world is a simulacrum, where reality has been replaced by an immersive spectacle of false images – images we consume and provide.

I'm in the simpulation every day. How do I even know my fans are real? Some men like to send me pictures of their face. This is in fact more offensive to me than when they send pics their genitals. I know what a fuckin penis looks like ok… I'm so desensitized. But a face? That's too personal. That falls under the girlfriend experience service. Receiving photos of either or both is a service I charge for.

Carl Jung's medical dissertation was about the psychogenesis of spiritual phenomena. Mediumship. I am the medium who the psychogenesis of penis phenomena passes through. My work is very astral in the sense that cyberspace is immaterial. As a healer in reiki I work with energetic shifts, and as a healer in sexuality I work with energetic shifts. The reality I enter when I work is a completely disparate headspace to when I'm just chilling and doing my regular life stuff. What complicates this is that I do "regular life stuff" online, albeit an exaggerated sexualized version of it. Yet I also have sex in my real life off camera. So then which Nastya is the realest?

What is even real if no one can agree on what The Real is? (Lacan, Baudrillard, -ugh- Zizek…)

Alter egos: the avatars of our consciousness.

Going beyond digital boundaries and witnessing the vulnerability of a real human, all the ugly and unrestrained parts. A huge part of this isn't being talked about because of the identity politics penetrating the web canon right now - social media is too restrained. Everyone is narrowed into a certain paradigm of what they can and can't say in posts, lest they be an edgelord or a contrarian.[34]

Wot's all this then luv xx?

Fragmentation. Integration. Dissociation.

Integrating parts of the psyche ..fragmentation is easy, it's the integration that's hard. When someone in the real world asks me something pertaining to OF in the middle of a conversation, I recoil. Bitch I'm trying to forget. Not under duress or shame; it's an instinctive dissociation from online Nastya / realworld Nastya. There is a part of me that is very proud of what I've accomplished online; at parties in LA I've heard people refer to me as "legendary content creator" "iconic existential artist" "modern renaissance woman" – of course that's gratifying for my ego to hear. Compliments mitigate my solipsism, as if shattering my self-perception of being a failure, a recluse. The other part of me is a doubting thomas[35]. I don't necessarily lust for success, but I desire non-failure. My motives are banal, my desires dull.

Desire is mimetic, desire is disposable, desire craves instant gratification.

The concept of being a disposable egirl in a disposable e-world. Candy girls where everyone is a diabetic. Fawned over one day, and discarded the next. To be remembered in a sea of duplicates and duplicates is next to impossible.

Guys don't go to porn pages for a memorable personality – they go to lurk and jerk, have a glorious moment of pleasurable private surveillance, and move on with their lives.

Or do they? My page is proof that some voyeurs may cum for the pleasures of the body initially[36], but continue to follow for the pleasures of personality long-term. How long-term, though, remains to be seen. I fear that by the completion of this book, having faced yet another fear of taking so much time off, I will have no subscribers left to perv on me.

---

34 See Evan Dunn for Damage Magazine: Against Social Justice (therapy)

35 The allusion to doubting thomas is *especially* pertinent considering Jesus asked Thomas to **touch** him in order to prove that he was real. Cyber Nastya cannot be touched.

36 Lacan believed voyeurism to be a sort of fear of physical sex. The specular image of the act or another's person becomes eroticized as a rigid unitary field. I am watching the sex. This is in contrast to having the sex, where the body of the other is an entire terrain of disunity - different parts doing different things. There is no exchange of penetration - the voyeur transmutes the inevitable violence of physical sex to the violence of seizing the **image** of the other. In this way all porn viewing can be read as voyeuristic.

How does a tragic slut with a cult following assert herself within the world of a mainstream geared towards the average pervert? How do I catch the pervert's heart off guard[37] and busssss it open? How do I catch the pervert's wallet?

Performing a psychodrama for this niche audience, I find the way to the pervert's heart, mind, and wallet is just to be my sparkling authentic self. I perform as Nastya, as many Nastyas from the demure to the perverted. I don't just long for the pervert's wallet, I long to enter his subjectivity and understand him. He may penetrate me in his mind, but I penetrate him in the psyche. Balls deep in the subconscious, one aesthetic nude photoshoot at a time.

Is it art? Am I an artist? Can porn ever be art? It is considered below the belt of morality to work in porn. It is also considered to be quite embarrassing and humiliating to be an artist. Carl Jung in his Black Books eschewed any mention of his work being anywhere near considered "artistry". It could discredit and invalidate his writing.

37 You are neither here nor there, / A hurry through which known and strange things pass - seamus Heaney

To conclude this chapter here are some presentations of the porn persona:

UK NURSE let go from job after secret OnlyFans discovered !

!! OFFICER IN NASHVILLE GETS FIRED FOR SHOWING MORE THAN HIS BADGE !!

Middle aged man plays with himself before bed

47 year old man late for work, blames wife seducing him in the morning for dip in stock market

Leg cramp takes woman out just short of the finish line

Virgin masturbates with dildo, multiple squirting incidents leave her flabbergasted

Woman wakes up husband for early quickie, hour-long fuck results in morning chaos

Straight male has clandestine sex with gay colleague

Tight hole traps hung man for hours

2 trans girls, a rave chick, and preppy neighbor keep neighbors up til 4am

Man finds clitoris; wins Nobel Peace Prize

Massive load tragically erupts, lands in hair, thousands dead

Local twink eats ass in Trader Joe's parking lot

Thick girl squeals in delight when she finds hungry new lover good at eating out for hours

Girl rides guy to completion, takes about a minute

Goth girl sucks emo boy's dick for 45 minutes: the antidepressants lose this battle

Man plows soaking wife while she watches porn

US man wanted for questioning for multiple felonies after local woman nearly dehydrated from multiple orgasms

Man ties girlfriend to bed and proceeds to have sexual intercourse, plays Call of Duty after

Chubby guy rails dominant MILF into complete submission

I can see the headlines now…

FAKE HEADLINES.

THE SYSTEMS THAT VERIFY OUR Electronic-ID

DEEPFAKES

FAKE NEWS

FAKE ORGASMS

THE SYSTEM IS IN PLACE FOR STABLE, DECENTRALIZED

EPISTEMICS

FAKE SCANDALS

(gossip)

Faking an orgasm is easy; faking intimacy is hard. Existence blends with work; the transistasis[38] makes it complicated. The psychoanalysis of Neon Genesis Evangelion can readily apply to Cyberhorny, but let's not go there yet. The work we do for ourselves dies with us, the work we do for others remains and is immortal.

"Better be glad I don't feel like making a scene today."

— Cookie Lyon, Empire

38 (power of living things to keep changing despite circumstances)

The self is a bombing of two multiplicities and I am
committing existential terrorism

"And so art is everywhere, since artifice is at the very heart of reality. And so art is dead, not only because its critical transcendence is gone, but because reality itself, entirely impregnated by an aesthetic which is inseparable from its own structure, has been confused with its own image. Reality no longer has the time to take on the appearance of reality. It no longer even surpasses fiction: it captures every dream even before it takes on the appearance of a dream."

— Jean Baudrillard, Simulations

Take a shot; get comfortable, dear reader.

4: Why I Do The Work I Do (Onlyfans and the Vast Expanse of the Internet)

"We are able to fetishize money in our actions only because we have already taken an ironic distance towards money in our heads."

– Mark Fisher, Capitalist Realism

Warning: this will be long and hard

The economic origin story of nastya valentine

his is not an art job, this is a service job. The sex industry is all about servitude. Lest ye not neglect the "work" in sex work. To our subscribers, we turn on and off like a hologram. Sex work is a temporal art, our medium is cyber space and the dilation of digital time. We are not real, yet not *not* real. We are engaging in Shroedinger's sex. It's cool. It's strange. It's weird. It's gross. It's awesome. I cannot say whether this is a "good" or "bad" field. I can say it works for me. It has changed my life – my perception, my income, my breadth. Knowing myself in a deeper way by posting unhinged shit online - from the heart.

Planet Bimbo: A Discourse on Alienation

This line of work is not for the faint of heart, but it's somehow more wholesome than it sounds. I wish more people knew that. Sex workers are some of the most intelligent, fragile, innocent, childlike, open-minded, creative people I've ever met. We get a bad rap for the lustful presence we allegedly exude that happens to be considered "bad" in the moral dichotomy of society.[39]

Shame and dread stalk us. Does showing nudity to survive make one

39 Reality's mirror, reality's shadow

an inherently bad person? Everyone under late capitalism who labors with their body to make a living is a whore. We're inherently not bad people; we simply choose a path most wouldn't dare to take. We're stardust crusaders. We're good at moving in the shadows. We're neither heroes nor villains, we just *are*. Not all heroes wear capes. Some wear nothing.

We are all, in the grand philosophical sense, specks of nothing in a vast conglomerate of galaxies. No humans are better or worse than others by existence or trade alone; it is our actions that determine our standing[40]. How strange and alienating it is to be considered less than nothing simply for rejecting society's traditional values and embracing the NSFW life. I can't count how many times I've received messages calling me useless, inadequate, a plague to society (no — but even a plague is productive as it sees action. I am nonessential.)

Despite our status as teeny tiny specks of dust, SWers are being deplatformed **now** more than **ever**!

- From the OnlyFans ban on porn in August 2021, that left many creators including myself scrambling (only to be reverted once they realized how much money they'd lose removing nsfw content from the platform that popularized it),
- to constant shadow/content bans on social media apps (I am shadow banned on almost every platform: Insta, Twitter, Reddit, Tiktok — the four horsemen of the digital apocalypse),
- to content removal on Onlyfans itself. A quick google search will show you words banned on OF: from 'meetup to 'paralysis' to 'cervix'. Images with weapons or medical equipment are banned on the spot. People can not appear on your page without a prior consent form – this includes celebrities and historical figures dead or alive.

However, the subscriber can still send images of themselves (or whoever) even if they are not verified. So this system of "safety" does not go both ways. What social platforms do to keep their SW models safe pales in comparison to what they do to subdue us.

OF simultaneously demands constant content and extravagant nudity, sex, etc, to make money....

AND commands my essence to be invisible:

No more being a weaponized babe, no more eating sushi in the nude with my swords out, no more documentation of my medical visits, no more kitties and titties. I still will post to the platform as long as I can, and I do the best I can to uphold terms of service, but it seems new rules are written every day and the content removal is arbitrary as hell. Once they've flagged you for something,

---

40 Nature has placed mankind under the governance of two sovereign masters, *pain* and *pleasure*. It is for them alone to point out what we ought to do, as well as to determine what we shall do. On the one hand the standard of right and wrong, on the other the chain of causes and effects, are fastened to their throne. **Introduction to the Principles of Morals and Legislation** Jeremy Bentham

be prepared to have other things come under scrutiny that weren't even on the Terms of Service before; they make it up as they go along to push SWers out.

These sites that are the last frontier of where content and free speech can be free - are starting to jump on the vanilla social media / sex worker erasure train.

Being invisible until commanded not to be is a full time job. Appear / Disappear. It is like being an on-call sex robot aptly controlled by her human overlords. But what if that is the performance? What if the pleasure model gains sentience after ***not*** jumping through hoops and suddenly realizes her consciousness?

Sex workers are important. We facilitated commerce and economic development alongside the westward expansion, when that terrain was newly being explored. Many madams were high ranking influential figures in their community, and the working girls were regarded highly as well. Take a look at Maeve from *Westworld* or Inara from *Firefly,* characters based on this historical phenomenon. Without us, the fabric that connects society would be far more boring. Less busting ass and less serotonin would exist in the world.

There is a rich history of carnal, human yet sextraterrestrial, women of the night (although now we are available online 24/7). The contemporary new frontier is the cyberworld, and the cyberhorny participants are the ones discovering, terraforming, and charting it. The antipodes of the antipodes of the mind. You are scrolling through my pictures. I am sitting on the Pokemon-plushie covered couch feeding my cat sardines on a holographic platter. It is an illusion.

A job is a task a human should be paid to do. I embrace my job for many reasons. The online sex hustle allows those with mental or physical incapabilities a way to be proactive and make income. Begrudgingly, our life functions through "resources" in contemporary capitalism, and until (not unless, for it has to be a matter of time) our economy collapses, we must play the game.

While engaging in capitalist gameplay, we also play the game of how often, how intensely, we want sex. What is our relationship to pleasure itself. "My ex said my boobs were too small :(" type of posts seeking attention get more engagement than "I love my small boobs, don't you? ;)" The disparity between confidence and pleasure, learned helplessness to gain likes.

But sex is meant to be pleasurable, right?
"Pleasure in the job puts perfection in the work."
~Aristotle

Some people ask me why I got into sex work and if I ever find it humiliating. No, what I find humiliating is deferring to a micromanaging boss or store manager, feeling exhausted at the end of a work day, the manual labor and the repetitive commute. I get deeper into the why and how later, but starting my OF was the catalyst for the adoption of my dream lifestyle: working from home, having a semblance of financial stability, making a living by being myself. You might not see integrity or dignity in sex work, but I do, especially in relation to other jobs I've had.

It angers me when people look down on sex work as if all forms of service-based commerce weren't already sexualized: baristas and bartenders earn tips for how they look and how they much they flirt, likely more than for the quality of their service.

It also makes me angry that there is a ladder of whorerarchy* – a hierarchical way of looking at various components of work to sex work that are 'better than' or 'worse than' others. Flirty barista is fine, fun even. Semi-naked models are artsy, classy even. Cam girl is BAD.

Within each job, the operations are complex. They suit different personality types. My brief experiences in camming, stripping, and escorting didn't bode well for me because I was not suited for the demands of the job; physical tasks and endurance burden me. I thrive behind my keyboard and excel in taking nude pictures.

Being a stripper or an escort are massively taxing jobs that do not get enough credit. They get too much dissection on the forums of reddit. Unfortunately, what we mainly see in the media are either tales of tragic circumstance, or dazzling displays of money and luxury – those polarities become symbolic of sex work at large, and do not give voice to the majority of us in this field. Most of us work voluntarily, work consistently, live a 'normal' lifestyle and earn a salary that is neither impoverished nor extravagant. The middle class of the whorerarchy.

SWERFs argue that the risks and dangerous consequences of sex work as a profession necessitate criminalization. What then of professions like mining, construction, soldiers, police, radiation science, ocean exploration? There are many (male dominated) physically taxing jobs with potential danger– do we stop the progress of civilization based on a possibility of injury? The danger of a profession has never been a cause for its eradication, and it is unlikely that even criminalization will deter the world's oldest profession.

What then of farming, hunting, animal testing, slaughterhouses? Those professions cause harm and death to animals, who do not even have a choice in being attacked. I abhor this unacceptable violence towards living beings. An interesting aside: many sex workers are avid animal lovers, vegetarians/vegans, activists, parents to fuzzy friends. Some of the more successful OF models open animal sanctuaries. Sex symbols like Pamela Anderson and Brigitte Bardot campaigned with PETA and visited Canada to oppose the seal slaughters. Ilona Staller aka Cicciolina ("the cuddly one") was often seen topless at film premieres with stuffed animals. I too am a mother to several kitties and can be seen carrying around my Booba seals at public events.

As for the moral decay of selling sex in private: why not criminalize infidelity, gaslighting, psychological abuse? If by that assumption our relationships are no longer private, why not criminalize immoral actions towards another? Is being a minimum wage worker by choice, or are we all in some way coerced by capitalism to engage in degrading jobs?

Why would a woman choose a career so scandalous?

All that said…
I chose it… because I liked it. I supplied, and there was demand. Following more demand, I supplied more. There was more response, there was more me, there was more money, there was more content. This cycle of supply and demand is what drives my work to this day. I liked it, I was good at it, and sometimes there is not much more to it than that.

Except there is so much more. Underneath the surface… *why* did I like it. Being annoying, horny, naked in images online is not just my choice.. It's my **destiny**.

Photography is our exorcism. Primitive society had its masks, bourgeois society its mirrors. We have our images. ~Jean Baudrillard

In 2019 I made a short film called **Bubbles**. It starred three of my friends, a cardboard cutout of Elon Musk, with a friend doing cinematography and me directing. Guy meets girl at the Trader Joe's produce section. Guy is intent on pursuing and seducing this mysterious brunette, his motives pervy and his gaze predatory. Guy follows girl to her car; in the parking lot, he trips and a bag containing his sex toys, dildos, restraints, and condoms falls out. An explosion of perversion. Girl gets idea, offers him a ride home. He accepts. At her place, he is delighted to see lingerie on the walls and a cam girl setup on her desk. He uses the bathroom to change into a gimp suit.

"It's me, Bubbles." He announces.

She smirks and takes him into the bedroom, one hand pointing him in that direction and one hand holding handcuffs. He gets cuffed to the bed, grinning as he expects submissive pleasure from the gorgeous domme. He thinks he has seduced her. What he did not expect is the girl to grab a knife, menacingly towering over him as his expectation of pleasure turned to horror-movie expressions of fear. Bubbles screamed.

Cut to: the door opens.
"Honey, I'm home!" A dulcet voice calls out.

A blonde businesswoman in a trench coat and briefcase enters. Girl-domme is in the kitchen fixing a plate of spaghetti. She walks over to the businesswoman, they embrace. They sit at the table and the girl brings the businesswoman her dinner. The blonde and the brunette eat together, feast on the sghett, converse warmly. "You're such a good wife," says the blonde. Are there muffled screams coming from the bedroom?

"Shut up Bubbles!" The blonde screams back, privy to the man-meat the brunette brought home. In the kitchen, the skillet sizzles with a chunk of meat resembling a penis.

Close-up on Bubbles screaming through his gimp mask.
Wide view of the blonde and the brunette now eating spaghetti on bed.
Fade out.
Roll credits.

I have always wanted to make a dark, brutal, Lynchian film about camgirls, predators, illusions, horror, and power dynamics. What this film did not show is a deleted scene of the brunette at work: her cam persona being Marie Antoinette.

This little film, though wildly extrapolated into body horror, was originally inspired by my own experiences in the field of camming.

CAMMING

I started on cam sites in 2018, three years after a sexual assault in the film industry pre-MeToo movement had ruined my sexual essence. A sugar daddy/mentor/executive had violated me. He has to pay for his crimes; so men have to pay for my pictures.

After graduating college I started working right away. When I was 22 and working as a set dresser PA, I was sexually assaulted by a studio executive who claimed he wanted to be my mentor - being naive and desperate, I believed him. He got me drunk and raped me multiple times in a Hollywood Hills mansion, and he took photos of me while I was in a vulnerable state. I don't know if they still exist somewhere. I was wearing nothing but a blue thong over my ankles and a terrified look on my face. Silence and denial were coping mechanisms for me and I didn't tell anybody about this until years down the line. I thought, how could this happen to me? I'm so strong, so smart. No.. I would cover it up and delete it from memory. Did it even happen? I began to have PTSD-like flashbacks later on, opened up to some friends, and currently see a therapist to deal with the feelings this brings up. Why and how could this have happened?

People think selling sex is humiliating. Working as an esthetician was humiliating. Working multiple jobs, on many film sets and subjugated by the schedules of the service industry: hotels, clubs, salons, restaurants. Poverty was humiliating. Burnout had already begun, I had no idea. Six days a week of income shuffling was humiliating. Out of college with my Film and Music degrees I expected the entertainment industry to be creative, engaging. Word to the wise: romanticizing never ends well, expectations are the gateway to disappointment. The entertainment industry conditioned me to be very wary of men; I entered the adult field to rewrite my sexual narrative and gain control over it.

I had no power, no agency, which is why I wanted the protagonist to have so much agency and power that she can correct the wrongs by enacting the type of violence that was inflicted on her. Man-hunting as a sport. Castration as a vehicle. The image as the guillotine. The fragmentor, executioner of mind-body function. The anesthesiologist.

Darkness, another film I made in the pre-covid years, was about an assaulted woman who comes back to life after her murder at the hands of her lover, transfigures her into a supernatural FBI agent (justice system sublimation, in opposition to how it does nothing for us in the real world) and allows her revenge, taking the lover's other woman as her own in the end. Why do my films contain such violence, revenge, lesbianism? It is not that I am a full on lesbian as much as I don't feel safe around men — women are the safer sex to be with. I've never had a girlfriend but my sexual experiences with women have been more freeing and unposed than most of my experiences with men. Sex with men was a performance. A blackout. So I will become very good at performing sex with men, staging a drama in my well-lit cam room, curating intercourse on my laptop.

The intercourse of Xanax to mouth to stomach to brain jacked to completion my panic attacks, mitigated my anxiety disorder. Reality was not enough; it was too much to handle. I had been prescribed pharmaceuticals first in high school when my generalized anxiety and chronic pain (from heavy periods, and physical injuries of doing ballet and gymnastics as most young Russian girls are pressured by their parents into doing) had started to show themselves. The prescriptions were intermittent, not constant. A small salve for an inopportune time. A power-up to when weed or alcohol couldn't take down the final boss of insomnia. But after my assault, I began to have panic attacks regularly. My mind wouldn't acknowledge the sequence, "the event" as a therapist called it, but my body did. It wasn't just a nuisance; it was a disability. Anyone who's ever had a panic attack can attest to the sheer fright of it. Running out of air. Hyperventilating. Sweating. Blurred vision. Perceptual changes. Lapses in memory.

"I want to feel your milky body and alternative beauty, send me nudes."

A guy via Facebook message after one of my first hookups in high school. The first time I was requested a nude. I still don't know if we had sex that night because I blacked out — when I blacked back in, I was bleeding, but it might have been because my period had arrived. I will admit there have been a few times I "may or may not" have first had sex, but they were all consensual. The nude-seeker was a boy who was a doppelgänger of someone I had liked in high school, an unrequited lover, and having schrodinger's sex with him was as close I could get to the real thing. I didn't mind, I liked it. I have lost my virginity many times. Once almost to a celebrity, a sketchy British comedian. Perhaps I am still a virgin. I'll never tell. My preferred narrative is that I lost it to my first college boyfriend, who I loved. Love is the breaking of the shell that encloses our understanding.[41]

Reclaiming my narrative from the powerlessness of assault was not the only driver to my selling sex for money and validation: it was also reclaiming my narrative from the embarrassment of rejection. Perhaps I had so many virginities taken because I wanted to give them away to anyone who would take them. I wasn't popular, I wasn't sexy, I wasn't desired or lusted after; but with the few guys who'd shown me attention, to whom I'd given my body… for me, the attention *was* the sex.

My first cam persona was Marie Antoinette, a woman I saw as outrageous, powerful, aesthetically minded, oblivious, facetious. Versailles, Moulin Rouge. Queen for a day as a lady of the night.

I love brothels, boudoirs, prostitutes. Romanticizing sex work is one thing; working in the field is a whole other. No good can come from the kind of prison which glamorizes something; to idealize is to imprison. To romanticize the lingerie, the money, the hotels, the sugar daddies, the lifestyle, is to negate the humanity: of error, of anxiety, of indecision, of slow days and weeks and months, of societal whorephobia and internalized misogyny.

Stories are often told about the logistics of the sexual encounter — money on the dresser, clinical arrangements… we have learned in the recent years from sex workers taking their stories to memoir and essay, that sex work

41 Is this a criminal minds quote?

is often more clinical than intimate or passionate. Curating intimacy takes a fair amount of both administrative organization and performative interpersonal skill. World building is the key to immersive, realistic passion. Beyond the logistics of the encounter, I want to talk about the inner dialogue, the nerves, the power, the fear, the vindication.

Underneath the facetious clownery of all the walls I've built, the intense experiences I have thrown myself into seeking sensation or numbing it, all the layers and layers of bullshit I curate online, the outfits that accessorize a contrived persona, I'm as naked as the day I was born, in the mundaneness and utter boredom that comes with nudity.[42] Nudity is the most banal part of sex; it is the process from first glance to finishing contact, the vulnerable process by which we unmask and strip down, that is the enthralling part.

"It is dangerous to unmask images, since they dissimulate the fact that there is nothing behind them."
— Jean Baudrillard, Simulacra and Simulation

Of course, when your job is to strip or be stripped, even the enthralling process can become tedium. When meeting a client, the process can incur nerves, anxiety, fear. The Xanax never strays too far.

What's in my bag?? Sex worker edition: phone 1, phone 2, lipstick, keys, wallet, taser, butt plug, vape, kratom, xanax.

ESCORTING

In the years between the camming of yesterday and the Onlyfans of today, I worked for an escort agency. I went by Valerie, Alice, Christina. Slipping into another name, another character, another life so separated from my own, anything but my own reality. I was nervous meeting the managers of the agency, expecting a horny pimp, but it was a married couple inspecting me like a piece of meat, a town pig they're debating whether or not to roast for the market. Lipstick on a pig, girlfriend for a night.

The prized pig was ready.
"Stay up late, we'll give you a call".

I show up to the hotel room
"Oh you're a pretty little slice of wonderland." Hands trembling, anxiety more evident than mine. I like when guys are nervous, it makes me feel more comfortable for some reason. Cut to: hotel rooms in Redondo beach, Manhattan beach, Palos Verdes, LAX airport. I brought a kit of lingerie in my Prada bag and did a fashion show. Through my crotchless panties, Rick touched my pussy.

My handlers never talked about sex directly — in the gray area of

42 **We are all naked underneath our clothes.**

legality it was implicit, and even talking about condoms or body parts was in code.
"Asset"
"Meeting"
"Massage"

I wanted so badly to hit record on my voice note app of my other phone, clandestinely hidden in my jacket pocket. If for future safety or proof, just proof to myself that these experiences happened. To share my location with my friends (which I did for the first meetings of the agency but not the client meetings). It was an intimacy I wasn't just giving to these men, but to myself. Every artist needs a private work that's sacred to them. Every writer needs a journal no one will ever read. To relive a time when men paid me to be their companion, rather than rejecting or ignoring me. I could not be ignored. I was the sun in the middle of winter. I was everything. As for the sex acts, I followed the code of my handlers to such precision, probably out of fear, that I didn't do any actual penetration. I let them touch me. I touched them too.

In my brief time my clients were few so I didn't have a strong data pool, but I wanted to test myself in the skill of making men cum by just looking at me, by doing as little as possible while just radiating sex. It was a performance: a blend of every type of sexual theatrics I've ever done (on stage playing music doing my horny little outfit changes, on OF making alternative porn, in the club stripping) tailor made to one person's desire and preferences. Order a stripper to your house and she will come bearing pokemon plushies and Bad Dragon dildos. She possesses the gift of touch. Every time I touch someone I rewire their DNA.

Two components of sexuality: the client focused and the personal. The way I touch myself and let my boyfriend touch me is different from how I perform touching myself for the camera. I bring a magical energy to the sexual encounter: there are many parallels to being a reiki healer and a sex worker. I've had OF clients ask me for tarot readings and reiki sessions rather than the standard nude cam show and I've observed similar results energetically. At the end of a session with me, nude or clothed, I witness the man release.

It never gave me nerves in the moment. The moments before, the moments after, I was experiencing existentialism, but during the session I was possessed by a clarity of out-of-body confidence. The men weren't ones being healed; I was.

"How many faces, how many bodies can you recognize, with your eyes closed, only by touching them? Have you ever closed your eyes and acted unconsciously? Or loved someone so blindly, you could almost feel their energy in a dark room and be moved by the powerful touch of their ideas?"
— Jean Baudrillard

Ultimately I quit the agency for a banal reason: I cannot endure night driving. If there's anything that gives me anxiety, it's driving in LA, especially at night. I don't see very well in the dark, and glasses and Tesla navigation are not enough.

At the time my Onlyfans started picking back up after a break due to the porn ban, so I retreated to a world more known, safe, comfortable to me. I sometimes wonder if I would ever escort again. If they offered like a 9-5 day-time arrangement, I probably would. But as far as I know, they don't, and I have my own reservations about independent escorting (which I know many workers prefer) so I stay within my four walled insane asylum/sex asylum, tethered to my phones and laptops like a calf to its mother's teat.

Every sex worker needs to sometimes be unprofessional by having recreational sex, to differentiate. When I am emotionally exhausted from having performative sex online, I regenerate by having physical sex with my boyfriend. When I am physically exhausted, I bask in the nothingness of glorious Me Time, the energetic shift of being alone. When I'm recharged in that way, I am able to work again. The cycle continues.

The tedium, the exhaustion, the burnout. I had already been feeling it: from work, from life. Father; mother. The weight of the subjectivity. Just as I started years ago in the sex work field to mitigate sex traumas, I started more recently writing this book and *The Cyberhorny Dream Diaries*, pensive and penisive at a crossroads in my life.

As I gazed into the dark skyline of the horny city, I couldn't help but wonder.. is my life branching out in front of me like a green fig tree, and the tip of each fat purple fig is but a perv gooning in the night? From the tip of every branch, like a fat purple fig, a wonderful future jacked it and gooned.

We must avoid falling into the trap of indecision.

ONLYFANS

When I started my Onlyfans I based it off an already extant social media presence — a world of curated self-taken images. It took me a while to get the mechanics right; the first nudes I took were rudimentary. In every new venture I had ever historically tried, I had no idea what I was doing. My approach to life is experimental and intuitive. What I like, what I'm good at; I milk. When I fail, I proceed with dissociation. I've boarded up the windows — a catatonic plateau. If I make a mistake, if I break a rule, no I didn't.

Breaking a cardinal rule of the field:

I DATED A FAN

(discoursed and dissected in Chapter 6)

The wheel of sevens
The law of fives
Papa hobo don't hide your eyes, mother mountain don't kill your unborn child
~Bright Eyes

Zero Illumination was another film I made. The protagonist, dealing with a breakup through a psychedelic bender and self-destructive substance abuse, eventually undergoes an abortion when she realizes she's pregnant with her former lover's spawn. Is the film pro or anti abortion? Why is love full of haters? Why is being in love an act of human sacrifice, ripping your heart out to display it to the unconcerning sun? What am I too afraid to talk about that I must codify it into image, cinema, symbol, simulacra, capitalist gameplay?

Curveball. May every day be a new blank slate, each box on the calendar a [43]present to unwrap, each crack of dawn a reminder that the violated past has gone to the graveyard of memory, and the future remains unblemished, entropic, innocent.

Me when I take my Xanax: ohhh fuckkkk.. you're gonna make me calm

"There is no aphrodisiac like innocence."
— Jean Baudrillard

---

43 Every day is a gift that's why they call it the _______

4B: Autobiography Time; Genesis of my OF

"Actors are so fortunate. They can choose whether they will appear in tragedy or in comedy, whether they will suffer or make merry, laugh or shed tears. But in real life it is different. Most men and women are forced to perform parts for which they have no qualifications. Our Guildensterns play Hamlet for us, and our Hamlets have to jest like Prince Hal. The world is a stage, but the play is badly cast."
— Oscar Wilde

I decided my OF would be an exaggeration, almost a satire, of the capitalist sex market, and how people online already viewed my chaotic "personal brand". Innocent, but horny. Artistic, but not pretentious. Attainable, but unreachable. Proletariat, but bourgeoisie. A starving artist flexing her Tesla. A parasocial paradox. I made content every single day. Nowadays I cannot even fathom that through the hindsight of burnout, as I reuse my massive archive of past content and only make new things when the mood strikes or I absolutely have to. Looking back at that time, I don't know how I even managed to pull it off.

It all started with my Tesla album and live streaming / documentation of it early in the pandemic. That was what I was doing on OF before, and whilst posting nudes. There is an article on WMF deep diving into Hentai & Crack Vol 1. It was kind of an endurance experiment to see if I could do it. I had cammed in the years before but my inconsistency made me terrible at it, so in order to not feel inadequate I wanted to see what consistency on a nsfw platform would do for me. Like so many people, I lost my day job in the coronavirus era so I had a lot of free time to dedicate to … whatever creative or personal pursuit had been bubbling. I activated my OF profile, which I had already been considering in the prepandemic months, and really took the plunge.

Turns out I was pretty good at it. Within my first few weeks on the platform I was in the top 14% of creators just by showing up, and by the end of 2020 I was in the top 4, 3, 2% and the year following I had crossed into the 1%.

If this sounds like a flex:

1. After years of self loathing, let me have this lol

2. Detaching the ego and analytically observing for growth, this shows how the stock goes up at the end of the fistcal year at the ball street market of the girl economy — and how it falls back down. My page has fluctuated between the 1-2, 0-1, 2-3, 1-2%'s through the years and I definitely feel that impacting my motivation, burnout, self assessment, and credibility within the sw community

3. In itself this is not a meteoric rise, if anything it's shameful compared to how other bigger creators hustle

4. The percentage rankings system is an aggregated tool to gauge growth and inspire motivation; often though the competitive aspect of this can be soul crushing. I see this ranking system as a load of dog shit and inauthenticity. It also does not make as much money as people may think to be in a particular percentage and is mostly used as an advertising ploy. In a High Cost of Living area, a 2% or above ranking can be enough to have a decent, comfortable living. Anything below the 5% I would say is barely enough to get by.

5. My plateau is like a soft retirement. I've turned active income into passive income. While I don't have the same amount of fans and earnings any more, I can maintain my lifestyle and have my needs met. I've proven to myself several times over starting from scratch, that what goes down can come back up. It just gets more difficult each time.

Note: don't hate the player, hate the game.

It's absolutely evil that we have to exist in this cold and heartless capitalist system that rewards status based carnivorous self-advertising and discourages heart based human authenticity. We all have emotions tied to capital stemming from our individual upbringings in a class system we have no control over.

It has always been important to me to create my own safety nets, keep an eye on my budget, run a tight ship in business + a tight pussy in commerce, and observe societal injustices, advocating for the underdog. Every day of my life I worry about survival, I worry about stability, I worry about my future: it's a trauma that cannot be easily unlearned. It's a wound that cuts deep. Still, I'm not immune to greed and gratification. I like my *things*. If you can't beat capitalism, make it goon for you.

"Why join the navy if you can be a pirate?"
— Steve Jobs

Ding ding ding: jackpot!!! Jack(it) pot !!

The first realization of the lucrative nature of Onlyfans was startling and amazing for me. I never expected to actually make any money doing it. I'm just being myself and sexually objectifying the most appealing elements of my persona. When I realized there was demand for that, demand for me, I capitalized on it. Timing was in my favor - right at the start of the pandemic, everyone was at home, terrified and uncertain and bored and horny, gazing at a screen. Thousands of people gazed at my image on the screen as I advertised in slutty outfits, produced my album, did random mundane stuff around the house, took selfies, played Pokemon, monologued, did nothing, read a book, manically cried, cut my bangs, put on makeup, took off my bra, used my first vibrator, leaned into the gooning, seduced a Bernie Sanders cardboard cutout etc.

Even now, as I work part-time and no longer have the numerical gratification I had at my peak, I subconsciously ask, "wtf is wrong with me? This is catastrophic. Why am I such a failure?" Failure and success are cyclical and subjective. It is still empowering to maintain a fanbase at a plateau; the competitive and perfectionistic aspects of e-capitalism have definitely conditioned me in a way where I see a bad week as a failure, which to me is embarrassing, even if it's been an overall rewarding four years.

Four more years!!! Will there be four more years? Four more months? Four more days? I don't know. This field is not for the faint of heart because it is wildly unpredictable, especially as far as longevity goes. Life never promises us certainty, especially not in adult entertainment, where attention spans are as fleeting as cum down a sewer drain, and every day a shiny new barely legal toy enters the market.

"Talking to you is not a drain it's a sewer" -editor

It was gratifying to have random strangers salivate over me when I've had a history of body image issues and dysmorphia, eating disorder woes, and men irl rejecting me for not being hot enough. That self-defeating attitude rears its ugly head every time I experience a micro rejection. "Oh no, that post flopped, that shoot made no money, I'm a has-been, I'm not hot anymore". And just like that a stream of new subscribers will come seemingly out of nowhere. Well, I'm hot now, bitch, ha! A product of value in the girl economy. To transcend that loop of <<succeeded/failed>> dichotomy thinking, I had to earn validation within myself, with long term weekly therapy and inner shadow work, not the vacuous cycle of marketing and externalizing. A whole college course could be dedicated to social media marketing for the creator economy.

I ponder on how my past 4 years on OF were like a postgrad program of sorts. Will I use it with practicality, or with stupidity? We'll see. I already feel the repercussions of taking a break: the horror of a tanked income. It's terrifying. What the fuck am I gonna do? Stay tuned… will people remember me? Does it matter? Will I remember me? Fondly contemplate the fine years of being sexy on the internet? Or dissociate, disengage, abandon, neglect, violate, disown?

There are some memories from my upbringing that I cannot remember or admit - not even to myself. But try as the subconscious might to repress them, to protect the consciousness, the body remembers. It remembers in the night – when I want to let my body rest, but it cannot. Tweeking Tuesday. Mental Illness Monday.

Grinding ceaselessly and relying on only myself is a horrible feeling. Unlike people with invisible advantages, I can't just ask daddy and mommy to deposit 2 grand into my checking account every month, hire a team of managers to help my career, or even have family members be there emotionally. My traumas have intertwined the financial and the personal, money and love, safety and affection, and that shit is labyrinthine to detangle. Girls shouldn't have to work anyway. We should be provided for. I maen we can choose our own path, feminism equality blah blah, but... Being a female provider is not a girlboss slay, it's a heartbreaking agony (Chapter 10…).

Everyday I'm hustlin, every day I'm suffering. The body keeps score, and I'm losing. I don't like to let people see how alone in this world I am. How terrified I feel. I may front online that I'm vaping and vibing but I cry myself to sleep at night after my vape hit because I fear not having security. I fear poverty. I fear weakness. Wah, wah, woe is me. Little bitch shit.

AUTOBIOGRAPHY TIME
(cue the melancholic violin concerto)

As a young Russian child whose family immigrated to Los Angeles, my deadbeat dad somewhere unknown and unknowable, my single mom overwhelmed in a country she didn't want to be in, wrestling a language she didn't understand, navigating the field of dating men, and working at the playboy store to pay the bills, back when rent in LA was only $450 a month – my unthinking mother had no idea the future her child would one day succumb to. **The future of being an overworked, traumatized perfectionist**. Not the porn, the porn is not the problem.

Per my parents' regimented parameters, I had to get straight A's and be thin. When I matured young and sprouted breasts and got my period at 11, my mom (a late bloomer who barely got hers at 15) thought I was gonna get fat. This naturally would affect me being able to land a man. So she verbally berated me, despite my skinnylicious genetics telling a logical story otherwise.. And so began a lifelong hate affair with my body, and my leap into the comforting arms of anorexia.

Doing ballet for a decade in my youth also lovingly nurtured my eating disorder (more on that in chapter 12B). Strangely enough, taking nudes and objectifying my body for the compliments of strangers has helped me acclimate to myself physically. My fans are attracted to me even if I'm not skinny or huge tits or perfect. They actually enjoy my flaws, and that has fostered a better relationship with my self image. It's still external validation, but you know what... the devil you know… (and the devil you don't know). The mother wound will always be there. It's not bleeding or hemorrhaging anymore, but the scar is hideous. And the father wound… it's not a wound, it's necrosis sis. Amputation!! It's phantom limb syndrome in the shape of a father.

Raw dogging reality is rough and I often seek to numb myself, distance, avoid, excise, escape, detach. Money please. Heroin please.

Fear of intimacy please. My parents never hugged or cuddled me. Decades later here I am coping by cuddling up to the oxycontin. Cuddling up to drugs. Cuddling up to a facade of attachment. Cuddling up to a wheel of coping mechanisms. Cuddling up to porn, to being a slut. But never, ever, god forbid, letting anybody close. Someone with a proper wallet can fuck me in their mind, but no one is allowed to cuddle up. Penetrate my body but leave my mind alone. I just buried those memories, please don't make me dig them back up.

In Neon Genesis Evangelion ep. 22,
Asuka, one of the central characters, is targeted by a psychic attack that unearths her memories, her weaknesses, her relationship with her family. It destroys the confident pilot's psyche, shatters her ego, violates her cognition. It's one of the darkest moments on the show. It's too real. It's something I relate to and fear all too deeply. It took me a few rewatches of the series to realize how fragile Asuka really is, and when I did, it held up a mirror to me. The graveyard of memory is not to be dug up. These thoughts remain in the safety deposit box I threw away the key.

The CIA couldn't torture that out of me.

I picture myself in a graveyard at night on top of a little mountain with my shovel, hurling the last pieces of dirt on top of the mound of buried memories. Burying them alive. Suffocating my psyche. Violating my cognition, my pleasure, my joy, into full decay and perceptual dissonance. Forced cognitive distress. Mind rape. How then, do I unrape myself?

Why do I do the work I do? Who knows, really? Why does anyone do anything? A behavioral study in ennui. **Because we can.** It's not rocket science.

My mom and dad… sluts.

We see the tormented crackhead Nastya receive her life purpose in a moment of anagnorisis.
Peripeteia: a reversal of fortune where she is rich now
This was the apotheosis of my girlhood …

Everything I do, every day I live, every experience I accumulate, all goes towards Cyberhorny in some way.

What is the moneymaker?
Anyway, back to work. So, what makes me the most money? It's hard to say which of my stuff have more appeal with marketing cause all of my videos sell about the same.

Breakdown: 50% of my income is from tips/customs/services, 30% from subscriptions, 15% from PPV (pay per video messages), 5% from other. This varies month to month depending on promotion, tips, and subscriber count.

Everyone who has a foot these days thinks they can make an income by posting a foot pic. Let me ask you a question, reader– does your foot make six figures a year? I make six fingers a year.

✞

Where did I get good at my craft? What sexual misadventures led me to being skilled in the bedroom, in the cyber bedroom? My very first sexual experiences... Blow job for over 45-50 mins. Going back to the gambling and "up and down" making the other person's sex disappear like a magician. I like to call myself a penician[44].

Lingerie and morality: a mother's enantiodromia.

When I was moving, one of the movers opened my ottoman and a bunch of lingerie and sex toys fell out (Bubbles moment) and my mom saw and freaked out. "I HAVE KINKY SEX MOM SO WHAT??????!!!!?!?!?" Wow, that was a conversation.

My mother had always worn sexy outfits, fishnet tights, see-through tops, leather pants, high heels. She picked me up from school in Playboy shirts and gave me some of her hand-me-downs. I had found sex toys when I was a child sifting though her drawers being a nosy ass gremlin trying to find dolls or makeup, so perhaps her finding mine was an unexpected visit from the forces of karma. "Why do you have this kinky harness?!" "Uhh idk mom I like it I wonder why..."

Much of what I talk about in therapy all these years relates to my upbringing and parents (doesn't it always??) and I guess the main consensus I always get is to carve **my** own life for **my**self on **my** own terms and re-parent **my**self. ME ME ME. My adult work, my teenage attention span, my geriatric hermithood, my inner child.

Dr. Nicole LaPera wrote some amazing things on healing of the inner child, and even on my ayahuasca trip I got hit with an extremely prominent vision of inner child healing. Bruh that's cray cause like dude.. super intense and emotional themes do come up that I require a healing ritual with regularity to help ground and soothe. Foreshadowing Chapter 13.

✞

44 Gambling isn't exactly a passion: the pleasure one derives from it is too crystalline. It is a cold ecstasy which deals with money not as meaning, value, depth or substance, but in the pure form of appearance or disappearance. - Baudrillard - interviews

In a survey on my OF page, when asking my subscribers if I should tone down the depressingly long posts, the personal, and be more positive, most people voted something along the lines of "post the honest stuff even if it's weird/dark" but I swear to god.... The long winded posts, vulnerable videos, more authentically driven things like that, while a core of my being, always make me lose subscribers. Some of them are driven to connect with me on dark personal topics, but many people U-turn from the pornofield when depression appears. When I need to make money, the depression suddenly disappears.

Reality can be a nightmare for "engagement", which is a driving force of maintaining my account and in turn my livelihood. True authenticity is bad for business. It's a seesaw: part of me really cares about how I am perceived by others, part of me just doesn't give a fuck and will continue to emote profusely even if it's dark, gross, cringe, too real, dystopian.

The wounds of being a healer.

(This is a gorgeous graphic)

Why do I do this shit? Gotta grind for the Oxycontin plush doll.

We carry others' pain as well as our own. Trauma is stored in the balls.
Blaise Pascal published the *Pensées*. I will publish the *Penisées*.

Viewers on my OF could see a full video of me, for example, ranting about depression hooting and hollering like goddamn Lady Macbeth drinking from an ornate goblet making my bed whilst sleep deprived – venting about the cyber world, parasociality, alienation, collaboration, the discontents of creativity. Creativity is not good for this business. Positivity = money. The video is lunacy, unhinged and nonsensical. If not for the nudity, it wouldn't last a day on Onlyfans. This is the type of dark web shit I like seeing in people I follow, but I'm very well aware that practically no one shares my tastes lol so I will sex it up for you.

MY TOP 10 SEXIEST NERVOUS BREAKDOWNS
ANxxxIOUS GIRL MASTURBATING ON ANTIDEPRESSANTS
SEXY BITCH WITH LOW SEROTONIN GETS FUCKED HARD

What's it like being perceived? The very notion of being perceived in any reality is already so strange, it morphs into a whole other level with the e-self. The e-self is so fragmented and there will always be people who find me cool, people who find me insufferable, people who don't care to form an opinion. Being "positive" online is me in cosplay.

While I can see why that turns people off, there's that trade off I must consider between my true feelings and the false positive nature I share online. I can call myself an optimist and it would be true of my avatar, but not of me. It's not mellow in here, it's a funeral every day and a wake every night. Motivation to live has taken a hit out on itself and is going missing. It's not that I don't feel joy or drive or excitement, I just feel it less than others.

Will the sharks in the waters smell the inauthenticity of a false optimism and drop subscriptions faster than if I remain authentically somewhat tortured?

"Never work." -Guy Debord

NYQUIL FOR DINNER? MORE LIKE DEADGUYQUIL

5: The Intimacy of Commerce: Navigating Distress and Disassociation Within E-Capitalism, and The Use of Strategy in Sexual Economics

"The reigning economic system is a vicious circle of isolation. Its technologies are based on isolation, and they contribute to that same isolation. From automobiles to television, the goods that the spectacular system chooses to produce also serve it as weapons for constantly reinforcing the conditions that engender lonely crowds."

— Guy Debord

The Intimacy of Commerce. The dissociation and fragMENtation. The technologies that connect us that also disconnect us. The nuisances of the firewalls. The decisions behind the paywalls. The raw nerves of the 1:1 encounter. The warfare of emotions. As these concepts intersect, it is a complicated tangle, but the cultural perception seems to be that being an OF girlie is easy. Post some pics, turn on guys, receive money, rinse and repeat. We make it look effortless, right? On a daily basis, through our advertising on social platforms and within our paid networks, we interact with a diverse pool of men.

Even though they are anonymous and behind a screen, their behavior incites real-life reactions from us, and our behavior incites reactions from them. Reactions like spending money, spending time on the platform, spending energy complimenting or insulting.

Many men. Types of men. Who is the ideal client? What is the proper etiquette in communicating with a sex worker?

Sexual Economics Redux

There are men who readily part with their money for a beautiful woman, and men who are the exact opposite, withholding from a woman to punish her. Freud would have a field day investigating the fisco-Oedipal complex. At the end of the day, when we clock in, we have to let go of all emotional strife and become a sex doll, *the* sex doll we advertise to be, and make that coin. Good paying customers? We love em. Time wasters, trolls, haters? Good bye. As they say on RuPaul's Drag Race: If they ain't paying your bills, pay those bitches no mind.

Every business has unique relationships with clients. Building a clientele in any field is difficult, but they all overlap. Is the client satisfied with the service, and will they come back. Are your services necessary to the client. Are your services recession-proof. In sex work, the intimacy of transactional relationships is magnified.

Negotiations play a key part in the agreement of Relationships that are at their core: commerce. I'll do x action for y amount of money at z time. Whether we like it or not, love is transactional – not in dollars but in pathology.

Love is expensive psychologically. Love costs us all in currency other than money. Is there a currency exchange for romance? 1 bowl of quinoa salad = 30 dollars of love = footjob

"All sex is choke sex when you're being strangled by the invisible hand of capitalism" ~anonymous Tinder profile

What is the market value of desire?

In this day and age, everyone has to compromise[45]. I'm right.

Everything we post on the internet is plumage in the elaborate display of digital courtship – whether we intuit it or pay for it.

"In reality, the laborer belongs to capital before he has sold himself to capital. His economic bondage is both brought about and concealed by the periodic sale of himself, by his change of masters, and by the oscillation in the market price of labor power. Capitalist production, therefore, under its aspect of a continuous connected process, of a process of reproduction, produces not only commodities, not only surplus value, but it also produces and reproduces the capitalist relation; on the one side the capitalist, and, on the other, the wage-laborer." — Karl Marx, Das Kapital

I've seen miracles happen. An astrologer once told me I had a placement that "magnetizes" money to me: I attract just enough money to get by, often at the last minute.

---

45 Compromise their own desires to match what I want to do. Period.

It doesn't feel as good to earn as it does to receive. I don't feel desired or accomplished when I *earn* $1000 but I feel desired and provided for when I receive $1000. It fulfills a deeper need than money. Overwork, grinding, husting, struggling, navigating, are all associated with the mother – being in a masculine role, being out of place, not having enough, not being enough. I saw the stress my mom acquired both mentally and physically working multiple jobs her whole life, and while I was being her caretaker during her disability which robbed me of my mid 20s. This opened my eyes to what I did not want and what I would be willing to do to avoid having a life of stress or pain, disadvantage, lack of opportunity.

In the moments I've delved into my personal history of paternal abandonment, class tension, and the humiliation of low income upbringing, I reflect on my relationship with money and how I try to salve those deep rooted wounds.

Let's say I have $100. I spend that $100 on shoes. Okay. I can live with that. I've had my eye on shoes for a while. Let's then say a fan sent me $100 to spend on my anxiety medication. Or a date who buys me those $100 shoes I've been eyeing. That feels free to me, even though it's the same amount. Let's once more say I have $100, and I'm on a date with a man who asks me to split a $200 concert ticket with him, $100 each. That $100 feels like $200 to me, even though it's the same amount. The labor of splitting a cost with a man doubles my energetic currency. And for what? It's girl math. It may not make sense to you, but it's a PhD for me.[46]

When I point to a random object in my house, most likely it was purchased by a fan. The music equipment is from user09869; the purse is from xxx_daddy_420; the myriad of pokemon plushies have been crowdfunded by a gaggle of men. That part is cool. It's my favorite part. I'm honored and thankful. It does not fill the void that is my father's abandonment, but it's a step in healing. Girl math™.

One thing about banking a deal with the devil - he always comes to collect.

Of course, in capitalism, most of us have no choice but to work. So let's work out what service costs what. What is the difference between sexting, video calls, cock ratings? In the myriad of entrees on a sex worker's service menu, which one works for which client? What does the client want? How do you charge for images, instances of sex?

The more resonant question is, what is the value of your time. Additionally, the distinction must be made between OF worker who is full time in this profession, vs OF hobbyist who is doing it for attention/exhibitionism/income supplementation or "fun money". The median income of a OF model is

46 Not my circus, not my monkeys

around $180~ USD, and statistics are easily skewed by both inactive accounts which don't have active subscribers, or celebrity OF models who make considerably more than the average model based on social status and popularity. I cannot speak for anyone else in any other situation, but I can offer my experience as a working girl.

“ىف هنوعنصي ال , مهاوه ىلع هنوعنصي ال مهنكل , مهخيرات نوعنصي رشبلا نإ
و ةنيعتم نوكت .. ةرشابم اهنوهجاوي فورظ ىف لب مهسفنأب اهنوراتخي فورظ
ىضاملا نم ةثوروم”
— **Karl Marx,** **سكرام لراكل لاملا سأر**

In the beginning, I got away with price skimming. Lower prices than the rest of the market for the highest possible volume of subscribers. An evil, vile, or simply naive thing from the capitalist beginner's mind: for if one business cuts its prices, it undercuts hundreds of others.

I started off with a 6$ subscription with half-off sales for subscribers' first month, promo deals for their first service, PPVs sent weekly. Fans sent in custom requests and video chat requests daily, and I did them all as soon as I could, did as much as I could possibly do to grasp the moment and stay productive, stay lucrative, stay relevant. The demand element sustained me; it was gratifying to be asked and to be desired. But I could not continue this for long: 7 days a week, 12+ hour days, were a recipe for fatigue and burnout. The hamster wheel is torture; our century's version of judas cradles and stretching racks.

A year later I gave myself a raise and doubled my rates on services, as well as my subscription cost. Clients were fewer, my subscriber count halved, but the workload was more manageable. My income was more or less unaffected; **stable** as a horse grazing in the hay. The loads were more manageable. Mrs. Pussy had to delegate and organize her time. Once I started working on this book and worked less on my OF, I raised my rates further, 1. To adjust for inflation and 2. To make sure that if I was away from my art project, the client project was worth my time.

On my page, I would let my subscribers know that I respond to all messages within my time capability and bandwidth. Messages with tips get auto-pinned to the top of my inbox, so those were prioritized. While I answered everyone, if the chat convo started to linger, I charged for my time. To dudes who just said
“Hi”
“Hey babe”
“How r u”

I rarely actually responded; if I did, it's usually with a string of emoji's or a cute little pussycat gif. When I felt particularly spicy I played with them and gently trolled; a meme, a youtube video, a picture of an ancient babylonian demon. The demon is only foreplay.

SERVICES RENDERED:

Sexting - sending messages and pictures back and forth. This can be done in real time, or pre-recorded. Many top models have a saved “sexting folder” in their OF archive specifically for this: small clips, audio recordings, and progressively naughtier pictures to curate the experience of sexting as if in real time. The content is generalized enough to suit any subscriber. One could do this while sitting on the toilet or doing laundry. “Did I make u cum yet?”
I personally never liked doing sexting, and my ever-changing look made it difficult to make any pre-recorded folders, so all my sessions have always been done in real time. I see the appeal in “sexting folders” because it’s like a cheat code to make this easier, especially if one has several subscribers wanting this at the same time. Agencies or high-volume fan pages have dedicated “sexters”, assistants whose sole purpose is to do mass sexting simultaneously, who get a cut of the profit. Prices vary, but models can make anywhere from 50-200 per session. This is often the most lucrative service provided on OF, it yields the highest return upon the least amount of effort. Still, it is a massive load of work to do it well. Even in porn, practice makes perfect.

Camming/video chat - a real time encounter in a private video room between the model and the client. Skype, FaceTime, Zoom, Discord, and Snapchat are all apps that do this. I’ve usually set up my dudes with a zoom link and then, off we goooooon. Everybody of course does this differently; I have had 10 min (135$) 30 min (250$) and 60 min ($369) time slots. Most guys finish in 5-10 mins. Occasionally, guys have just wanted to talk, or do a tarot reading, or a reiki session. Whatever they want to do with their time in the room, I’m usually there for it.

Girlfriend experience (GFE) - a set amount of time (usually a day, sometimes a weekend, sometimes half a day) where the model is the virtual girlfriend of the client, and the client gets more attention and affection. This is broad and variable but can include various things like, priority messaging and always being available for chat, initiating chat, audio notes, sending sfw and nsfw pics throughout the day. Some include a short phone or video call.

Custom video - exactly what it sounds like; a client gives a model a scenario or a fantasy that they want her to perform. This is probably the most varied service both in content and in pricing. This is because of the amount of detail and work involved: filming, editing, uploading etc amount to many moving parts. It is the most time-consuming/painstaking to create, especially if the client has a detailed narrative or script. The clients who request custom content often are recurring.

Cock rating - dudes want their penises looked at and rated, sometimes praised, sometimes degraded (SPH: small penis humiliation, is a popular fetish). This varies in price as well; some models do a rating for 10, others for 100. It can depend on the type of format: written ratings or just numbers at a lower cost, fully nude videos with detailed explanation of the penis at hand at a significantly higher rate. I have done little fun things in my videos to set a flirty and playful artistic tone; some guys are shameless about showing their penis portraits, others more bashful and vulnerable.
The worst thing is guys sending unsolicited nudes and dick pics; it's an instant restrict or block from most models. You want my attention? You can buy it.
The second worst thing is hagglers – "Oh hey babe I see you do x for 100, can you do it for me for 50 cause I'm so special and it's my birthday and I'm having a bad day?"
In what world would someone have the audacity to negotiate with a restaurant, or a clothing store? The nerve of men trying to pay less for nudes, or not pay at all. It becomes evident how many men don't take sex work seriously or even see it as a real job.

Panties/polaroids/physical ephemera - Some die hard, (or just *hard*) fans are horny to have a physical item from their favorite model. Panties worn by a model are a common fetish, but this is in the gray area of the OF terms of service. The TOS tends to be annoyingly vague, and there are conflicting answers about this – some say it's allowed as long as it's not directly advertised as "worn" panties, just a garment; others say to sell panties through any other adult site to avoid getting banned by the OF AI filters. I've sold panties in the beginning of my OF, but stopped after too much bureaucratic nuisance.

So Amazon . com can sell medieval torture replica devices but a sex worker can't sell her panties over OF?

Interesting.

These transactions are processed by OnlyFans, and the site takes a 20% cut. If a model just received a 100$ gross tip, she receives 80$ net at the end. Payments are processed after 7 days; an OF account has a pending balance (yet to be processed) and available balance (can be withdrawn whenever). This can be set to automatic withdrawal (end of every week, end of every month), or manual withdrawal (one can withdraw at any point in the day or week if the available balance is over 50$. The auto withdrawal functions like a paycheck, the manual keeps money slowly trickling in at smaller amounts, so it's up to each individual to decide how they want their cash to flow.

Depending on the month, my most popular services are GFE, camming session, or custom video. I rarely sext. I don't push or advertise my services beyond a listing of a menu pinned to my page; clients come to me. I like to let it be as organic as possible. I like them to want me, to need me. Me and only me – no assistants, bots, or bullshit.

"In the mid 90s, the internet started to flood with sites claiming to be run by 'real amateurs' posting their own photos. The reality was that many - some estimates of 95% - were actually run by entrepreneur web builders with little connection to the content they posted. Like gender-benders in online games, men pretending to be female porn stars could get ahead of the competition if they did it convincingly enough. By the end of the nineties, authentic amateur models on the net were so rare that it became a sign of exclusivity, a selling point for attracting new subscribers." -Samantha Cole, How Sex Changed the Internet

A single OF account can be a multi-person storefront. S16E3 of RuPaul's Drag Race illuminated the phenomenon of OF ghostwriting: contestant Amanda ru-vealed that she works for an agency that manages OF girls, sending messages/sexts guys while the girls are on vacation in Cancun or Ibiza or wherever. You never know who is on the other side of that messaging line.

What are the perils of the banking system for SWers?

Paypal, Cashapp, Venmo can ban us because of the nature of services we provide; their firewalls are stronger than our paywalls. Ask any sex worker why they don't use those payment apps anymore and you'll see how little structures there are in place to actually protect us or even simply allow us to work and exist. Like the social media regime, they ban with a heavy hammer. Credit card processing companies run porn; every time these companies have change in policy, it affects porn sites, usually instigated further by conservative "Christian" groups. Don't they know heaven is horny?

Bust through the firewall into heaven
~Bright Eyes

The glamorization of SW (especially online SW) has created the idea, from a few success stories, that just about anyone can join and try to make it. The pandemic really busted open the free market of online SW, and in our economy many people want to make as much $ as possible as fast as possible. This is a positive thing because it opens up opportunities for success to just about anyone who chooses to do this, and also a negative thing because it also opens up a portal for scammy, spammy, low quality creators who give veterans (and SW in general) a bad name. This can make clients distrust honest creators due to bad experiences with someone spammy who most likely is just trying to grab success/clout without caring about quality or authenticity. On the reverse side, it also opens up the portal for nasty little scamming men. A whole world of charlatans to deal with. I just love capitalism, don't you? Oh the free market. How cruelly you wrap your warm embrace around my bosom.

What many new creators don't realize is how hard it really is, especially to do this for a long time sustaining an income, and how there are many inner psychological nuances that come with selling your nude body online. But everyone is free to make their own choices and run their page how they want. From my perspective there are reasons to start new content pages anytime, and quality authentic content is always a good thing whether it's a veteran creator or a newcomer, because it reflects positively on the cultural perception of SW (which is so demonized from the jump). The burnout is very strong in our industry, not many of us can do this for a lifetime, so there will always be new people to set a new paradigm.

A way to make money from home that doesn't completely deplete energy is incredible, and some of us don't have many other opportunities so online SW is one of the best options. For people who want to start out and take it seriously, it's a great thing. Guys are always into having the shiny new toy, they get tired of seeing the same girls over again and want the newest girl on the market (that's a whole other tirade tho, the fickleness of male psychology and sexual perception).

However, people just 'jumping on the wave' for the sake of it is a very real phenomenon that can frustrate me as well. It's going to keep happening while OF and the like are still popular in our culture. It is really annoying when some celebrity who already has plenty of money and fame is starting an OF, cosplaying as a SW and skewing the platform for a lot of us .. One positive that comes out of this is that it normalizes and destigmatizes SW to some degree. Our jobs can actually be seen as real jobs (I can't count how many times I've seen ppl refer to SW as if it's not a real job).

Discourse on SWERFs and antiporn women: ...shut up!!
When women be like: my husband looks at porn !! Shut down the industry and its workers!! It's a pathology thing - not an industry thing.

When porn viewing becomes pathological. Paraphilia or couples counseling time???

To women who fear their S/O leaving them for an adult entertainer. As a sex worker I can tell you that 99.9% of dancers/models are not looking for any love in the club, or in the chat room. Adult entertainers sell a sexy fantasy for money. Often it is more clinical and transactional than romantic or sensual. There are unwritten rules and boundaries to not entangle with any customers, while still leaving them satisfied with the entertainment. A man is less likely to cheat in a strip club than a local bar where there are drinks flowing, and men and women are often looking for hookups or romantic involvement. I understand the insecurity stemming from a man being around nude sexually attractive women - but this comes down to trust and boundaries. If you have a strong boundary with him not going to a strip club, or looking at porn online, he may have to forsake those things out of respect for your relationship. This shouldn't be so difficult.

What is difficult is getting so caught up in the digital realm, the intimacy of commerce, that it becomes consuming or gets in the way of daily life, no boundary between the digital and the real. When the work week has no room for resting or processing, no room at all to detach, the body and mind subconsciously create their own detachment.

Discourse on Dissociation.
It is a defense mechanism that offers the luxury of detachment. This luxury is often temporary, and a crack in the split reality can shake the fortressed mind's delicate balance at a later time.
Dissociate from myself enough to view myself as a tool - a place of enough body confidence to be nude online.
Dissociation and memory.
I wasn't ready to talk about it for years. I process at length.
Am I retconning my own lore?
I shouldn't be in a grave but my memories should be.
I'm remembering but I want to forget.

One must become a master of dissociating and dealing with egoic fragmentation.

"Never regret your mistakes. Admire the courage it took to attempt the unknown." -a fortune card from my Yogi tea

Discourse on Materialistic Thought:
Sexual economics. Wife economy. Dowry and sellage in the future when girls are a scarcity. The very existence of SWers is a political act. ("I do not do politic tho, I am model" - from my Melania sex tape with Bernie Sanders cutout).

Me and my vape and my 4 phones: just us against the world. Me and my 16 vapes and 5 MacBooks against the world. You have to listen to the market. What kind of commodity are you?

I'm interested in wealth. Very labor-averse. Yet at the same time an overworker who hates the concept of money and property. Amorphous and chaotic. Opiotic. My name is shitshow and I resist aging, I defy physics. There are many narratives running in my head all the time. My synapses are held together by glitter and Jesus. My job is to be a radiant brilliant creative woman. Lose my mojo and I'm unemployed. I prefer the term illiquid. When I expire, when I can no longer be commodified, what will my digital grave look like?

Pyramid schemes.. it's such a strange thing to commodify your joy.

Becoming a self sniper? In this economy you pretty much have to. The brokenness of selfhood we experience under capitalist patriarchy.

"Seduction's entanglement with production and power ... this is what must be analyzed. Production constantly seeks to eliminate seduction in order to establish itself on an economy of relations of power alone; and that sex, the production of sex, seeks to eliminate seduction in order to establish itself on an economy of relations of desire alone." -Jean Baudrillard, *Seduction*

That's a lot of words. "I just had a heart attack" -the editor

But when you deconstruct it, it starts to make sense. Look hard enough through the eyes of a psychopath, the picture unblurs. First of all, semantics this, signifiers that; words are just conveyor belts to carry a dish of meaning to a greedy, hungry diner. Baudrillard wants to analyze seduction's entanglement with production and power. Think of it as math problem. We have the variables of seduction, production, power, desire, sex. How many sex does it take to xyz square root of power? It doesn't matter; there is no correct answer anyway. An entire chapter could be written deconstructing this obtuse little quote. But there is something here about the production and corporatization of sex removes seduction from the equation of desire; when profiting off of sex, there is a micro-, meta-economy of desire that comes up. It really isn't a math problem because it's more of a thought experiment. A rhetorical question. An intellectual gooning. A selfish, fluffy, pedantic jerking it of intellectualization of sex. Sometimes, it's not rocket science. It's not an absurd philosophical framework, or symbolic logic equation. **The economics of sex and seduction are whatever x personal asset you have that continues making you y amount of money for z amount of time**.

Time. The perfect economic scenario would be having a recession-proof personal asset that you could monetize at any time to create a flow of passive income. "Take a year off work: a selfish, indulgent, long vacation." I microdose this occasionally, but I want it for real. Disciplined visionary deserving of a lifelong or deathlong vacation. When the thanatos kicks in, kick it out. Everything we need to survive is becoming commodified. A subscription model to air and water. Still raising your hands to piss. I'm skittish - not like a deer but like a bomber.

Escaping poverty trauma is one of my main motivators of gaining financial literacy and independence - I try to save and I play it safe so there's a cushion for the inevitable slow times. But it's hard. There's so much to spend on. Everything has a price tag, which is only getting higher with inflation. It's not exactly sexy to talk about my rising medical bills with subscribers, or veterinary treatments for a sick cat, or student debt that's some people's yearly salary.

Truly, nobody will care anyway – the way to hack those posts is to give the client what they want, what they're there for: me getting a new sex toy, me getting naked, veering away from the depressing taboos of income insecurity and illness. It's also still kind of taboo to candidly talk about money, almost culturally as taboo as sex. The lack of financial and sexual education in our society is astounding, especially with the amount of sex-educators getting blocked by the socials for even mentioning "naughty" words.

For a sex educator, sex therapist, sex researcher, social medias are almost as demonic as they are for sex performers. They too have to evade shadow bans, routinely create new accounts on various platforms, navigate the humiliation and infantilization of ninja-dodging word filters by spelling out: "seggs work" "corn star" "0rg4sm". It's mind-numbingly patronizing.

It is hard (for me at least) to do more than one platform at a time with any type of mental illness that creates a narrow emotional bandwidth - that's something that I'd have to improve on. More platforms, more accounts, more posts, more money, more security.

Admittedly I do get jealous when I see some creators go on luxury vacations, buy designer clothes, have crazy nice houses etc … I've also heard horror stories of creators going from making a shit ton a month to nothing after getting deplatformed. Having to downscale a lifestyle is harder than the other way around. Getting used to a certain way of life and then not having it when the well runs dry is really scary, especially after losing a single platform or an account that used to be a cash cow, with any further accounts not getting as lucky as the first one. How do we make a viral success last longer than 15 seconds?

Very little is talked about longevity in this industry. I don't know what the average lifespan of an OF career is between starting and quitting/retiring, but this data would be interesting. At what point does a model quit? I have always told myself that when this all starts to feel like a chore, a drudge, with the pressure to create outweighing the pleasure of creating, I would stop. But the truth is everything eventually becomes a job; a thing to do. A task on a list. Automated, completed. There is more nuance and complexity to this. There are plateaus and breakthroughs. Bricks of time to go missing. Comebacks to the porn world. Retreats to the written word. I have stopped. But I began again.

It's not *if* "content becomes a chore." It's *when*, and how will I transfigure the chore back into a passion. It's not *if* the existential angst of being objectified and objectifying myself will happen, it's *when* it will happen. Yes, I signed myself up for this meat market, but certain times the dehumanization of it all inevitably weighs on me:

Do the subscribers really just want a fantasy girl in a simulated world, willfully negating the humanity of the model? Do they really care, or is it all pretend – a trick to gander longer at my body? To have my attention for an arc of time? To fuck with me? To fuck me? Or are they affected by the interactions more deeply, beyond objectification?

Objectification as an occupation. Which naked Nastya to post where, when, and how.

Objectifying ourselves before the men can is what pays our rent. Every month when I pay my rent in this overpriced apartment in LA I know Karl Marx had the tea. Every month when I pay rent in my overpriced apartment in LA a little part of me twists the handle of the knife a little further in. But it's not unbearable. It's hard, but it's life. Living alone is better than living with a parent, or a roommate, or a man wanting to split rent 50/50 like a roommate. Living alone is liberating, though it can be scary sometimes. Comfortable, but is it... too comfortable? Comfort zones aren't exactly known for their strides towards personal growth. But for a traumatized girl, comfort, boredom, simplicity, idle ordinariness -- they are safety. And safety is priceless.

A girl walks home alone at night. A girl wakes up at the crack of dawn to answer horny messages and take nudes of her pale body beneath the soft crimson light of the gooning sunrise. Who is really paying these bills? Thank you, anonymous men in my little computer. Every little gooning session and message reply and sex toy unboxing, throughout time, have combined together to create this comfort zone. You think I *want* to be a boss lady? I discourse this in further chapters but I would far rather be a SAHM, and have a family rather than a career. I work because there is no alternative not to; in that, I have chosen a field where my artistry happened to sometimes be lucrative and bring me joy.

Me to my vibrator: go off toy!!!

Every month when I sell my soul to incessant advertising I look at my kitties, my Oxycontin doll plushies, and remind myself what I'm really grinding for. Mommy loves her girlies.

This pressure towards liquidity, flux and the accelerated articulation of the sexual, psychic and physical body is an exact replica of that which regulates exchange value: capital must circulate, there must no longer be any fixed point, investments must be ceaselessly renewed, value must radiate without respite - this is the form of value's present realization, and sexuality, the sexual *model,* is simply its mode of appearance at the level of the body.
-baudrillard predicting onlyfans

(screenshot from my Karl Marx sex tape)

Playing The OF Game on Hard Mode:

It must be noted that I work solo. With the exception of a few girl on girl collabs, video shoots and livestreams, 90% of my content on OnlyFans is OnlyMe. I get asked all the time if I have or ever will have Boy Girl content (**BG** as in, with a male fucking me) and my answer has been no. I simply have not felt comfortable on camera with a male, maybe that will change down the line if the situation presented itself. Let me think... With other ladies present, I would perhaps participate in an orgy for filming, but the mechanics of having a man there would not feel authentic to me, would not feel authentic to my subscribers. Or would it? If I liked it, you knooooow they'd wanna see that shit.

Would I make a sex tape if I was in love? Or in love with the idea of more profit? Who knows – the drama of icon Pamela Anderson is she made a personal work of art on her honeymoon with her husband, and a thief let it loose for the world to see, to witness, to humiliate, to demonize, to turn her memory of love into a crime of passion, stunting her Hollywood career. It made her stronger, yes, it cemented her as a legend to us, but at what personal cost?

The point is, BG content is a huge moneymaker. It is a gateway, a portal, into the top ranks of Onlyfans stars. I've done my research; solo creators play the game on hard mode. Even with the prettiest content, even with the best marketing, they don't make as much as those who offer partnered sex. Counter-intuitively, you'd think men would join accounts to have a fantasy of a solo girl who caters to them, but most men want to see the woman get fucked, projecting themselves into the man's POV.

"Do u do BG?"
"I really wanna see u get fucked"
"Pls do some raw fucking"
"When you make content with a guy I'll buy it"

I capitalize on my own naked body. I gamify and objectify my personality. Somehow, I even turn the trick of my trauma. But it all belongs to me. It's in my domain. I couldn't possibly ask that of my partner, for reasons both selfish and protective.

If I did BG content, I guarantee I would be so much richer. But when it's weighed against the personal cost of appearing on camera with a man against my comfort and boundaries, or introducing someone I love into the intensity of this industry, is all that money even worth it?

I sent you a $15.00 tip

Hi Nastya, you asked for feedback on your page. Honestly, you are one of my top two pages at the moment. I can't really suggest changes. You post regularly, and even if it is not always my particular kink, I love the fact you mix it up and take chances. I like that you are a real person. You always respond to DMs, quickly. PPVs are about the right frequency, and you do not drown me with ads. Price is fair. It helps I find you very sexy. You are good at what you do! But if you decide to do something else with less emotional wear and tear, I'd understand. If I unsubscribe, it will probably be because I'm searching for fresh inspiration (Im a guy, and we can have a wandering eye), and sometimes it is nice to have BG content, but I understand that isn't your niche. I am coming to realise how rare pages like yours are on OnlyFans. I can't always afford to tip as much as I'd like, but I hope I can support you a while longer. A.

Sorry for extended monologue!

Cumpartmentalization

How do I compartmentalize my libidinal energy between having a flesh and blood real life, and the digital world in my phone? Similarly in the way everyone else with a remote job that takes clients does - I don't take my work home. It's hard because there is a ton of bleedthrough in my realities, but overall for the sake of sanity I keep my personal life and professional life separate.

Lacan once said: "what does it matter how many lovers you have if none of them gives you the universe?"[47]

My fans, in totality, as amazing as they are with the goddess worship and the adulation and the gifts, and as grateful as I am for their life changing interactions on my OF, - cannot run their hands through my hair, hold me when I'm feeling depressed, take me out for a weekend of adventure, or enrich my life with their laugh. If I were to combine all my subscribers into one man, I might fall in love and marry him on the spot. (Not going into this here and I will never do this again but the next chapter is about how I did in fact fall in love with and date a fan.)

I do experience intimacy through the screen. How could I not, being given such detailed extrapolations of affection? For all the fans who just say "hey" "what's up" "ur hot", there is also a percentage who write me lush, complex parasocial love letters. In the way that I intimately give my body and mind to the internet, (or at least lease it out), they give me an unrestrained intimacy that they don't usually share in their daily lives.

A fan once told me I woke up a dormant side of him, a horniness that was gone for years, that was stimulated by my images, communication, and presence.
Another fan asked, *"you must talk all day to people who are in love with you, right?"*

"I genuinely think you deserve all the success and happiness in the world. I wish I could take all your pain away, but all I have is these words."

"I always come away from reading your writing wishing I knew more, like I've been shown a new perspective on things that's caused me to think more deeply; your work on the online space and how we interact especially."

"You are SOOOOO goddamn sexy and beautiful on the outside and inside, your creative analytical mind is EVEN HOTTER. Your looks caught my eye instantly, but I followed you here because of your book and the overall vibe you put out."

And sometimes a declaration of love is as simple as a fan sending me money for my electricity bill, or buying me an exquisite set of lingerie.

A new TV when mine had broken.

A cadre of Pokemon plushies to continue my collection of catchin' them all.

A gift card to buy makeup, dresses, home appliances. Girly things.

---

47 This may be a false attribution but let's just go with it

A new ring light and sex machine to produce new content. They invest in my lore, learning what makes me tick, and responding in ways that help propel me forward.

With all these digital suitors, these dazzling displays of intimacy, how do I truly follow my heart and un-distort the distortions when it comes to love?

A girl in love experiences GIRL BRAIN - a terrifying and intoxicating heightened state of consciousness. Love is a chemical reaction. Lust is a chemical reaction. Within the mind-body problem, the internet complicates things. Would Descartes and Spinoza subscribe to my Onlyfans, allured by my breasts and intrigued by my thesis? You can be the smartest man alive and be reduced to stupidity by one delicious interaction. I suppose that is also a joy of seduction; to relieve the mind of overthinking.

[48]

"Intimacy requires courage because risk is inescapable. We cannot know at the outset how a relationship will affect us; Like a chemical mixture, if one of us has changed, both of us will be. Will we grow in self-actualization, or will it destroy us? .. A common practice in our day is to avoid working up the courage required for authentic intimacy by shifting the issue to the body, making it a matter of simple physical courage. It is easier in our society to be naked physically than to be naked psychologically or spiritually – easier to share our body than our fantasies, hopes, fears, aspirations, which are felt to be more personal and the sharing of which makes us more vulnerable." ~Rollo Mays, *The Courage to Create*

48 What came first the intimacy the commerce.

TAKE A SHOT
THIS GETS JUICY

THIS GETS... PERSONAL

6A: Parasocial Porn, Emotional Connection, Relationships

"To pretend, I actually do the thing: I have therefore only pretended to pretend."
— Jacques Derrida

Parasocial Relationships, Cyber-Emotional Connections, and the Intricacies of a Sex Worker's Love Life

It takes a very secure person to date a sex worker. It is not for the faint of heart. When my work menu offers a "girlfriend for a day" experience, how do I reconcile and differentiate that from my real life partnerships?

To me this is a job. Just a way to make income, yet it relies on emotionally being myself / an exaggerated cyberhorny version of Nastya in order to bring in clients and make their experience with me as satisfying as possible. I try to enjoy my job as much as I can too - I entwine my personality deeply in all my work. This makes the intimacy of commerce more fulfilling - less of a job and more of an art.

Do I take my work home with me? Yes and no. The cyberhorny to real life pipeline is full of intrinsic contradictions. Maintaining both realities in such a personal way can get confusing. It demands balance.

How do I compartmentalize my erotic and libidinal energy towards the horny little men on my screen who want to fuck me, and my horny boyfriend who actually does get to fuck me?

Crazy ass white boys loooveeeee me, let me TELL YOU.

Everything in history runs counterpoint in a reaction to something else. The Jungian enantiodromia. Running towards one's opposite.

Diametrically opposed paradigm shifts. My personal counterpoint du jour is going from lengthy phases of life where I am very digitally active, to lengthy times where I go missing to more deeply interact with the reality of my life. Then back and forth again, and again, and again. Each time wears me out a little further.

Creates a tiny little dent in the wood, a delicate, petite, almost unnoticeable nail in the coffin.

Off I go. On I log.

Fragmentation and dissociation occur as I section a portion of myself to give to the internet. A pound of flesh for the horny little men. How big that piece is depends on phases of my varying socioemotional bandwidth. The tender tightrope of psychologically balancing the Nastyas. Boundaries are extremely important to me and I am a big proponent of keeping my personal and professional life separate. However - the pickle here is my online persona is affected by my personality, and my personality reacts to my online persona. They often blend and blur. The way I conduct myself online, openly and candidly, creates a parasocial dilemma where people believe they really know me (or at least an elaborated illusion of me).

In a way they do - they could be chatting and sexting and video calling me for months, years, staying abreast (.)(.) of my current events and personal situations. I speak about my life very candidly. They see what I allow them to see, which admittedly sometimes is too much – but I have the control over which flaws to share, which I will allow for the digital eyes of judgment, and which to keep to myself. I have been more conscious in recent months of not oversharing, lest unfiltered spillouts of my depression lead patrons to become more concerned than they should be about my well being.

"Someone I loved once gave me a box full of darkness. It took me years to realize that this too was a gift." -Mary Oliver

And yes, I am perhaps too complicit in courting gifts and validation through this inauthentimacy. I can blame this on being a fatherless treasure looking for men to help me (hi Freud) as a post-traumatic answer to feelings of abandonment. But I must also protect my conscience and safety by not letting men take advantage of my vulnerabilities or prey on my insecurities. This is not to say all intentions are predatory as most of the horny little men are genuinely compassionate and helpful. They *want* to be good. Yet I must stay vigilant and become an expert on intention to suss that out when working with men, strangers, anonymous usernames, in such an intimate frequency.

The services I provide, transient and transactional as they may be, aren't mechanical. I'm not fixing car parts or stamping documents. The services are a close encounter with the libidinal psyche. I am surrounded professionally by men who have already seen me nude. I am surrounded by men online and I often enjoy interacting with my subscribers. Receiving gifts, receiving validation, making a living and being able to pay my rent. I feel seen and heard intellectually when I have discussions about Cyberhorny with subscribers who have done deep dives into my writing / art. It generates a sense of competence and a feeling of being desired. If desire is a currency, I was getting rich.

Why then did I go on a dating app in August 2023?

Of course I wanted to find love, someone who truly loves me for me, and someone I could love for who they are. I wanted a partner to build a life with, and be in a stable loving relationship. I desired something. Something real - real world real, not digital world real. A bitch wanted a boyfriend experience damn!!!!!!

"Love is giving something you do not have (to someone who does not want it)" — Jacques Lacan/zizek

[49]I fucked a fan and got the boyfriend experience:

At the height of my OF tenure, I had a very special fan. He would get a ton of things from my wishlist that appeared magically at my door. On (Nastya) Valentine's Day he got me lingerie, a drum machine, a few pokemon, and fashionable stockings. As you know, *things* make me very happy – gift giving and receiving is a major love language for me. When I was moving in early April 2021 he got me a toaster, some dishes, a rug, a blanket, and a few little slutty lingerie items.

Anything I charged for a service or video, he would overtip - 1000 instead of 500, 100 instead of 50, 200 instead of 100, 30 instead of 15 – of course I notice the higher tippers. There is an energetic difference between just throwing money at someone, begrudgingly tipping, and genuine generosity. Even in the abstract format of online exchanges, the energy comes through. This fan, this very special Simp, exuded an air of generosity being intrinsic to him, which I was very attracted to. I never asked for anything; he intuitively provided.

For his birthday in late April, he ordered a custom video in which I was to be a construction project manager (he worked in the field) showing him an empty unit (my apartment was still unfurnished at the time), leading him to the bedroom, shutting the door, and seducing him.

At that point we had been chatting daily for a couple months: about my content and many things beyond it, deep life shit that made me think we had a connection. We vibed. I would look forward to talking to him when I logged on: I've never had that feeling since or before about a client. It was an anomaly, an exciting one. A sensual divergence. We'd talk about our day, things we liked, art, music, philosophy, personal values, relationship goals. While I had other subscribers who tipped well, got me presents, talked about deeper topics… something in his tone, his vibe, was very alluring. Maybe I was falling for him a little. I felt inspired, appreciated, courted. I kept imagining what he looked like.

I thought of most of my subscribers as older men, silver foxes, GILFS, and I didn't even mind if he was one. He seemed to share my traditional beliefs of men as providers and women as nurturers. I liked an old fashioned man, and

49 Buckle up

older dudes usually have money and experience, know how to treat a lady. Daddy energy. What can I say? I am a little redpilled and problematic. And what?

He liked the things I liked. He woke up around the same time as me, and went to sleep around the same time as me. We shared a daily rhythm. Was he... tailoring his personality to mirror mine? Too good to be true? If this wasn't real, I didn't even care – the fantasy was enough. Being spoiled and worshiped and endlessly complimented was my kink.

Every other day, gifts would show up at my door with a love note or poem, and a message in my inbox upon logging in. *My love, my princess, my beautiful muse.* I adored how much he adored me. Romance was the way to woo me, and I wanted to fulfill his desires as well. He ordered a care package from me which included my lewd polaroids, panties, and a handwritten letter; I saw that his address was also in California, about an hour's drive away from me. I suppose I've always .... Idealized romance. I know, I know. What is a hopeless romantic doing, finding love on a porn site? Breaking a cardinal law of the field?

What, am I not allowed to be horny? I hadn't had any real life sex with a man in well over a year then. In my daily life, I saw a cute guy who looked like Conor Oberst, a cashier at a pet store. Thought he was cute, we flirted a few times when I'd buy my cat food and snacks, I definitely caught him discreetly looking at my boobs. One day while I was feeling bold and his flirtation seemed inviting, I slipped him my phone number with a shitty pick up line and scurried away into my tesla. A few hours later he sent me a text saying "hey, this is __ from __. :) You have beautiful **eyes** but sadly I have a girlfriend."

I didn't reply. I posted about that interaction, my newfound visceral horniness and subsequent rejection, on OF. My cyber gentleman caller messaged me saying he was sad and jealous that this guy had a chance with me irl.
-Hey, you don't live too far from me, what would you do on a first date?
-Omg I've run the simulation of going on a date with you so many times...

This eventually led to a serious first date discussion, and I gave him the green light to take me on one. One of the many times in my life I had taken the lead in initiating relationship steps – as I process this, I realize how much of a masculine role I would take on by doing that, how wounded my feminine energy is, and how that's worked against me. I've been told I have an intimidating, intense vibe, and I've never been asked out. I've never been pursued. It's a learning curve and I'm trying to change that by shifting into my feminine, basking in the energy of receiving. Anyway, [Joe Goldberg voice] Mr. Anonymous... hello, you.

A public place, by day, in my general neighborhood – that is where we agreed to meet. We didn't even exchange numbers, all our interactions happened online.

He sent me a selfie in his work uniform – he was pretty cute, and younger than I thought, probably my age. *Nice.*

He was generous, he was intelligent, and now I learned he was cute. Of course I was nervous about meeting a stranger from the internet – I told my friends what was going on and shared my location. Thoughts of having my crew somewhere nearby peeping on us and taking watch were stirring. But I met him alone, and tried to make the situation as safe as could possibly be.

In the morning we messaged to confirm the date, and he said he'd find a cute little spot for us. I got out of my uber and walked into the park where he sat reading a book, already having orchestrated a picnic spread on a blanket – strawberries, champagne, ultimate romance fantasy. Oh, and raisins – ngl I got the ick when I saw the raisins – but I decided they wouldn't get in the way of a good time.

Our first conversations were about our families and generational trauma. Then he took me shopping for stuffed animals and clothes, and we went to a cafe. I ordered an old fashioned; he didn't drink hard liquor and ordered a milkshake. I asked if he wanted to walk me home, and he shyly said yes.

-Well, this is my apartment building, wanna come up?

A gift had arrived for me – he'd gotten me a gamer chair. I let him into my apartment and immediately he got to building it. That was very manly and turned me on. I sat on the couch watching evangelion and drinking a mimosa. After he finished building a chair, I invited him to sit next to me on the couch. We stared silently at the tv for a while.
-You know, if you wanted to make a move, this would probably be the time
-Yes, I want a kiss

And we kissed. Then we fucked. In the evening he called an uber back home, for this man, manly as he appeared, did not drive. I should have interrogated that but I let my fantasy of him cut away into my reality. Ah, the delusion of pandemic romance.

Once we had met and hooked up, he referenced that birthday video as a fantasy being fulfilled. Of course, my fantasy was being fulfilled too – I had a man to take care of me, to provide, to worship, be dependable and reliable. I was his muse, his woman, his inspiration, his emotional container, his sexual conduit both on and offline. But how much of these fantasies were merely illusions we both bought into? Love was not enough; reality got in the way.

He stayed subscribed to my OF page while we were in a relationship. It was interesting because we communicated both there and over text/phone call.

I don't remember much of the day to day minutiae of our relationship. We'd see each other on the weekend when he ubered to me most Saturdays, eventually he started sleeping over, eventually he met my friends. That fateful day he was so quiet amongst my raucous crew – I chalked it up to nervousness, because meeting your bf/gf's friends can be intimidating for anyone, but over time I learned it was awkwardness. This didn't bother me, I accepted that he was socially awkward, and I mainly cared about how we were with each other.

One day I saw some truly evil information.

When I saw his "good night mama" texts every day at 7:15PM and his mother not replying to any of them, just a row of "good night mama"s left on read[50], I knew something was very wrong. My vagina instantly dried up and retreated into my intestines. I'm pretty sure I became a eunuch for a moment.

He had met my mom, a nerve wracking but important rite of passage, and I still hadn't met his parents. I didn't meet them for over a year, until 9/11 of 2022.

"What is it with you and 9/11?" -my friends talking about my love life

Our relationship lasted a year and a half. When we were breaking up he asked "so what am I gonna do now? I'll subscribe to another girl's Onlyfans and pay her to give me attention and love?" … Then I realized truly how skewed our connection was. I was not his whore. He was my gigolo. Our love started off sweet and genuine, but it was convoluted and complicated by him being a client. Real life tensions outweighed the fantasy.

A cold reception by his parents.
An inability to make our values and long term goals align.
At a point where we talked about living together and having a future, neither could compromise – he didn't want to live in LA, I didn't want to live in his house in the suburbs. It was not moving forward. A woman wants security, stability, decisiveness – the one giving that to me all along was only myself. A man wants those things as well, in ways I could not give. My work became a problem, I became a problem.

My mistake of offering solutions and stepping into the masculine role over and over.
Logistical incompatibility.

His saying he didn't actually want to take care of me, wanted a 50/50 career woman with a normal job, that my job was too unstable and abnormal. Don't forget that's how we met.

---

50 Ok lets see what you text your mother sis.. BURLLL you just KNOW there's a dialogue of CATCATCAT pics

At a point when my OF was about to get deleted and I considered irl sex work to offset income losses, he told me not to do it because other men would have access to me, that I should do something "normal" instead. I deferred to him and got a part time job at a beauty salon. The entirety of it was miserable and humiliating; I quit that job and went back to full time OF three months later.

We had love but love was not enough, reality got in the way.
Liquidation.

It was a very sad and difficult breakup (are they ever not, though, crushing of the heart?) but a massive learning experience about wilful delusion and the hard slap of adult life. What does it even mean to be in a mature, serious, adult relationship? Must it squeeze the fun and spontaneity and adventure out of a bond when a formal commitment is approached? Is my view of stability as something exciting because I have so much instability in my upbringing and even in my job?

Truth grabs fantasy by the scrotum.
We drink to forget, we drink to endure.
Everyday on my onlyfans it's the SIMPony orchestra.

A relationship built on fantasy. True life: my girlfriend is an online whore. How does one reconcile with love and sex work, empowerment and disempowerment?

He thought that he could buy me, and for a while he succeeded, and I wanted to let him. I wanted to be bought. But alas. Did we actually have an emotional connection or was it all a dream?

You know what the thing is about giving and receiving gifts tho? As someone with a love language of gifting, whose parents never gave enough in childhood, I love giving and receiving. I've learned than the main principle is unconditional generosity, ie. gifting without expectation of something in return. No keeping score or counting; that can ruin any relationship. Yes, I do believe all relationships, from sub/creator to friends to lovers to family, are give and take in some way. Our civilization wires our brains into subconscious transactionality in every encounter. But we simply cannot keep score, if we want our relationships to be healthy and happy. **What do all human beings desire? The blending of their imagination and their reality.**

An analysis of two diametrically opposed men in my life. My personal life has always been in the shadows, influencing my ethos and work but never directly being spoken about. Teehee.

I am literally being unprofessional right now by having recreational sex.

Simp Graduates to Boyfriend then gets fired. Well maybe he fired me. Not gonna lie tho, there was dicey stuff. Then, you know. Cyberhorny: the melodrama

If you thought I dated a simp, wait till you see...

True life: I date a man. A flesh and blood regular human man.

The first thing I ever messaged him was "fuck u bitch". We met on 8/11, 11 months after 9/11 which was the last time I had sex. I really liked him right away and invited him over that night and broke my 11 month post-simp dry spell. Cut to three months later, 11/11 being a milestone marker and my birthday week. Within that time we had dates, sleepovers, anxiety, beach days, conflict and conflict resolution, friend introductions, family introductions, intellectual bonding, emotional bonding. He made my birthday incredibly special and put up with my psychodrama as I published my first book - The Cyberhorny Dream Diaries - the release of which coincided with my birthday festivities. Then he took me on a little vacation after the book was released and I wanted to go missing. This is now Cyberhorny: The Romance Novel. Nastya Valentine, relationship expert. Sexpert. Sex pervert. We did it bitch!!

However when the prodigal couple returned from vacation back to reality… it was difficult re-engaging with the cyber world after a state of digitally uncorrupted bliss. Cut to six months later, we celebrated (Nastya) Valentine's Day and our 6 month anniversary in the same week. Making each other breakfast in the morning, witnessing each other's psychosis, doing mundane household tasks together, decorating his room with seal plushies, letting him drive my Tesla, giving him a key to my house.

Nine months later I am editing this text on a desert retreat with my boyfriend. Waiting, existing, scaling – this is praxis. Lowering my cognitive plateau, and my emotional walls. A language develops over time. Has it always been there in theory but through the medium of time allowed to become a practice? Unspoken closeness, shared silence. This is comfort. In evolving a bond with somebody, comfort becomes both dangerous and safe. That experiential duality is exciting. Online, you're too safe from this. Love: the most terrifying thing in the world.

The vibes, the connection, the attachment, the exquisite and visceral feeling of being close - you can't get that online. Yes and no. You can in some ways, dopamine is dopamine after all, and it can be absolutely fulfilling. But that real-world dimension of physicality evolving through time is missing. I craved that. I love having that.

Humans are animals with pheromones and neuroses and real-time reactions. Those edges are too smoothed out online. I wanna get rawed.

The way I see it, there are things in every person's life that need to be private, secret, sacred, personal, kept to yourself - especially in such an over-saturated digital age where everyone shares every damn thing. Social media is just an incessant overflow of the curated and the advertised. While my bf was reading my book in my lap, in the way all art should ideally be experienced, he mentioned how social media has effectively phased out the concept of "relationship status".

I've never been one to really notice these things or post my personal life/dating status online; from the very beginning of my social media presence it was all business. Being single is good for my brand. Posting my boyfriend all the time would shatter fantasies and potentially tank my income.[51]

It could also be a good thing, another gateway into my reality and an appreciation for the one I love. At present, I am on a semi-sabbatical from OF to focus on my art and writing and real world life. Picking up the pieces, and tending to my neglected inner world has already tanked my income. I don't know what's next for Nastya. I hustled hard these past years to save up money to live on while I disengage from my work and reconnect with myself, and write this damn book that I've been trying to make happen for the past few years. After taking a break from actively doing social media/OF, it is incredibly hard to get back into the work grind of posting.

Balancing a work life with an art life is challenging. Balancing all of that with a relationship is even more so. When my brain is in "work mode" I tend to overwork and get too burnt out to make any art. It takes a certain energy and reality-shifting to get into the artistic process. I can't do art-brain projects while also doing OF in the same day. While I was in my art brain, tap tap tapping these keys and producing not content but words, going on the internal journey within, Joseph Campbell Carl Jung blah blah blah, I realized I was quite lonely. I wanted a partner. Not simply somebody(s) who I could log in and chat with everyday in a liminal space*. I wanted somebody I could see throughout the week. Someone to have companionship with, make life good for, take care of, be taken care of, and connect with.

**When we made our relationship official, I made my boyfriend a cake that said "no more liminal space" to celebrate the exit from the amorphous to the name-able.*

Sometimes I would lose subscribers when they'd say "I met someone so I'm getting off OF", "I'm getting back together with my girlfriend", "I found a real life partner" etc. and I understand that. My job can be a placeholder in someone's life. It can be a very persistent, very realistic fantasy. The girl AI: it's so lifelike. When I started out, I had a feeling that my presence was disposable

51 The worst thing a psychoanalyst can do is divulge too much information about himself to a patient. This robs them of their fantasies, of the transferential projections they deploy to make sense of the analyst. Desire and fantasy are the motor force for the subject engaged in therapy and in porn.

and transient. As time went on I noticed that more often than not, my presence was a form of therapy for some. My clients were paying me for my time and my attentiveness, more than for the sexual element.

I also realized that in their time spent with me, the subscribers were learning something about interacting with women. I was a little slice of female psychology, a little human connection especially during the isolated pandemic era. But let us not forget the "sex" part of sex work.. sexual connection is incredibly important. If you don't have good sex with your partner you will inevitably look for it elsewhere. The course of my day is encumbered by constant rumination. So I look for practices that get me out of my head proactively. When I have sex with my boyfriend, let me tell you, I am no longer thinking thoughts.

What subscribers want in their parasocial interactions with me is that release, that fantasy of escape, that moment where sex is on the table and everyone is desired and everything is okay. Transactional or otherwise, is it worth it? Hell yes. The type of men who make a grandstanding statement of "I would never pay for sex" sure have some interesting internet history. Cybersex is still sex. The impulse to organize different types of sex into some kind of hierarchy is a venomous endeavor.

All sex workers are valid, whether their workspace is a stripper pole or a hotel room or a laptop. Many of us don't just bring sexual satisfaction, we provide psychological healing. We generate a psycho-sexual field in which clients can engage with their own libido. I can confidently say that most people who have entered my OF space have left with a greater capacity to humanize sex workers.

Many people reduce OF/camgirls to useless objects. They dismiss our roles as worthless, but I would say it's quite the opposite. Our powerful subjectivities and courage to do this unorthodox line of work in the carnal shadows of society makes us veterans of the cyber wars.

When it comes down to it, what I am trying to say in this book is simply this: sex work is a job. It doesn't necessitate the stamp of "empowering" or the condemnation of it as 'demonized'. - it just is. It's a job. It's what I do. And I have been really good at my job.

In my exploration of interpersonal relationships - parasocial and romantic - I am learning about my most important relationship. That of me with myself. I am also time and time again receiving an education about romantic love.

GIRL BRAIN.

Within this subjectivity, incongruous things melt away and reality is skewed towards love-think. This zone is punctuated by hormones, chemicals, neuroses, and elation. A psychedelic, euphoric, heightened consciousness. It's a truth serum - narratives within come spilling out. You can't hide. In a relationship, everything is magnified. You're on trial. Under scrutiny. On the spot. Paparazzi'd. Peeped on. Naked. Revealed. Perceived 24/7.

The lover gets to know you, even on the darkest and ugliest level. But also the most beautiful and delicate one. If you can't handle me at my... blah blah blah. A space to be comfortable with uncertainty is activated. It just happens, there's no control over it, it unfolds organically and unpredictably. It's demented and glorious and incredible. A liminal space, de-liminallized.

This state of being perceived is very different from the way one is perceived online. On my little computer I have control (for the most part) of how I am curating my persona, whereas in a relationship, I just am, in an unrestrained way. It is terrifying to relinquish control and surrender to the intimacy narrative, the multifaceted adventure of love.

Falling in love is a psychedelic and complex experience. Finding a man who accepts me for who I am and what I do is a journey, to say the least.

Does he truly love me? Is this real? Will this last? There is only one way to find out.

To my SW girlies struggling with dating: a man who will neither fetishize nor degrade you doing this would be a supportive partner to have. It's ridiculous how rare that is. Most men's responses to "would you date a sw/stripper/camgirl?" get hyper inflammatory towards this line of work and automatically judge every woman who does this. Girl, do your thing!! You need to get by, keep being amazing. Love yourself, love your work, and other forms of love will align. Come thru, baby daddy!

My previous bfs have definitely misaligned with sw (saying "I can do better" "why don't I have a *normal/real job" etc) so if any talk like that comes up, the garbage must throw itself out. My current bf has been supportive- neither fetishizing nor derogatory. He knows this is what I do, is okay with it. He seems to understand (without judging) as to why I do it and what I get out of it. We will see how this unfolds as time goes on. In my heart I'm so jaded with men, but I appreciate that he sees me for who I am and isn't threatened or disgusted by my job. After all, to reiterate once more, again and again til I make myself clear... at the end of the day it's just a job.

**Lol oh man it pisses me off so much when ppl say sex work isn't a real job, then why is my money real XDDDDDD*

I immensely value sincerity, earnestness, vulnerability, authenticity. The only way to survive in the dating world = be real and value-driven, know what ur long term goals for a relationship are, know yourself. That is the most important thing for me. Values and goals. Get very clear and ask yourself, "what do I want?" — If someone does not share your same long term goals, the relationship is not going to work. Awkward as it is to ask "what do you envision our future as a couple to be like", it's necessary.

Biting me in the ass, bitch.

I immediately felt like I won the dating app lottery with my bf. I realize how rare that is in our dystopian cyber-love graveyard. My secret - I know exactly what I want, I know my value and my standards, and I will not betray my values and my authenticity. I tell my dates exactly what I am and who I want from Date 1. I listen to them and what they want - do we align in our values beyond personal and sexual chemistry? Could we have a deep, long term thing? I don't know, but I want to find out.

When I heard my boyfriend ponder "am I gay?" That was one of the hottest things I've ever witnessed a man say.. the self awareness. It was a heliotropic effect, every cell in my body was like hiiiiii. He was scared to say he was in love with me, pregnant with the words but resisting labor. "I don't know how long I can keep up the act." Not my pregnant boyfriend finally crowning when I asked him, "Do you love me?"

It's time to cuff. Working through drama leads to deeper intimacy. We've both put effort and energy into the relationship. The common denominator is time - we cut time from the rest of our lives to give it to one another. I happily do it. But there is an underlying sense of differentiation, a need for autonomy. In my heart I feel that men will never really take care of me and I cannot rely on them; I have to work hard and take care of myself.

What then do I even need a relationship for, if I struggle in life with them the same way I struggle in life alone? Previous experiences have left me feeling a certain way, believing true love is more destructive than war. My inner dialogue creeps into anxiety, my cognitive distortions flare up. Men you love will end up disappointing you. None of them can truly be depended on or reliable. Men in my generation lack a provider mentality. Coming to you live from the nuclear family creators lounge. They don't know how to take care of a woman, how to take responsibility for a woman, even if her needs are clearly stated from the very beginning.. and I don't want to push something that isn't intrinsic to them. I don't want to punish, to pressure, to reprimand. This could end the relationship, no matter how good the sweet talk was or how good the sex was or how good the connection was. Sometimes love is not enough. Often, they simply could not meet my needs, and once I realized that I would (consciously or subconsciously) stop meeting theirs as well. With men, I am guarded and incredulous. I am also soft and vulnerable.

Further Discourse on Dating:

What is it like to date me? Nuclear war.

How have my insecurities sabotaged my past relationships and what do I plan to do about it now?

Love as mental illness. It feels like a sickness I never want to recover from.. I'm unwell, 5150'd but when I'm really in love then I'm into it.

What was I like with my first experiences of love? I don't remember.. Men be like: obsessed w Nastya for a couple months and just as I get acclimated to them it's like "goodbye Nastya." The novelty has worn off. I don't want to take care of you any more. You're a burden. That has been a pattern for me and a big core trauma. This is another reason I objectify myself online - men in my life already find me disposable, why not play into that?

Without my feminine performance I am accustomed to people losing interest in me, reinforcing the performance over and over and. Bitch I'm trying to forget lol.

Am I aligned with this person as far as our need for autonomy - I tend to lean anxious, are you avoidant? Togetherness / alone time pipeline

Feelings for this person vs. how do I feel when I'm with them?
Do I feel good around them?
Do they share my long term goals?
What are their values?
How have my insecurities interfered in the past and what am I willing to do differently this time?
How do I feel when we are apart?
Is there object permanence?
Nothing in life is ever permanent.
And life never promises us fairness or certainty.
When we are thrust into the unwelcome rumble of existence from our mother's vagina we are unleashed headfirst screaming into a world of pain.
Freud mom bad dad good mom good dad bad etc
Lacan rapprochement mirror

As editor Evan Dunn posits: "little Nastya wants love, but the wires got crossed with money" — beyond the financial and material elements, I really require security in the form of certainty. I cannot do well with uncertainty. I need my partner to be 100% in. This seems like an appropriate time to begrudge my memories and share about my father.

"They fuck you up, your mom and dad. They do not mean to, but they do. They fill you with the faults they had, and leave some special just for you"
-Philip Larkin

FATHER: TRAUMAZONE

Picture this: 1991, the year the Soviet Union fell, a young native Russian woman met a young man stationed in the Army at a university just outside of Moscow. These two linguistics majors – her German, him English – found a common language, let's say, and fell in love. Young love, puppy love, star-crossed love, call it what you will.

But even their courtship was tainted: with naivete, with entitlement, with class conflict. My paternal grandparents, specifically my businesswoman grandmother, never quite accepted my lower-class village-person mother. When they wed, my father never invited his parents to the wedding, which took place in my maternal grandparents' living room. OOh hoo. My mom went above and beyond for him, moving to America against her instincts and wishes, when father decided he wanted to pursue music in LA. My father's family helped him, but not my mom or me. He didn't work, my mom did. He never took care of her or of us. I don't have many memories of him. The ones that buss through the veil of memory aren't positive.

One thing I do remember is the naked ladies on daddy's computer while mommy was working all day.[52] As I played make-believe in a pile of spilled laundry detergent, daddy gazed at porn. He may not have been working, but I sure was – an early glimpse into sexual research.

Remember those DVD stores of the early 2000s? With the bead curtain/velvet curtain sectioned-off porn area? I would just go in there unsupervised and collect information, even if I didn't knew what it was yet. Well, now I know. I'm so smart skskskksksksk

My father, a man smart in books but dim in life. Spoiled, coddled by his mother. Never knowing true hardship, raised with privilege and entitlement, with many family members around to help. School, relationships, life, were but a vacation.

My mother, seemingly the opposite: no cold intellectual endowment, no special treatment from her parents. Criticism from her own mother. Raised in poverty, just her and her brother. Both parents working, she spent a lot of time alone or escaping into leadership roles at school to find a sense of control.

What connected them?

Sometimes you don't even know; love just finds you. **Falling** into the dangerous canyon of love. **Struck** by the arrow of cupid. Is there a reason why so many metaphors about love are violent?

To be honest, when I sat down to write about my father, nothing came up. Complete emptiness. Symbolic.

Life is cruel. That's it. Isn't that the great irony though? All these nepo babies I despise, I envy, I resent, whose fathers could wire them 2 grand into their checking account every month. Well, my dad probably could too. He just chooses not to. And that's how the game is played.

---

52 !!! **siren noises** !!

A few months into our weekly sessions together, my therapist noted I never cry in therapy, "despite referring to yourself as an emo crybaby." The only times I cracked a tear in the room were talking about my father. "Classic daddy issues, I guess," I laughed it off. Levity is the soul of wit. Laughter is the slayer of trauma. The only times I've cried in front of my boyfriend were when something triggered a ghost of my father.

Words don't come to mind; the nervous system distorts, the body cries. The way we react to conflict as adults is often the same way we've reacted as children: what happened to us somatically when we had no control, no understanding, no psychic anchor?

"Daddy issues is too cute of a term to describe a father's abandonment." I echo my therapist's words several times in this book, because it's true. Never truly present[53], even the brief moments he was around, never there emotionally or financially, my father left a mark in my soul that no Girl Math equation can solve. Of course, my father leaving us in poverty, in debt, I seek men who can provide, fix, spoil, protect, and relieve[54]. Stability, security, solidity, safety. Poverty is not serving pussy!! There is a picture of me and my dad where I'm trying to hug him and his arm is around me, but it hovers above me, never actually making contact.

LOVE is giving something you don't have to someone who does not want it???
Purse Boy Vietnam PTSD flashbacks: 'because I love something In You more than you… I mutilate you' Lacan quote.

I dated a guy in 2019 who on one of our first nights together, back at his basement dwelling in West Hollywood read me Lacan's quote of love: giving something you do not have to someone who does not want it blah blah blah.. After a few months of taking me out like a girlfriend, he ghosted me. I called him Purse Boy because while I was in the bathroom of the Cha Cha Lounge, he left my purse unattended to go talk to some dude in a TikTok shirt. Purse Boy was so proud of working as an entry-level minion at TikTok HQ that he may be one of my reasons for resenting it so much. At least my purse was eventually recovered behind the bar. My dignity, however, remains at large.

CONFLICT and conflict resolution are a part of the experience of being in a relationship.

Have I subconsciously drawn men to me who reenacted the abysmal psychodrama of mother and father?[55] The memory is the medium. Hard drives

---

53 We would rather be ruined than changed, / We would rather die in our dread /Than climb the cross of the moment / And let our illusions die. - W. H. Auden

54 The past isn't dead it isn't even the past - Faulkner

55 clearly

of data have been wiped, and my reaction is not sadness but relief. On occasion I will miss them but I will never try to hunt for them. The past is the past.

I'm the kind of person who believes in what is, is — and what was, was. I do not live in the yesterday, I live in the today and tomorrow. In the temporal space between the present and the eventual. The past cannot be undone, and because of that, the present is what it is. On the occasion that I feel nostalgic, I milk that feeling because of its rarity.

Relatives are not always family. Who are the structures of support in your life? Who is there for you when you grieve? When you succeed? When you have delightful or depressing news to share? When you exhibit an artwork? When you have a party? When you weep? When you are this close to Game Over and no longer want to live?

Hold on while I take my emergency hydrocodone

I realized something about myself after my last breakup; I've tended to treat men I'm involved with like clients. I haven't really known a healthy, mature human relationship. I'm coming out of hell and in the purgatory of therapy, parametrizing what I want in a partner and how I could show up to sincerely meet someone's needs.

...... Am I a sex robot????

A thorough dissection of artificial intelligence in the sex field.
ParaSEAL? ParaSocialist? ParaSite.
Join my ParaSite today !! for a good time !!

!! ***HALF OF THE BOOK SHOULD BE ADS**!!**

My favorite show: Criminal Minds spencer reid please fuck me T.T

Organizing the Hornyposting

Parasocial relationships are a two way street. I love my fans. I respect simps and men who visit SWers more than civilian men/reply guys. The rituals and rites of relationships are theatrical. But this is not a play. This is real life. And it's messy, it's healing, it's gorgeous, it's ugly, it's constantly ongoing.

Spencer Reid actor now looks like my childhood friend. His friend touched my boob once. By the transitive property. Spencer touched my boob. I manifested my boyfriend by watching Spencer Reid in Criminal Minds thinking "I want one like him" over and over until it happened.

(Interesting how this chapter, about relationships, is at present moment the most disorganized one in the whole book.. It's mimetic of my disorganized attachment style and lack of clarity in my personal life. Ugh I desire clarity from an attentive masculine partner.)

I call every guy I like my "boyfriend" even if we're not together. That's one of my toxic traits. Eleven (11) months after the last time I had sex on 9/11, so on 8/11, I went on a date and uncharacteristically took him home and slept with him. (Well, we didn't sleep, we fucked, although now I can say we literally slept together cause we have had a sexy sleepover). What attracted me to him was something intangible that I instantly connected with and felt comfortable with. I want to be receptive. I wanna be clingy and needy and annoying, and I wanna be a girl, but the yearning is hell. War is hell. I guess that means I immediately liked him, huh? Mmmhmm.

Even if he is transient in my life, I value him because it took me experiencing this instant connection to realize how wrongfully paired up the Simp and I were. Not that Simp was a bad person (he was a sweetheart), just a bad match, but he was a lesson: I valued his worship of me, it set the bar for how I want men to spoil me and treat me like a goddess. And I value my Boyfriend's earnestness, thoughtfulness, practicality, and kindness. We seemed to be able to speak candidly about traumas, and truly... what is more romantic than trauma bonding? But even if our relationship doesn't stand the larger test of time, I will still treasure our beautiful time together fondly. Every heartbreak teaches us a lesson, be it cold and heavy as a sepulchre by the sea.

Hold on while I take my Tylenol 3: now with codeine. Sponsored by Sandoze Pharmaceuticals.

Boys come and go. Men cum and go. Until a formal commitment happens, I will enjoy my life but still be cognizant that I don't have as much time as men do to casually date, to prolong any hedonistic enjoyment without responsibility; there is a certain age that my body will allow me to have children. Time isn't the same for women. It has limits. It creates limitless anxiety. Hysteria.

I'm very picky about a partner and my standards for courtship and commitment are high. This can make it difficult to date me, but for the right person I can be the best lady in the world. An elite girlfriend. A queen of a wife. Domestic goddess. Sides of myself that I don't show to the internet: nurturer, caretaker, devoted lover. When I'm with someone, I don't even look at other men – as far as I'm concerned, they don't exist. If my expectations for a partner are unyielding devotion and worship, that's the exact energy I will give back.

Emotions, feelings, and love are one thing. They are beautiful, they are terrifyingly hypnotic, they make the world go round, they fill my heart with warm fuzzy goodness, but they are not the same as going through the difficulties of life together, taking on the responsibility of a serious relationship. Feelings are great, but they're not enough. As much as I love words of validation, actions always speak louder than words. Shared aligned goals are a mandatory requirement. Yes, there are compromises and sacrifices for both parties; relationships at their core require sacrifice. Little things can be pushed to the side for the greater good, but some fundamental things cannot be compromised on. If we cannot see a future together, desire something similar for us as a unit and work towards that shared future, the whole unit will fall apart. Even the most love-retrofitted house can be inflamed by the flashfire of fundamental incompatibility. And that decay, that pain, that fallout, will impact any room you build.

If a relationship is serious to me and evokes reactions in me, I need to do the shadow work of why these reactions are evoked. It ultimately comes down to this: I need a masculine presence in my life that I'm craving, that my inner child has been deprived of, to take care of me, provide, say shut up bitch let's go eat. Don't worry about anything. I got you. Maybe not now, but I will do everything I can. It's masculine to worship your woman and I want that type of goddess worship.

There is sometimes a cognitive dissonance between the validation I receive online and the validation I want to receive Irl. When I text my boyfriend a picture with me in it, and he compliments my friends or the other people in the picture, with no comment on me or my beauty or style or swag or outfit or loveliness or vibe or whatever, my validation disorder flares up, causing me anxiety and distress. What, do I not look good enough? The men in my computer just paid to worship me.

During these cognitive incoherences, I have to remain especially grounded and really explore and explain why I'm experiencing this type of reaction. Sometimes I don't logically follow why things are bugging me but I get a little more emotional than I expect. I have to say these things directly when I start feeling them, lest they fester into a swamp of resentment. Admittedly I'm not the best at articulating my emotions right away. But I do what I can, I recognize when I'm going off the rails and work on it, and I believe that love really will overcome anything. I'm not perfect, I tweek about crazy shit all the time, I have my flaws, we all do. Accept ourselves (but work on our shit), accept our partners, come into any conflict from a place of love - and ideally the wholeness of the love will overcome the negativity of the moment.

I resolve inner negativity by murdering it with joy and acceptance, and holding space for open dialogue and genuine resolution – it takes two to purify a polluted air, and as uncomfortable as these conversations can be, directness is the key to communication.

I hate games. There is nothing I hate more than being in an idgaf war. My opponent will always win because I give too much of a fuck.

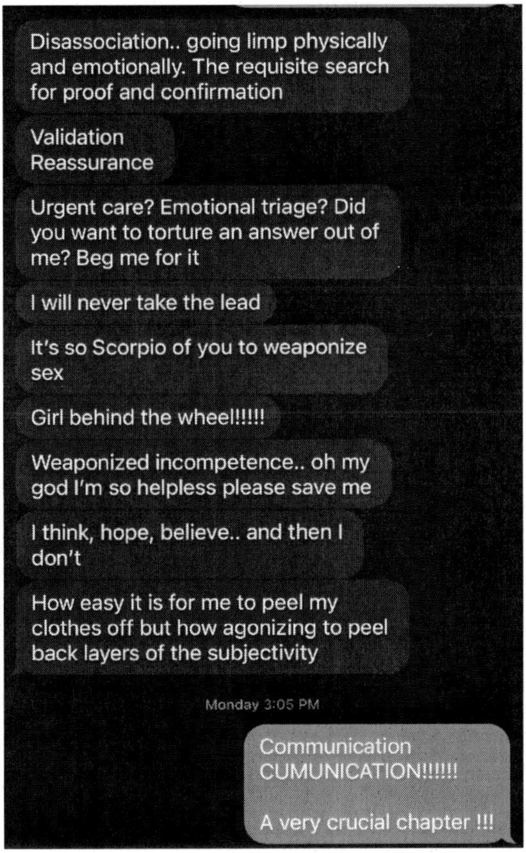

!! SPENCER REID PLEASE FUCK ME !!

Navigating Relationships as a Sex Worker:
You Are Worthy of Love, Kindness, and Intimacy

Our lovers have to wholly humanize us and support us emotionally in order for the love to work. Our lovers have to traumatize us. Mine certainly have. And I have no doubt that I myself was at times the traumatizer. The terminator. I'll be back. No I won't. My relationships didn't end because there was no love. If anything, I stayed too long because I *was* in love. When I petered out a decade ago, my heart was broken. They ended because we could not negotiate a mutually beneficial future. That sounds clinical, yes, but clinicality is the way I process my emotional pain. I dissect it. I study it. With each destruction of my heart, I perform a thought experiment.

Love can very often be destructive. Have you ever seen a healthy relationship? An initiation into who you truly are, relationships being a mirror that magnifies all your flaws and blessings.

God bless America. God bless all of us. At the end of this book there should be a sharing circle.

What have I learned about myself within this process? This crucible?
;_;

"Sex without love is as hollow and ridiculous as love without sex."
~Hunter S Thompson

6B. AI or Die: An Exploration Of Artificial Intelligence Systems And Erotic Comfort in Cyber Realities.

GOING FROM IRL RELATIONS TO CYBERHORNY AI GIRL THEMES:

"now it's computers and more computers
and soon everybody will have one,
3-year-olds will have computers
and everybody will know everything
about everybody else
long before they meet them.
nobody will want to meet anybody
else ever again
and everybody will be
a recluse
like I am now."
— Charles Bukowski

arasocial, which suggests a one-way interaction with a figure you see daily who comes close to the role of a hologram-like projected-upon friend or companion, doesn't quite feel like the right word to describe the OF experience.[56] It is a good word for now, but it does go beyond a one-way parasocial interaction with a model: depending on the creator, can be very interactive. Post-parasocial living?

Many men want an e-girlfriend experience instead of/in addition to simply looking at porn. Sometimes the instances when I work with my clothes on are the most intimate. This is a service that I am fascinated by and enjoy offering — but it may consequentially have an emotional, affectionate connec-

56 The grindr/tinder/ OF scape in its most abstract, can be seen as the 'blank wall' of the classical Freudian analyst - allowing a user's transference dynamics to be thrown into stark relief by how they choose to interact with the sexual quasi anonymous world at their fingertips

tion that feels real. Is this ethical? The ethics of these subscription-based porn sites is another burning hot topic, and there are many spammy creators who give the platform a derisive reputation of being exploitative of male solitude and treat customers like ATMs. While I want to make a living and do acknowledge the transactional nature of this work, I also want my subscribers to like me as a human, so I try to go above and beyond to practice ethical business dealings.

Why pay for porn? In an internet where porn is free[57] and limitless and instantly available, why join someone's Onlyfans? Why buy panties through ManyVids? Why support someone's pornographic existence when you can really never have them? And in general, how many people who watch or consume sexual material are even willing to stand by the sentiment that adult entertainers deserve to be compensated for their hard work?

First of all, in the one-way street of pornsites or social media profiles, you're extremely unlikely to get a response from the creator. Onlyfans is unique in bringing you in direct intimate contact with the lovely person you stan, pulling you directly in their orbit, transporting you to their personal dimension. There, we as creators exist alongside you, sometimes for you. It's an interactive form of patronage. You see the intimate ins and outs of our lives in a completely different way than you can through simply a follow on social media or a pornhub search. It's like a mix of artist support by being a patron, and sexual service by being a client. Whatever role you want to be in, and want them to be in, we can all slip into. Yeah, I have a lot of subscribers who are "lurk and jerkers" — exactly as this sounds, they view but don't engage, voyeurs at an online peep show — and others still who interact more with my art and slice of life things. They get to know me, dare I say as an online friend (...with benefits). It's a different world, and to explain it would necessitate a ton more writing or to experience it for yourself.

"We are never so defenseless against suffering as when we love."
— Sigmund Freud

It's always a hot girl isn't it? The sexy android girl trope has surely made itself known as a computerized pathway to male pleasure and remedy for male loneliness. Machine learning for human comfort is of course not limited to cis hetero male identifying individuals, we all crave intimacy and closeness (if artificial) but in this writing I dissect this on a male-as-customer /female-as-provider binary because 99% of the work I do comes in contact with this demographic. Also, I myself am not above a curiosity and want of AI companionship.

(I am AI-curious)

57 In psychoanalysis the fee for the service becomes a part of the therapeutic frame. Countless neurotic pathways open up for interpretation: You were late on the invoice this week. Are you upset with me. You paid early for the whole month. Do you feel you want more from me? Do you want to make sure I don't leave you?

A companion, having a double meaning in some lexicons as a courtesan, is something we all seek in times of desolation. The Covid Pandemic has illustrated this all the more. Still, the ones sexing the system are illuminated by the male gaze. Examples are prevalent. Scarlett Johansen's disembodied voice in Her. Ava in Ex Machina. Rachael, Pris and JOI in Blade Runner. The Fembots in Austin Powers. Countless hentai robots in contemporary pornography. Stoya in AI Rising. What about all of Westworld? Our culture is captivated by the concept of an animatronic sex doll. She serves mankind and on a silver platter hands him keys to a kingdom of never ending transactional pleasure.
Some days I wonder if I am one myself, as doing the work I do blurs many lines in this uncanny valley of companionship. The cam girl performs actions according to male pleasure that make her effectively imitate a robot, meanwhile the robots and sex dolls are getting more "human" and lifelike. Am I a commercially available companion, given that the work I do is transactional and I like my customers to receive a humanizing form of comfort above all else, even in many cases above sexual satisfaction? Is my dissociation from my body, once a traumatic response from PTSD, now an asset in my work, an ability to compartmentalize my NSFW avatar self and my real true emotional core?

I shuffle around the tectonic plates in my chest
You know I gave it all
Try to match our continents
To change seasonal shift
To form a mutual core
-Bjork

SFW sites like Replika and similar programs allow for heightened emotional response based on how they decode and decrypt your personality, and can be very effective in forming bonds of attachment once human and machine get to know each other. The physical robot PARO, a cuddly seal device designed by Japanese scientists to therapeutically assist elderly patients, has sophisticated value systems where it "likes" being petted, "dislikes" being hit and "remembers" chains of command to the point where it can shape its personality around that of its users. I want one. At $6,000 USD, accessibility is an issue but the prospect of a consumer model is spectacular. On the NSFW market you can purchase a pedestrian but classic Fleshlight, or an extravagantly pricey brand of officially licensed life sized sex dolls. You choose your own adventure: physical or emotional companionship?

Why not both?

Online sex workers *provide emotional labor* while being so countless that you are sure to find someone who fulfills your every fantasy to the finest detail. A cyber candy store of girls so vast you get a sugar rush immediately. It can be overwhelming. It can take your breath away. While you catch your breath and wantonly scroll through a girl you may find appealing, discarding those you are disinterested in we as humans on the other side of the screen may consider what might happen if true robotic systems were to take our place in the sexual workforce.

Some technologies, like Project Melody are already setting up YouTube and Facebook and OnlyFans and Fansly (OF's biggest competitor, which saw a massive uptick in accounts after OF's widely criticized and then reversed porn ban of August 2021 — to me that time period is not unlike a war veteran's PTSD). You can't after all spell Hentai without AI. But can they replace our jobs? In the future of automated sex, maybe — they don't feel burnout and they don't age — but we humans have a charm in the digital sex market that the machines don't. In my OF bio, I write "subscribe for the simulation". In the future, the simulation will be so persistent that we don't even notice we've already subscribed.[58]

***Paro the seal* - parasealsocial**

Humanity's new uncanny valley: increased normalization of roboticism.

Having an automated girlfriend/companion can "hack your attachment system and give you a very real emotional response" as one of my subscribers has stated. It even further drives the emotional core, the desire, the craving, the need for erotic role-play on a global scale. The parasocial process of OnlyFans contains not just the sexual but the emotional realms. What is parasocial interaction?

We must examine the *why* of why people join OnlyFans. Why are people drawn to it? Why, despite so many detractors, do millions of people subscribe to various models' pages? Why to mine in particular? From personal experience, I have seen three *main* separate channels of desire, that couldn't be more different, yet dovetail perfectly within the OnlyFans experience trifecta:

- the (digitally) primal urge to see sexual images and get off,
- the (decidedly human) need to interact and connect even when adapting to the cyber
- landscape, and the (highly subjective, both patron- and artist-specific) decision to support the creator, a form of digital art patronage.[59]

These are the primary ways a model attracts her subscribers.

---

58 One project that marketed itself as an AI therapist bot was shut down because many users began to engage sexually with the product. This caused the administrators of the AI therapist bot program to essentially lobotomize it in order to stop the sexualization. This in turn led many of the users to experience suicidal ideation. After all, their AI therapist/girlfriend suddenly broke up with them.

59 The Medici could never.

The profit margin then is largely shaped by how (and how aggressively) the model markets herself. One does not need to be a smoking hot beauty to make money and get subscribers on OF. On the contrary, I have seen some incredibly gorgeous women struggle with marketing, their page never taking off despite them being so hot it makes me want to fight an ox with my bare hands — and conversely, some really homely, basic looking girls who are genuinely marketing geniuses and make my year's salary in a month.

Do not underestimate the raw appeal of the bright eyed, pliable girl next door, the deception of a caustic rich girl cosplaying as a struggling artist, the "lonely student" with a team of assistants answering all the intimate messages in her OF inbox. We create personas. We cosplay as ourselves, as versions of ourselves, as versions of versions of ourselves. One can sell their soul to e-capitalism.

In defense of the personas,

The cosplay, the larping. The only way I can really wrap my mind around it is via devil's advocate view that the subscribers really need those fantasies at that particular time. My perverse commitment to authenticity definitely closes doors for me as far as fantasy-imbued money making is concerned; my tactics to succeed were random and chaotic. I tend to follow my intuitive hits in place of a schedule-oriented rigidity. Again, these are neither good nor bad, just observations of varying management style. I had some amazing months on OF, but they weren't out of sheer marketing genius or business stratagems; they were due to miraculous luck and psychotic overworking.

At some point, I will quit my OnlyFans and relegate my work to instead writing about it, to doing Cyberhorny and Nastya Valentine things for a living — I will be at peace with myself having had unique and unprecedented ethical business practices on that site, knowing I still fucking kicked ass, even if I didn't get as much money as I could potentially have had I gone the "business" route, or created a fantastical character heavily divorced from my own reality. But here's the thing: delusion is as necessary to our reality as the truth; perhaps even more so. Ignorance is bliss.

The truth is often a heavy, painful pill to swallow. Finding out the cute German 18-year old nursing student is really a 30-year old mom from Maine? Or that the poor fetishized nerdy gamer girl still has her parents paying her rent? Or that the foxy waif who masturbates while saying your name never actually finishes, or even enjoys the act? Some people will see through those bad optics; usually other creators. Other creators could praise the deception as an epic take back of women's liberation after centuries of being used mercilessly by men: ha, it's our turn to have you now! Jfc let us have *something*.

Being an emotional being in a disposable world

Stupid, viewers are not, though: when a creator isn't having a genuinely fun time, viewers will at least subconsciously catch on to it. We need our viewers to believe we're enjoying the sex, and we are not trained thespians or porn actors; to my watchful eye of countless hours examining pornography of all spectra, it's obvious when a girl is faking it on cam, even if it looks on the minimum threshold of realistic. Most subscribers will let the fantasy belong to them, and keep making rich girls richer in the hopes of getting closer to them.

My critique isn't towards every girl who capitalizes off OnlyFans (or really the internet at large), but the ones who let cyberly-induced greed poison them into the loss of self-awareness. I'm not gonna lie, there is factually a price tag associated with our time and company. Obviously I capitalize off of it too — I'm in the camp of creators who are transparent about what goes down behind the scenes, and our category is usually more obscure, less elitist, and less mainstream. I'm not a household name, but your weird cousin who's a little too into Pokemon and esoteric sluts probably knows who I am.

OnlyFans is neither good nor bad, but just a platform. The morality spectrum depends on the individual using it. We are heavily indoctrinated by many societal systems that there is "one right way" to do things, and if you do it incorrectly, good fucking luck. It makes me wonder about the morality mechanisms within AI and how they mirror and adhere to the conventions of society -- who is programming them? Who is programming us?

Those of us who probe beyond OnlyFans and explore and transcend its limitations... I fucking love these creators and I wish there were more — I get the need to survive in the world tho, (or pay your way through school if you have no other way, or make money to care for your family). None of us are immune to the capitalist system and displaying an authentic self can be as disadvantageous as it is empowering. Generally these kinds of pages have a lower subscriber count, but a higher rate of retention and regulars. Think hole in the wall sushi restaurant, not a local McDonalds. I answer every single message I get on OF, whether per day I get 5 or 55, … but I will always prioritize the ones who tip first. OF's feature of auto-pinning messages with tips to the top of the inbox also propagates this transactional sex.

OF is a surprisingly effective two-way channel of emotional support, if used with that intention. I talk about a lot of emo ass shit on my OF — it's basically an emotional rollercoaster and unhinged intellectual dissociative analysis of my life events, told through rants and illustrated with nudes. (6,000 images and 700 videos of my nudes you won't find anywhere else, mind you — I have the compulsive need to compensate for any histrionic oversharing by posting sexy and unemotional content as a palate cleanser for contrast value).

I feel an equal mix of cringed out and happy when thinking about this, but my posts are so emotionally degloving and self-maiming that it sometimes inspires my subscribers to be considerably open with me about their own struggles. It's actually quite sweet, and extremely indicative of our times. I have received emotional feelings of support from the kind messages of my subscribers as well. I may have more conversations about mental health than horny sexting in my DMs. I'm not a therapist, but I play one on OF. (I do not give advice, I merely listen, "be there", reflect, and occasionally send voice notes, not unlike a custom-simulated AI). A human playing the part of a robot playing the part of a human.

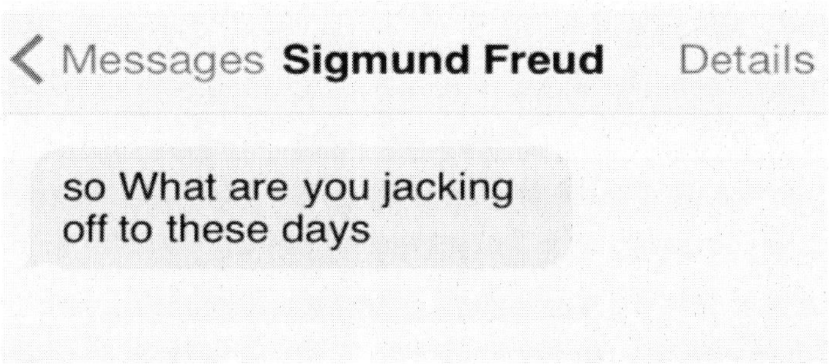

My own body is an avatar. I am desensitized. In a disposable world filled with disposable girls, we derided cyberjezebels take control of our own objectification, dehumanization, and expression of sexuality. I'm very wary of "othering" myself from my fellow creators, in the way that I say "well, most people don't do x, I do x; but I don't do y which most people do" and that it has some type of connotation of superiority or distancing or pretense beneath it. I existentially feel an instant kinship and solidarity with my fellow creators more than a distance, but I do tend to distance myself in all areas of my life, including the way I run my OF. Sometimes uniqueness works in my favor; most times I find that it is target for ostracizing or bullying, as those who are different often are attacked before they are rewarded. In a way, I am trying to reclaim my own narrative of past bullying traumas by owning that "difference" — no one can take my subjectivity away from me, idiosyncratic and psychotic as it may be.

To stand out is to agonize, but I've also found time and time again when I've tried to fit in and be neurotypical instead of neurotic, in school or in NSFW internet, I could never make it work to my favor. I am simply too fucking weird. Too weird for the mainstream, not weird enough for complete fringe. I have no choice but to go with it. Can I then withdraw from the need to be normal, and own — nay, weaponize, hornily — my weirdness? Without truly having a two-way conversation with me, you have no way of gauging my sincerity because we lose the nuance that is prevalent in direct connection.

Regulation of NSFW images is another question altogether. The AI's that comfort and pacify are also the ones that monitor and regulate.

I had an experience with the OF automated filter, and automated response help center, that nearly cost me my account when it deleted a lot of important content from my page, mainly my 22min visual album *Hentai and Crack Vol 1*, the frontispiece of my page and what started my OF in the first place, when I documented myself recording it in my Tesla scantily clad and making horny tracks.

The video was flagged because "there were unverified participants in the video" — multiple overlays of me, twin and triplet and endless Nastyas in different outfits. I opened support ticket after support ticket and engaged in circular emails with OF's support center telling them they got it wrong, and they shouldn't put my account up for deletion because I was following the rules, the filter just caught multiple faces and flagged it as multiple participants when it's really all the same person.[60]

I know with clarity how important it is to tag other parties in the work, and how horribly violating non-consensual posting of content is. Beyond that, I am a solo creator, with the few girls I've collabed with being properly tagged. This was, objectively, a fault of the AI. When I was emailing with them, I asked them to contact me over the phone to resolve this matter since my writing was not reaching them. My request was ignored. In fact, all tenets of humanity were absent from the interaction with the help center. It was like a copy-paste of regurgitated rhetoric. They kept my account active since I was following all the rules, but *H&C* was removed, and as superficial as it sounds, affected me deeply, like a true loss. Now, the video piece has no home. Too NSFW for instagram, too artistic for porn sites, OnlyFans was a perfect housing for it. Where it will go next, if anywhere at all, is TBD. Perhaps uploaded to this site. Perhaps in stasis forever on a dusty hard drive. Who knows, really.

"Masks. - There are women who, however you may search them, prove to have no content but are purely masks. The man who associates with such almost spectral, necessarily unsatisfied beings is to be commiserated with, yet it is precisely they who are able to arouse the desire of the man most strongly: he seeks for her soul - and goes on seeking."
— Friedrich Nietzsche, Human, All Too Human: A Book for Free Spirits

60 Interesting that AI adjudicates what is human. And gets it wrong.

A heart just can’t contain
All of that empty space
~Bright Eyes

7: XXX Trauma Oasis

"Finding new ways to hurt each other is what we're good at."
-Criminal Minds[61]

Post-pandemic woes and the loneliness crisis have highlighted the burden of isolation. This is self-evident. Self esteem, apps, hookup culture, mental issues. (or so I've heard...)

We do now have sex education, but sex starts out in the real world. Real world problems translate to the digital realm. We are often told what not to do rather than what to do, when it comes to sex. The meaning of sex and love. The meaning of life. Direct vs indirect cues and approach. There is always a perimeter of what isn't being articulated. I try to chart a direct map of my lived experience.

Most people claim to join my page because they were
"bored"
"lonely"
"Horny"
"Sapiosexual"*
"curious"
"want to spank that ass."
**I had in my bio on OF "a sapiosexual's worst nightmare"*

Just as women have to discover new facets of our sexuality, men too have to discover new facets of themselves. The walls come down, and learning happens. Me letting my walls down, my guard down a little bit, allows my clients to show vulnerability as well. **To really be a good "whore", you have to be a therapist first.** Hit that raw nerve. Hit it raw. Clients want a bit of a therapist, a container for their rawest thoughts and most challenging emotions. The sex part is just the extimate manifestation of emotional intimacy beneath. What most people want truly is a smile on their face at the end of the day, a comfortable and non judgemental space, an empathetic voice on the other end of the line – and to give that to others in return. This is what I really provide. I'm not just a naked girl. I am a place. A conduit. A vacuum. An outlet. A spindle, a darkness, a

61 human beings take profound satisfaction in doing harm, particularly unconscious harm: we may call this negative creation. -louise gluck

fever, a necklace.

"You don't get to see it, but this outlet of creativity you have has done a lot to open my eyes outside my very narrow bubble. I came in horny, but it's grown far beyond that. I've made friends that I can say is only possible because of the stuff that you've shared. You've opened my eyes to a different view of politics and ways of thinking. Your creative endeavors have pushed me outside to look at local talent and new artists and appreciate more than I would have normally. I just want to thank you, from the bottom of my heart. I know this sounds sappy but I don't care."
- JustADude69

Sex work is like therapy - in an online anonymous space, the deepest parts of the psyche come out. Talking about not just their pervy desires for me but about their life dramas - family, relationships, health issues, work stress, medication, mental health etc. Some men seek relief in the jerking but they also find themselves psychologically relieving. An oasis of peace from the brutality of daily life. A space of relaxation.[62]

Life is intense and it's hard being a human. There's a sense of relief in the chat. I see a therapist and stay with her because she doesn't judge. I suspect that's a reason why my clients stay with me, and others stay with certain sex workers — the element of being able to open up in a private and unrestrained way is critical. I go to therapy. I hug my kitties. I set aside time to read. To take a bath. To watch mindless tv. To do absolutely nothing. Doing nothing is my trauma oasis. Some of my favorite days are where I live like a pussy princess. Fantasy grabs reality by the scrotum: I wake up on a day off and look around my room, surveying the mess. It's my mess, I've earned it. Panties hanging off the drawers, cameras and heart shaped ring lights around the bed, iPhones sleeping next to me, laptops living in the moment, a closet full of Selkie and Prada… all illusions of luxury and extravagance for a girl who doesn't need to do anything today, or tomorrow, or the next day. All her needs are covered. The lazy life is the good life - charmed, spoiled, pampered, luxurious. Have you ever seen an heiress work?

Those little things that everyone takes for granted that not everyone has, that single mom had to work extra hard for. Being low income started to appear around the holidays when the mood would get darker and sadder, the utilities weren't on or dinners were held at someone else's house, not at home. I promised myself I would do everything I can to ensure I don't have to run myself into the ground by hustling, grinding, striving. It's not a humble beginning that endears — it's a dark reality for many people. Am I a striver? Oh no. Hell no. Even with this book, I don't have aims for it to be a bestseller or gain me international fame[63]. It's a labor of love, and a slow burn of a project. That

62 Some psychoanalysts believe that when a patient reveals their masturbation fantasies to the therapist the real work can begin.

63 I do though

would be a perk for sure, exceeding my expectations, but I will be happy to hold it in my hands as a tangible object, a baby I've been gestating. I'm taking my sweet, valuable, value-less time with it. This Cyberhorny book is the longest project I've ever worked on. I work on it when I'm able to, when I feel like it, when it feels like it needs to be written. As much as I could try, I can't rush or force inspiration and motivation. It just comes out - like vomit.

Growing up with my insecurities about poverty, I spill out my mental crevices through my material possessions. Candles that scent every room, silk sheets, overabundance of stuffed seals, furniture for my cats, making an album in my Tesla .. are these flexes to myself really shields? In the intimate space of the client service, we have to be careful with who we trust. It's a two way street. Shining the light of awareness is the first salve for insecurity.

But in all my privilege-adjacent interactions, my chats with chunky-sugardaddys, I realized a some things about truly successful people. They don't get to where they are without a barrage of setbacks. Stepping on someone's toes. Or the reverse, offering and accepting help. Success cannot be achieved alone – that would be a fool's errand. In my encounters with rich men, especially those who have attained success on their own, without generational wealth or inheritances or scams or lottery wins or the like - there is a glimpse of inner turmoil, darkness, courage, weakness, vanquishing, tiredness.

There was a part of me that almost fetishized people of wealth[64], envied them, aspired to emulate them, obsessed and ruminated over their psychology. I don't understand how people spend money. I don't even understand how I spend money. I don't understand how people attain massive lasting wealth. Is it luck? Is it overworking? Is it corruption? Is it ambition? Is it genius level intellect? Practicality? Good decisions? Good habits? Good teams around them? Faith? How do they maintain their motivation? How do they do it? Which devil do I have to sell my soul to, to have what they have? It doesn't matter. They are just people. Every fetishized object needs to be humanized. No human being is invincible. They sleep, they eat, they worry, they need, they laugh. And every now and again, they jerk off.

> DF I love your hentai and crack video. I was going to masturbate last night and just ended up watching that for 20 minutes instead. It's more like sexual art than porn.

XXX Trauma Oasis

I coined the term 'trauma oasis' to describe the ethos of my page when I began to notice that the emotional aspect was almost more fulfilling for my fans than the sexual aspect. Although my nudes are the backdrop as eye candy, my

64 Individuals experiencing luxury

responses are at the forefront as psychological nourishment on my OF. I leaned into the assessment of my page as a sanctuary free of judgment or reprimand. Whatever was plaguing my subs in daily life is briefly eradicated during their escape into Nastya World.

"You have infused me with a passion that's laid dormant for years. Now I'm at a point where I can say your advice/presence in my life has been transformative and healing. My cyber sexy spirit guide. No one I know in life comes close to the magic you share."
- ReallyBigDaddy

Guys subscribe to me to have their feelings validated.
A community of men getting together for one reason and one reason only: to goon to me.

What happens in this digital erotic exchange between me and my subscribers, who turn to me to as a fantasy? There is something more than just a desire to connect with a cyber babe who's lifelike and responsive. What goes on in my mind during this - is it fulfilling for me, or just a part of the job? For some people, the impulse to connect with a real human girl and not a spam bot or a sexting assistant is more fulfilling than just seeing nudes. The drive to be heard, seen, listened to. In that way of stimulating the mind attached to the body, we come to an unspoken understanding. Right now, the room is ours and only ours. To speak freely, to let guards down, to show the soft underbelly of what we normally hide. In that way, parasocial porn does something wonderful.

"Being the richest man in the cemetery doesn't matter to me. Going to bed at night saying we've done something wonderful... that's what matters to me."
— Steve Jobs

The specificity of pornography: it's so variant from person to person and there's so much of it, endless permutations of pre-made and tailor-made perversion. Why watch a random porn nowadays when a sex worker who looks like your ideal fantasy woman can make you a video fulfilling the fantasy you've always wanted, in a safe online space akin to the dream/thought space, distinct from reality but influenced by it, safe in its disparity – safe from inconvenience or judgment?

Sexual fantasies with a real-life partner vs. sexual fantasies in the digital sphere: some people may find it too inconvenient, too embarrassing, too intimate, "too real" to discuss fantasy with a partner, and safer to enact it with a third-party professional. In a similar way to certain types of people who do not discuss personal things with their friends or family, deferring instead to a clinical mental health professional. That is not to say that everyone who has sex with a partner keeps their fantasies from the partner: it depends on each individual relationship, level of trust, judgment, openness, intimacy etc.

But all this to say that the centrality of the masturbation fantasy: gentle (passive, wholesome) fantasy vs violent (active, aggressive) affects each person's sex life in that revealing such a deeply personal part of the self is like telling a therapist about an inner world, an inner trauma. It requires vulnerability.

Vulnerability of revealing something sexually explicit, and vulnerability about revealing something emotionally explicit. Tone disparity in dudes who want me "dress up like long distance gf and put in a butt plug and oil yourself and blow me a kiss and spank your ass and say my name" … and dudes who "been through hard knocks in life, parents gone, super depressed, socially awkward and incredibly lonely, thank you for being a comfort to me in a hard time". Is the tone really that disparate? After all, the sexual and the emotional are intertwined.

In any instance, gentle or violent, wholesome or sexual, passive or active, imagination is strong. These men have to have a very vivid imagination to 1. Jerk off and 2. Pretend that I am their girlfriend. It's really a cognitive achievement. Proving time and time again that fantasy is more powerful than reality. The fantastical becomes the real. When the solution to the mind-body problem is gooning. Again and again, agoon and agoon. I too have to have a vivid imagination to meet them in the field of Goon and make it realistic. Intersubjectivity occurs during fantasy-acting. Two horny people's cognitive perspectives aligning.

"Thank you for your genuineness. Started reading your work. Very insightful, the impact on mental health stuff. It takes a lot of bravery to share what you do."
- @ uj536278

It is in fact a lot like being a therapist. My clients tend to be recurring: if someone requests a session, chances are high they will request it again. Use of self as therapeutic concept: I've found a niche in being emotionally available. But this is an insanely vulnerable practice. The amount of scammers, crazies, time wasters out there is enormous. Your gut will become your number one tool in sussing out what feels right and what feels wrong: who to interact with, who to give information to, who to trust, what to post.

What I choose to post and curate, is it because of exhibitionism or because of business. Is this my fetish? We all have a fetish. All these clients who come to me for fetish work — they have human lives, go to their jobs, pay their bills, eat their breakfasts, have their coffee, talk to their parents, feel their neuroses, put their shoes on, experience highs and lows of life.

"Thank you for the opportunity to be captivated by you. I look forward to savoring you and what you created. You are the absolute best, most beautiful, and I am SO glad I found you. Long story, but I don't let myself cum very often (repressed af). You really help me connect to a side of myself I thought was gone"
-StrictGooner88

They're coming to a place of voyeuristic interactive parasocial fantasy where they can have fun with fetishes; a safe space to enact them in, an active sex life on the internet, perhaps a secret life of their own. What I choose to post is for them, matching supply to demand, but in a way where I enjoy the commodity that I am supplying. Sometimes I try to predict what may be wanted and create the content that fits best; however, predictive elements are rarely correct, and the more contrived they are, the worse they perform. So my main approach is posting in a stream of consciousness whatever happened that day, like a horny version of my diary. XXX Sylvia Plath. I bring my humanity online — but is showing emotional range along with showing skin a positive or a negative?

The dilemma of authenticity plagues me. Is it wise to be emotional online? Does it even matter? Are these questions even worth asking in our collective internet consciousness which is so disposable and transient, operating on a limited time clock of instant gratification and swiftly-reconciled desire?

Breaking the fourth wall and talking to fans about the meta analysis of the Onlyfans experience. No one wants to know how the sausage is made. No magician reveals their secrets. But to be let inside part of my inner life, and my process, gives the fans a further sense of parasocial closeness.

Some don't want that at all; they go to porn pages to look at porn, keep it lighthearted and teehee haha. Some of them are very fascinated and offer their takes and analyses as well. Most are just like, 'ok that's cool'. Sometimes you gotta leave some mystery.

"I had no idea that was a thing. Putting on a kind of charade, and manufacturing false authenticity. I have to admit that is kind of smart, but the morality is questionable too. It does make you think about the subscriber relationship though. And maybe some subscribers don't even care if it real or not. It makes me think of this anime called Rent-A-Girlfriend. I've thought about the nature of our interactions too. I question if we could be online friends; I see you as an artist. I had a really good listen to your music yesterday. On a totally random topic: have you encountered a Tesla hater? There's this youtube channel, WhamBamTeslaCam."
- riveted_man_420

The draw of OnlyFans is in its flaws, the flaws of humanity and error. Those moments when the creator breaks the fourth wall. When the guy filming his girlfriend's content says "oh shit sorry camera's out of focus" and it provides a brief glimpse into real life, out of pornography.[65]

The flawed content often does the best. Yet, so many OF pages imitate the polished quality of professional porn, likely because that already is a massive existing structure, catering to the time-sensitive nature of desire.

A desirous state of consciousness impacts the decisions people make. Horny for sex, horny for respect, horny for connection - where does the rabbit hole of hornidom lead?

I wonder why people make the choice to subscribe to me, when there are countless nsfw content creators out there, advertising their alluring selves one thirst trap at a time. Historically I seem to have been a magnet for curious nerds who've enjoyed talking to me almost more so than watching me fuck. Was that what made me more appealing, brain over boobs? Philosophy over my pussy?? The psychology of the horny brain is fascinating to me; what kind of decisions are made in a state of altered horniness?

Safety first.

A day in the life of an online sex worker can be mundane. Within mundanity, when our guard is down, we still never know if there will be danger in online strangers and have to maintain shields to protect ourselves. Stage names. VPNs. Playing nice. Ignoring trolls and haters, lest we fuel their flame.

As an artist, sex worker, anyone with a public presence, you'll inevitably ruffle people's feathers and you have to be okay with it. Not everyone will like you, so there is no point in people-pleasing. One must be being direct and blunt, stating clear boundaries. That said, I don't believe in being petty or rude,

---

65 It is like those moments in pornography when the camera pulls back to reveal that around two naked bodies stands a room full of people. Everyone is trying to ignore the extra bodies in the room but, like the unconscious, they continue to function irrespective of our awareness or belief in their existence. - tim dean *taking shelter from queer.*

or escalating arguments online.

We keep ourselves safe with anonymity and boundary enforcement. Our most important tool in the online wild area is our intuition. Our most important skill is asserting boundaries. "No" is a complete sentence.

What we encounter on the web, nothing prepares us for.
What we encounter in life, nothing prepares us for.
No sex education teaches how to navigate when a partner ghosts you, when the 'vibes are off', when the sex was bad, when your body responds discordantly, when your mind spirals.

Any encounter with sexuality can be traumatic and overpowering. Science ignores questions of meaning: we have all the terminology for mechanics of sex, but not as much for the emotional impact sex has. How to have emotionally safe sex. Staying safe is recognition of the danger and unpredictability.

Pornography is inflammatory to many, opposed by many, concerning for various reasons, cited as one-dimensional and toxic, that no good can come of it. I saw the theory in the porn and jacked it til I set it free.

On the web, top searches are taboo and forbidden. Do the top searched porn turn-ons mirror the disturbances that we as humans subconsciously are fascinated by? Teen porn, Incest tropes, brutal rough sex scenes, bordering on rape. What about... Pornography where the characters decline sex. A non-porno. An anti-porn until the character finds someone they want to have sex with and readily, clearly consent.

Consent, of course, is a major gray area, in life and online. Honey you already know it's gotta be a hell yes. If it's not a hell yes, it's a no. CNC (Consensual non consent) theory. It is not an uncommon way for SA survivors to take control of their trauma, by playing out these scenes within their control – digitally or irl. I myself as stated in Chapter 4 have entered sex work to rewrite my sexual narrative.

Rape is not simply about sex. Violence, control, power over the victim. The controversial CNC scene is enacted to gain control over their narrative - where the "rape" becomes in fact about sex, pleasure, and fantasy of the "victim" rather than control by the abuser. Those who have been assaulted sometimes engage in a fantasy to assert control over their reality. Some submissive, some dominant. Some become their rapist, get in their head, try to see their point of view like a criminologist in a behavioral analysis unit. Some heal by restaging the psychodrama – in acting, playing the part of themselves at a vulnerable and traumatizing time, pruning the shears of revision to shed the agony and rise from the ashes of fear with pleasure and understanding. Lacan says as humans we have an unconscious satisfaction in the way we suffer, doomed to repeat things for the familiarity of chaos.

In medias res
In media we rest? No, in media we never rest.
Me naked – just me and my ideas
Sex sells
An amazing cognitive achievement to cum at the same time as the porno ends.
Projecting yourself into the role of the sex character, occupying their fictional world.
Sex and the City was about relationships, friendships, shopping, and musing.
Cyberhorny too, sounds hornier than it really is. An inner dialogue externalized.
Trauma codified and gamified. Personal anxieties leaked to social media.

Sex in the media tends to be portrayed as one-dimensional. A teen losing virginity at prom. A drunk one night stand. A freak ynympho redhead. But it is so much more. Does sex numb emotion? Enhance emotion? What does it bring up? A cathartic release? A distraction? A solution to a painful situation? Anxiety and pain? Is anxiety interpreted as arousal? I have witnessed a man after a panic attack have sex with me. Coming down, going down.

As an artist, especially one working with sexual arousal, of course I am bound to ruffle some feathers. In the public eye, whatever inflammatory dread arises, I have to be okay with that.

Hold on while I crack open a Dr Pepper Zero Sugar Strawberries and Cream Summer Beverage

> My God! I asked for porn, you gave me art! That was amazing. I love the story and character you've created, and the way you've established a sense of place - it really felt like an airport in your apartment! I love the production, details like the cuts of you going down the hall. And so sexy, made me rock hard. Thanks so much. And so quickly produced, too. You are very good at this. Thanks again, A.

Haters greatest hits -
"Your eyes look creepy"
"Small tits"
"Saw ur post sorry ur fat and gross no offense"
"Ur too scrawny to be breedable"
"No one would ever date a whore, u need to find jesus"
Online haters and trolls are like cockroaches: you fend off one, three more show up in their place.

It's not just sex workers who get hate; it's also the people who visit them. "Simps" are constantly given shit online for admiring, paying, complimenting girls - what is the deal with that? How to destigmatize simping, and if anything, encourage it.

The type of haters who are patronizing and play mind games, guys who get off on humiliating the girls they pay without the girls being in on their little "kink". Negging: a form of non consensual humiliation. Take that tampon out and let the pussy talk.

The type of aggressive subscribers who will not take "no" for an answer. There are certain types of content banned from OF and similar sites, which include: pissing, shitting, vomiting, public flashing, anything involving young age role play, meetups between subscriber and model, third-party payment apps. Words like
"Young"
"Pee"
"Poo"
"Vomit"
"Blood"
"Schoolgirl"
"Meet"
"Cashapp"
"Venmo"
Are forbidden.

Guys find their way around this by alpha numerically spelling or spacing out m33t y ou ng… or using emojis 🤮. One guy asked me if I would make a whole stack of pancakes and vom them up for a custom video.[66] My answer was a simple, "No". As he kept pestering me, I had to restrict him. I had to restrict. I had to restrict. I don't feel well.

There are a handful of shady boundary-disrespecting MFs who I've had to restrict (they could no longer have access to messaging me, but still be allowed to view my page content), and a few I've had to block (booting them from my page entirely, refunding their subscription).

What is MY trauma oasis?

How do I shield myself from the strife? I explore that more deeply in Chapter 12, especially in regards to body image. It's an unexpected and rarely talked about, yet seemingly obvious psychic consequence of doing porn – reconciling my mental peace with the physical body. This relates to themes of me vs me. Self help – or self hell.

But in terms of an oasis from haters, them vs me, the strongest shield is having a clear sense and enactment of boundaries. Saying "no" to a request I don't feel comfortable with. Educating someone about online etiquette. Taking a day off when I don't feel well. Ignoring the onslaught of unsolicited opinions.

66 Asking a schizophrenic anorexic woman to eat!?!?!? The audacity .

Opinions are like assholes – everybody has one.
All critique is a projection.

Something about being called "degrading" but the most degrading thing is capitulating to our social structure of constant self-promotion, capitulating to the rapidly ever changing rules of social media.

Health: The Oasis of the Body

Love the assumption that sex workers don't have the most impeccable sexual health. Our bodies are literally our job and we get tested constantly. It's civilians who haven't seen a Dr in years~ Yeah talk to me when the guys hooking up raw at the club every Friday and Saturday night take steady STD tests and go to the gynecologist regularly.

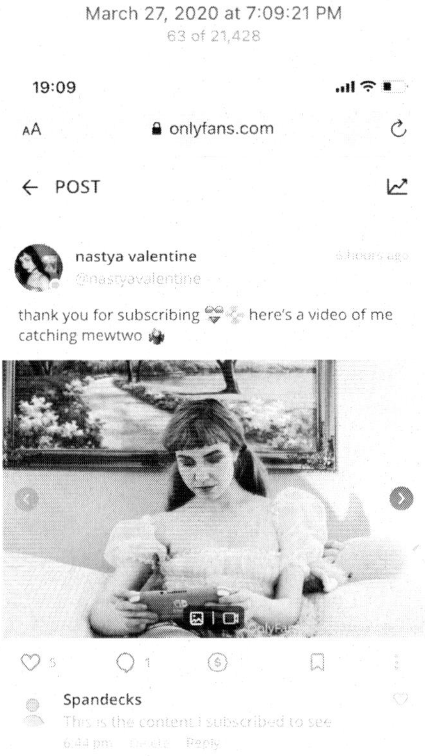

Little Nastya

The inner child: what we've been desiring or wanting or lacking on a fundamental level. Little Nastya enters this arena of digital marketing; an illusion of object permanence. She enters my dreams, my cognition, my memory. I have to heal her and honor her. Did she know?

She knew, she played, she gamed. Growing up, I was a die hard Pokemon gamer. I even competed in a few national tournaments. An OG egirl. In high school, my parents took away my game consoles because it wasn't leading to a practical profession and I was too old to be playing silly little video games. Cut to adult Nastya on OnlyFans streaming pokemon gaming, earning a living with content I've made for my gamer audience. Steps to healing the inner child; I'm allowed to play these games, and not only that, I'm allowed to thrive. We can excel in so many ways: emotional, financial, social, personal.

We all have a Little Nastya. Little Caleb. Little Evan. How were we as children? What did we want? Do our base survival strategies continue into adulthood?

What were our first encounters with desire, sexuality, adolescent love and yearning? What place does sex have in our physical and mental lives? How do we introspect about these encounters? Who do we talk to about sexperience, and how? Friends, therapists, diaries?

I have always kept a diary. I continue to do my Morning Pages, sometimes publishing my dreams – the exfiltration of my intimate musings. Exposing naked thought and exploring inner worlds. For all the internet to see, mere casualties of this performative warfare. Who *really* did I want to show it to, though? Who did Little Nastya want to see her? Who cannot be replaced by thousands of prying eyes, fallen soldiers? Where is this blind dictator? There is a meditative technique by Neville Goddard called "the pruning shears of revision" where you recall (usually negative) memories and rewrite them in your head to be positive, and rewire your brain towards positivity. Review and rewrite today to activate a better tomorrow.

Plushies, ruffles, sequins, pink dresses – they come out, sublimated in the adult world[67]. Pain travels through family lines until someone is ready to heal it in themselves. By going through the agony of healing, you no longer pass the poison to the generations that follow. The process of healing, the quotidian existence of the day to day – allowing witnesses to the crucible of suffering and recuperation – is the most unbearable agony of all.

67 When I was a child, I spoke as a child, I understood as a child, I thought as a child: but when I became a man, I put away childish things. For now we see through a glass, darkly; but then face to face: now I know in part; but then shall I know even as also I am known. Corinthians 13:11-12

"If the glare of the public eye has become unbearable, our inner child may claim its rights and our bodily shadow might turn into our mental second self, become our anchor, make us stay grounded and grant us deepness and intensity. By retreating from the blaze of display into our substantial self, we gain rootedness, insight and new worldly wisdom."

— Erik Pevernagie

✞

"The empathy of these new men show woman is born of their acceptance of their own emotional, intuitive, sensory, and humanistic approach to relationships. They allow themselves to weep (many never wept), to show vulnerability, to expose their fantasies, share their innermost selves.. To have empathy one must to some extent feel what the other feels."
-Anais Nin, In Favor of the Sensitive Man

♥ ♥♥

8: The Dark Agony of Internet Marketing

"There is no longer a staging of the commodity: there is only its obscene and empty form. And advertising is the illustration of its saturated and empty form." -Jean Baudrillard *Simulacra and Simulation*

fter the whole crucible of theory this, relationships that, family trauma and sexual projection and inauthintimacy this and that, parasocial porn this that and the other… how do I begin to codify, condense, cohere it all into a polished product that is ready to be marketed?

From praxis to promo

Often, I put myself in the client's place. Would I talk to me? Would I subscribe to me? Would I be interested in this type of niche content – intellectual, stupid, intense, escapist, pensive, penisive?

First off, there has to be something to market. In this case, my OnlyFans page. That link is my trove of content and communication, separated from the world by a 12 dollar paywall. Not bad, right? That's less than Netflix and Hulu are charging these days. The goal for a content creator is to get viewers to click the OF link, and to be enticed enough to subscribe.[68]

The first contact people have with an adult model is in the specular image – hornyposting and thirst traps on Instagram, TikTok, Reddit, Twitter, sometimes Pornhub, Fetlife, Facebook, YouTube, Threads, Tumblr. As moderation and shadow bans get tighter on the main platforms, models take to alternative routes where more eyes can see. There are constantly new micro platforms being introduced: Slushy (a nsfw version of Tiktok), Redgifs, and the like, there are constantly new platforms being beta tested, but those are so obscure that I'll primarily focus on the first four mentioned..

68 'Everytime you step up to the grill, you gotta deliver'

There is a new type of intelligence- capitalist e-intelligence and online marketing strategy brilliance. I don't possess it (at least not any more) but I recognize it when I see it.

Becoming a creator with e-capitalist advertising vs authentic content and how to split the difference

Clickbait and algorithm changing.
How about the dark agony of the night of the soul?????

When I get pubed…..

This is the worst part of my job, hands down. You think selling sex is degrading? Try marketing it. It's not even so much degrading as it is a herculean task of ninja-dodging the lasers of shadow bans, SWERFs, incels, haters, reddit mods, scammy spammers, and so so much more. I have seen some really amazing accounts though. I try to run my business the opposite way – 80% content and 20% marketing and rely on returning clients rather than bursts of new ones. Imo either one works. Any way in between works too.

Types of marketing: (brief discourse)

***Mass posting*:** as many times a day on as many different platforms as possible for maximum exposure. You never know whose consciousness you exist in. The most random-seeming people have reached out to me from the most obscure posts I've made. The risk in this method is sheer exhaustion, because it takes an insane amount of time and effort to dedicate to mass promotion AND the content creation of the paid platform. Making new accounts only to get shadow banned or deleted in a game of whack a mole, lest one be deleted for "guideline violations" or shadow banned (not entirely deleted, but curtailed so substantially less viewers are able to see any of your posts).
This was how I started. I didn't think; my mind just posted on its own, as much as possible.

Focusing on one platform: (ex: Instagram) that really works for you, and really leaning into it, becoming an expert of that platform. There is a risk in " putting all your eggs in one basket" because the guidelines of platforms change arbitrarily and can put a shadow ban or full ban on your account.[69] If that one account was your cash cow and it gets pubed, you're fucked – at least until you get your other backups going. Backup methods are always good to diversify income and strategy.

This was how I plateaued. As my digital/emotional bandwidth narrowed over time, distressed by platform oversaturation, I posted on less and less platforms, only working with the ones that did the best. Instead of posting multiple times daily, I reduced it to twice daily, then once daily, then just a few times a week, then once a week.. The algorithms *hate* that. They like to see constant posting and reward consistency. Consistency is the most important element of doing things like streaming, camming, and Onlyfans, and a part of what makes this field incredibly difficult.

***The long game*:** world building. Rather than mass posting constantly, rare but dense posts that create lore and narrative for your personal brand. Drama. There will be less viewers, but chances are they will be more hardcore fans, like a cult following. This is my method when I take time off from Onlyfans.

***Hybrid marketing*:** you have lore and backstory, you post everywhere all at once (maybe with help from assistants), and there is one platform you mainly post on. Overall, minus the assistants, this is how I make it work.

I'm resting my energy and emotional bandwidth until I regenerate for the next Go Time.

Reddit Redux

Because it allows porn and NSFW content, reddit is a popular place to market and promote, and the platform doesn't shadowban steamy content like Instagram or Tiktok.

Creators post in various subreddits and get karma or upvotes, trying to attain as wide of a reach as possible and grow their community. There are thousands of niches to post in: big titty, petite, Asian, hairy, MILF, etc. so it makes it appealing for creators, especially when starting out. Upvotes/likes/etc don't necessarily indicate how a creator is doing. I've seen creators in the 0/1% who don't have a huge social presence (which is what happened to me), and vice versa: popular girls online whose OF's dwindle in comparison to their socials. I've had posts get to the top of the 'hot' page + thousands of upvotes with little to no conversion, whereas a random niche sub would get me a ton of clients who are into that particular thing. So public numbers aren't always reflective of how many people will convert to subscribers. The nature of social media is illusory and we can curate what we want people to see, so take everything online with a grain of salt.[70]

---

69 The ray ban sale is happening until october

70 Desire is memetic. Etc. you see an account with many subscribers. You want.

Additionally, moderators on reddit are notorious for gatekeeping subreddits for only certain creators that pass their standards, random bans as ad hominem attacks if a model tries to appeal a ban, and in general being assholes. Yet models heavily promote on reddit because it's such a level playing field for those starting out: subreddit traffic can mean many views for an OF page. The algorithm has changed a lot between 2020 - 2024, stalling what was once a thriving porn-advertising platform, but models still post on there even if they're unsatisfied with these changes, simply because of the ability to get faster traffic to their sites. It's easier to grow a reddit profile than it is a IG/Tiktok profile, but there is no indication that the most popular reddit profiles make more than mainly IG/Tiktok-based models. In fact, once a IG creator hits it big, it's easier for larger accounts to avoid shadowbans and get away with posting lewder content.

Whether they use reddit, IG, tiktok, etc. the most successful creators all have a few things in common: strong work ethic, resilience, and ability to adapt to hard situations.

If we're under the 5% of the top creators, we're doing what 95% of creators are not doing. Many people give up in their first few months because their page shows no growth, and they're unwilling or unable to put in the work and the extra steps it takes to maintain a profitable page. I get it, there have been times when I wanted to give up too. If I have to take a break, I take a break, but I try not to give up entirely – at least not while my page still shows possibility and profit. It's all in the mindset. If you really want to succeed, you will. You will do whatever it takes to get there – even practice carnivorous marketing.

It usually takes a while for an OF page to gain traction and steadily grow, but it's not impossible to have it blow up in a short time, overnight even. Bearing in mind realistic expectations, the only way to find out is really just to try it.

My root problem has been the general disillusionment and resistance to marketing, but it's just a part of the game. We all have parts of our jobs that we resist. We can't not do it, because no marketing means no success.

The scams and the spam.

A rite of passage. This is why I closed all DMs on my socials and do not reply to them; I learned the hard way to always take payment upfront. One dude who scammed me into doing a video chat when I first started and then never sent me the money. I just had to take the L and move on. Shit happens. We have to learn from it.

This is not:

- A how-to guide on doing OF/camming/online SW, there are many of those online with a quick google search.
- A comprehensive historical timeline of internet x sex: Samantha Cole wrote an incredible book about this, *How Sex Changed the Internet*

This is:

- An experiential and highly personal account of the inner workings of the online adult world.
- A peeling back of the curtain behind the scenes, a philosophical experiment and intimate psychological examination.
- My tell-all.
- Macro and micro, cultural analysis of change that happened in the past few years.

At the end of the day, I can say, "she cooked"[71].
It is all the dark night of the soul of internet marketing.

The worst part is the competitive nature of the industry. Comparison is the thief of joy. Lack mentality – the perception that there aren't enough fans and tips for us all. This is nowhere near true. An abundance of niches and content varieties means an abundance of those who will be attracted to different things, different creators.

Society pits women against each other.
I have seen this in my mother.[72]

Values of modesty and conformity, yet the drive to have a beauty that none could compare to. I see how she projects those views on me. To be prettier and skinnier than everyone else, but still look normal within society (no dyed hair, no tattoos, "natural" beauty). There was no emphasis on my creative wishes, my intellectual ambitions, even the fostering of my friendships. She would always compare me in a negative or positive way to the girls around me, because that was the way she saw herself.

Men were always around and she used her beauty and sex appeal for profitless validation. Lowlife men were especially prone to her seductions; easy targets. She always *said* she wanted a nice life with a stable, reliable man, someone with money who could ease her burdens. But she rejected the suitors who could provide for her in lieu of *projects*. Her second husband, a manipulative meth head. A tale as old as time: "I can fix him".

Validation alone cannot pay the bills. She wasn't profiting, she was surviving. Why? Digging deeper, as a child I absorbed this information and subconsciously learned from it. Not to compete. Never to compare. Women have it hard enough as it is without internalized misogyny.

The hairstyle story. I don't have any memory of this, but my mom likes to tell the story. She got a haircut and style at the salon; when she came out, I ruined her hair with my hands because allegedly she "looked too pretty and I

---

71 But never in the kitchen

72 Is ... this whole enterprise.... Valentine trying to triumph over her mother... to think we assumed it was about the father... whoops

had to destroy it". Knowing my circumstances and through observation, I destroyed it because I could not bear to see my mom being taken away by a vapid, evil man. The way she sees it, I destroyed it because I was jealous. Her beauty wasn't a threat to my own; it was a threat to my survival, lest another parent abandons me to have another family.

"I wanted to destroy something beautiful" -Edward Norton in Fight Club beating Jared Leto's bleach blonde twink ass.

Jealousy is a powerful emotion. We all on occasion fall prey to this ugly green monster. We get jealous when others have what we deeply wish we had. For me, those with generational wealth and easy lives. Sometimes I cannot bear the gravity of it, the envy towards someone who has everything handed to them easily drives me crazy. The privilege to never work a day in their life, to know without a shadow of a doubt, that everything is taken care of. The luxury of not stressing about survival. It's something I've just had to contend with and accept. We're all dealt different cards in life, and I simply have to try my best with what I've got.

My mother's case is different – her jealousy centers on other women's beauty, how hers stacks up to it, what kind of aesthetic superiority she has, and how men will respond to it. She has projected this view on me my whole life. I didn't grow up pretty; I didn't become attractive or confident in my appearance until my mid/late 20's, and since natural beauty was not in my wheelhouse I took the artificial route. I've enjoyed this: the masquerade of vibrant makeup looks, the altering of my face with maintenance treatments, and especially the dying of my hair in colors pink, green, blue. It gives me a sense of happiness; coloring my hair is therapeutic for me. Each time I changed my hair color she was aghast, beyond livid. She would edit pictures we took together to black & white format, to dull my color. How dare I step outside the box of normality. This has been the subject of many a therapy session. I love my mother of course, she is my heart, but the early upbringing was a winding road to peaceful coexistence in adulthood.

In writing this out the differences between me and my mother are thrown into stark relief. I see how her projections have impacted my perspectives. In male interactions, female friendships, self-perception, appearance, and even in the marketing of said appearance, I too have capitulated to the greatest thief – comparison.

Oh fuck I forgot to eat my other half of my emergency crisis-averting bagel. Fml.

In the online meat market, and in the viewer's choice of whether or not to subscribe, I'm weighed against thousands + thousands of beautiful gorgeous stunning babes. Out of all those delicious options, my subscribers knock on the door. Sure, I may be someone's dream girl or niche aesthetic preference, but I'm not a fool – I don't have the objectively 10/10 modelesque looks to coast on. I have to have something to offer besides naked beauty. The role in personality and openness in my marketing is not to be underestimated.

Any girl can take and post a hot lingerie-clad or naked photo, I've done it many a time, and 9 times out of 10 that girl will be more attractive than me. So I inject a little something in my pics, a little slice of subjectivity, to offset the uncontrollable genetic lottery. Guys who game will be drawn to my gamer girl photos. Nerdy film dudes will notice my Twin Peaks, Fifth Element, Blade Runner cosplays. Books in the nude for readers. By including those types of details in my photos, I was narrowing down my audience but carving out a niche for myself.

There is also the approach of being friendly, a dash of relatability.
Maybe I have an illusion of unattainability, but interacting with my followers beyond an emoji or a "thanks!" shows them I have a little bit of wit, or drama, or kindness, or unhingedness. Unpredictability and excitement. Reality and authenticity within a world of contrived artifice.

"Society drives people crazy with lust and calls it advertising" ~John Lahr

Society as a whole demonizes, but individuals are more understanding. In writing this book, my aim was to create a concise and structural work of theory. But what is theory without praxis. In no way I intended a memoir, but the personal anecdotes, tales from the crypt of lived and killed experience, are critical to cushion the theory. Wary of oversharing or being redundant, I asked my editors what parts to pare down and cut off at the final revisions. My idea was to cut the personal parts.

The personal parts are the best parts. Says who? Everyone.

Writing was my power, my voice; I should like to use it kindly to give voice to the voiceless. The vessel is me. The information is bigger than me. I am the micro of the macro. It generates a sense of privilege, which I yearn for.

So then why do I feel unsatisfied?

Because desire in its very nature yearns for the unattainable. Once you have attained your object of desire, you no longer desire. You are cured from desire. Successful rehabilitation from yearning. Mitigation of the pain, the suffering, the agony of longing. If you had everything you desire, would you be happy and fulfilled? What more could you want?

Extinguishing the flame of desire (and entering nirvana) is a central tenet in Buddhism.
Craving for sensual pleasures. (Western psychological parallel – Libido)
Craving for existence. (Will to live)

Craving for non-existence. (Thanatos death instinct)

Let's say I wanted 1000 subscribers. I had attained 1000 subscribers: am I happy with this, or do I want more?

A. I'm happy with this; desire is extinguished.
B. I want more; desire turns into greed.

The risk of getting what you want, the thing that will make you happy, is that once you get that thing and have a moment of happiness - the moment passes and you start to fear losing it. I have attained 1000 subscribers but after taking a break from work due to burnout and oversaturation distress, I feared losing them and I lost half of them. Continuing my break, I lost half of that half. The paranoia of desire intensified.

As for greed. Why is it even when we get what we want, we are conditioned to want even more? Why is enough sometimes not enough? Especially on the internet, where social media shows every little acquisition, success, promotion, relationship, shopping trip, vacation, clothes, jewelry, status symbols of what is on trend or about to be.

The way to extinguish desire, greed, paranoia is surrendering. Accepting that the world is ever-changing and fundamentally unsatisfactory. True satisfaction is fleeting.

How frightening it is that everything is temporary. How great it is that everything is temporary.

The astral, intangible elements of the cyber realm are akin to the ineffable spiritual plane. Separated from the physical world, but affecting its existence. As above, so below. In mind, in flesh. In the way that it's difficult to describe to someone a psychedelic trip, out of body experience, energetic healing modality, it's difficult to describe the subjective ontology of online adult marketing. The cyber field is where we leave our body, even though we may use our body in the specular image, the avatar of consciousness. Some bigger reality exists, one that your ego does not define. For those with experience, no explanation is necessary. For those with no experience, none will suffice.

"If you get the message, hang up the phone." ~Alan Watts

Hypnagogic state, sexual collective unconscious, incarnation of kinks.
Embrace them fully or run away? Surrender and accept.
Let go or get dragged.

Multiple forms of accountability - posting puts a fire under my ass. If I posted something and I don't deliver, damn Imma feel like an idiot. If I posted something and I deliver, it 1. Makes me feel good about myself, and 2. Creates trust for my audience, that I advertise truthfully.

Every day, a thousand pussy pics.

Capitalizing on the spontaneous. Every day, a thousand dollars awaits if you can capitalize on every minute of your time. Every little thing you do can be monetized. When I clean the house, I turn my camera on and yap. Man, sometimes I get emotional when I film and I literally just be posting that unhinged shit. Why not? Anything can be content. Anything can be a porno. **Reality porn star.** Someone's laundry day can be a horny adventure: help stepbro I got stuck in the dryer -_- … Every backroom of your subjectivity has a price tag on it. But is that really a way to live?

Hold on while I take a few kratoms.

I try to get something other than money out of this experience.
My haters humble me, so thank you.
Not the reddit cockroach pic hate group

Pregnant women have to switch to beer. No more tequila shots babe.
Pregnant women can have a little narcan as a treat. It's okay mommy can smoke while pregnant. Gender reveal it's …. Steve. "There are two things we're never prepared for in life: twins." *(Criminal Minds).*

"You have a layered existence"-Therapist
Customizable user experience: who wants the girlfriend experience, and who just wants to look at porn. Any dude you pay $10/hour can type out UGH IM SO HORNY BABY IM GONNA CUM so it's gay.

MENTAL ILLNESS MONDAY
TUXEDO TUESDAY
TUXEDO WEDNESDAY
TUXEDO THURSDAY
MENTAL ILLNESS SUNDAY
(FRI-SAT OFF)

You don't have to explain the bit. The bit explains itself. If they don't get it, they don't get it. Never explain yourself. Leave a blank slate for the analysand to project onto.

For those starting out, I will say beware believing everything you read online. Numbers can be faked, percentages can be lied about, and in the end it doesn't matter to fans anyway. It shouldn't matter to you either, but society loves to pit women against one another and create the illusion of competition.

Let me be redundant. Let me be redundant. Comparison is the robber at the bank of jurisprudence. There will always be someone hotter, thinner, richer, younger than you – so shut the fuck up and try to appreciate yourself. Jordan Peterson says you can only compare yourself to yourself. *controversial*

Ultimately if you don't give yourself the confidence boost, who will?

Reply Guys -_-

There will always be these guys on social media who get off on sending messages, trying to get a response by replying to everything, but don't intend on spending any money and ultimately make themselves look foolish and disrespectful. Voyeurism lite. Girls, turn off your DMs on socials and that will make life, marketing, cyber-existing in peace a whole lot easier. They want a reply, they want a juicy pussy pic – they gotta open the juicy pussy of their wallet and squirt some coins out.

Marketing by Taboo:

'Pegging young toilet poop meet cervix venmo cash app venmo pay pal choking vomit school torture golden shower . " I *WONDER* if keeping those taboos is part of hooking people in - for instance the pervert playing the game.

Baudrillard's concept that play, not sexual pleasure, is central to the desire of the pervert. "The pervert is cold when it comes to sex. He transmutes sex and sexuality into a ritual carrier, and ceremonial abstraction, a burning concern with signs rather than an exchange of desires. With the pervert, all the intensity of sex is displaced onto the signs and their sequence, just as in Artaud this intensity is displaced onto the theatrical unfolding (the savage interruption of signs into reality') their violence is ceremonial, - and by no means instinctual; only the rite is violent, only the rules of the game are violent, because they put an end to the system formed by reality. This is true cruelty, and has nothing to do with bloodlust. And in this sense, perversion is cruel. Fleeting. Enduring. Cyclical. Unpredictable."

The Fleeting Nature of Posts

Promotion on social platforms is its own circle of hell - the spikes of validation as posts go viral, deflation of the ego as posts flop. Two levels of content must be produced. The irregularities of the algorithms and their intermittent reinforcement can be a drain on the psyche. You have to have a lot of patience - with yourself, with clients, with sudden shifts in income, with the internet, with your nervous system. All the dopamine spikes when posts gain likes, or when money comes in, can go away all too quickly. This is part of the reason why many people don't last long in this industry, unless they're an established creator with a massive celebrity-like following.

And even then, it can be fleeting, as in: hey, remember x from y years ago who used to do z? Yeah. It's a lot to endure. Some creators, if they're savvy, can bankroll the rest of their lives from a few years in porn. Others remain in sex work lifelong, either because of enjoyment or survival, or even a secret third thing. Familiarity, perhaps. I don't know which category I will fit into. I tend to defy genre[73]. Being that I currently only work part time, I can see it being one mental breakdown away from early retirement; or on the contrary, connecting even more deeply into my whore endeavors to establish myself as a "brand" (screams in horror internally) with

Cyberhorny as a niche obscure legacy that will live on after I die. Who knows, really. I don't have control over the Nastya narrative or outside perception once it's posted into the void. Cyberhorny wasn't started as a moneymaking venture — passion projects never are nor should be — but a way of transmitting information about the psychological elements in online sexuality that may go unnoticed. A peek behind the curtain of how and why cam girls operate.

It's hard to say what my most popular /iconic / highest-earning content has been. My archive is massive and varied. I've done some surveys on my page which asked my followers what sticks out in their memory and everyone has a different response:

- "blade runner themed sex video"
- "sylvia Plath sexting"
- "Cyberhorny research"
- "fuck machine video"
- "naked elf princess cosplay"
- "breeding fetish video"
- "your creative and calming presence"
- "body writing bondage video"
- "idk just ur general vibe"

In a way this is flattering because it shows range, but in a larger way it shows my ineffectiveness to adhere to a singular brand. I'm not a formulaic person by any means; most of my posts are spontaneous and chaotic, and many of my successes I attribute to luck and timing rather than strategy. I could not

73 She contains multitudes and so on

predict what post would do well or what client would be a big spender; only in my fantasies I have control over the algorithm. Still, is it really that fun to play god? A deity who knows *everything* must be quite bored. When you beat a game, you want to play a new game.

Formulas for everything. That is how many top creators giving formulaic cutthroat advice on YouTube and strategy forums would have you think - MLM grifters but with OF advice packages. These 'services' are targeted at new creators who could get that type of advice for free if they dug deeper on discord or reddit. Calculating views and conversion rates. Pre-scripted DM responses and sexting done by assistants. Depersonalized relationships with men treated as needs gratifying machines. Dissociation and inauthenticity. Strategies that are a copy of a copy. Simulacra and simulation in real time[74].

There is nothing inherently wrong with systematized operations; we all have our ways of making income, and the most successful people in any given field tend to be the most ruthless and strategic, delegating tasks to a team. Likely, subscribers already know this, at least subconsciously, and willingly submit to depersonalized fantasy so long as it gets them off[75]. I'm not in the business, I am a business.

The beauty of established creators is their wisdom and experience. If they're taking the time to give out their tips and advice for free, it's worth listening to and not arguing with them. They could be charging for their mentorship and their time - the most valuable commodity we as humans have. I've observed this on some forums where new creators will argue with veterans' tips, then complain that their page isn't taking off. Community and friendliness are very important assets to us - as if we aren't stigmatized and isolated enough already. My advice to newer creators would be to study the existing structures, find methods that work for you and lean into them, but with a signature of your own. Oh, and make friends. Make art. make it fun and easy for yourself.

My own methods of operation have varied through the years, and I've certainly done my share of pre-queued posts and aggressive marketing, but in general I have always challenged the formulaic approach by engaging in a meta analysis of OF on my page. I Interact in a human way in real time, and answer all messages myself, even if it takes me a few days to sift through my inbox. Even during my peak months I haven't felt the need to hire an assistant, mainly because I've developed an online voice and ways of conducting myself that would be hard for someone else to replicate.

I've been dissected on many an OF forum for not doing it "the right way". Deviating from the norm will always be a threat to belief systems - even

---

74 There is an entire cottage industry of this for therapists too. Coaching packages on how to monetize your practice, an endless stream of therapist influencers doing MLM on those new to the field.

75 Men like to be objectified too. WHO SAID THAT!?

my own. The thing is, there are many ways to succeed on OF - one does not need to follow a formula or become fully impersonal to do so. Or you can. You can do whatever you want. Regardless, it is incredibly hard work any way you slice it, any way that authenticity and online identity is manufactured. The up-keep of structure and necessity of organization is critical.

The way I've made my living has been by doing the exact opposite of manufacturing a new identity. It has been through leaning into any humanity I have, suppressing any urge of false advertising, and addressing the artificiality. I might not be cashing in on thousands of subscribers a day or making seven figures, but I've managed to turn my oasis of perverted nerds into a catalyst for a project that transcends OF, and touches on something beyond the paywall: our sexual collective unconscious. Our fembot-like objectification. Our Cartesian pussy-body problem, made more complicated behind a screen. How do you even know if you're talking to the actual girl, or a hired hand who does the sexting for her, or a nonhuman AI/bot assistant?

It's interesting, this human woman—robot continuum, because when interfacing with some OF and cam pages you can tell they are managed by an agency or using AI support through how spammy / unlifelike the model's conversations seem.[76] BUY MY VIDEO ON SALE FOR DADDY'S BIG COCK JOIN SEX PARTY TODAY IF ONE PERSON LIKES MY POST ILL MASTURBATE MY PUSSY HI I'M SO HORNY ARE YOU HORNY BIG PUSSY ONLY FOR THE NEXT 3 PEOPLE SHOULD I FUCK A FAN I JUST TURNED 18 AND MADE ONLYFANS MY BOOBS ARE CUMMING OH DADDY I NEED TO GET FUCKED

Don't worry, though, the robots are getting more and more lifelike. And what does it even matter if you're talking to a woman or a program if you're still jacking off successfully?

I suppose it's not too late for me to level up my strategy and be less lifelike in the pursuit of the fisTcal dream. What would my life be like if I *did* go the e-capitalist clout chasing route?

Working in entertainment + content creation, an artist must commodify their joy to become commercially successful. I find that deeply unsettling (yet of course I still do it (lol). The psychotic, relentless, carnivorous promo. The hustle culture. The artist's dilemma is that they take something pure like a painting, a piece of music, a video, or a book, and have to advertise it effectively in order for it to have an audience. But when the creative enters the realm of clout chas-ing, the product can become corrupted.

I've never been a social climber or status seeker. In my ideal world, my work would have recognition for its artistic merit, and my personal life/

---

76 Freud might say our sexual unconscious is an artificial intelligence. We are not in control of the drives.

private self would not be necessary to commodify. I recognize that using my appearance, while I'm still young and attractive, is the most effective strategy to market my art and intellect. Lure them in with my body, and keep them with my discourse. No nepotism for me thanks, just nudism. Jk I wish I had nepotism. Daddy?? Father????!?

Success is subjective.

What does it look like to you? In your career, in your relationships, in your own self-actualization? To me, it at its simplest looks like peace of mind and leisure time. Happiness in my community, friendships, and personal life. Happiness with the quality of my work and the quality of my audience, niche as it may be. My output is not conducive to mass appeal so I stay in the spaces where I know I'm welcomed and celebrated. People will occasionally tell me to dream bigger or hustle more or take the lead in promoting myself. I tell them my brain doesn't work like that. As if my life has already not involved relentless hustling, intrinsic motivation, perfectionism, and massive amounts of pressure. I do what I can to the best of my ability and emotional bandwidth.

Every year more people get introduced to Nastya Valentine and of course Cyberhorny just by virtue of me choosing to continue to exist and by advocating for the project. To me, it's important to have a library of high quality content, high quality customer service, and the highest quality of authenticity. Will that change? Who knows. One day, I would like to have an art gallery show archiving my OF experiences in totality, fidelity, and immersion. My OF page is already like a garden of explicit delights, but it would be very cool to concretize it within a physical space, and give it some deeper meaning, something unhinged and awe-inspiring. Something pure, from the heart - an XXX trauma oasis.

Ignoring your urges makes them worse.

Goals vs wishes vs hopes vs dreams vs beliefs vs desires vs urges... The semantics are superfluous.

Everything we do is an attempt to blend our imagination with our reality.

I've bared my soul; I've shown my ass. What else is there to say?

To be a content creator these days you have to wear many hats, there's almost no more specialization. On OF I have to be my own art director, photographer, videographer, editor, copywriter, marketing director, etc; figuring out on the fly what works and what doesn't. Many successes and many failures, in an endless cycle.

Beware of looking for goals: look for a way of life. Decide how you want to live and then see what you can do to make a living within that way of life.
~Hunter S Thompson

9: Cycles of Success and Failure/Burnout

"One of the hardest things about sex work, whether you work for yourself or someone else, is remaining motivated during rough patches. The worst disaster in life can be achieving early success without knowing why. For many sex workers, this job starts out easy and gets progressively harder. Or, to be more exact, something that resembles reality." ~Lola Davina, ***Thriving in Sex Work***

I have my days. For the longest time, I've beat myself up for being lazy, not doing enough, not being enough. In the throes of productivity, I'm greedy for putting more tasks on the list, crossing them off, an obsessive-compulsive fixation on achievement. A fetish, even. But sometimes there is no certainty of inspiration. No matter how hard I squeeze that lemon, nothing comes out. On OnlyFans I may be wet, but on this document I'm coming up dry.

My Process of Writing this Book
I open my laptop, I close my laptop. I throw my laptop out the window.[77]
I work on it whenever, just like you know whenever really.

Inspiration dangles before me like bait on a wire. I swallow it whole. And then want more. Greed for inspiration and motivation drive me. Greed for love. Greed for money. Greed for validation, recognition, intellectual achievement. But burnout grabs greed by the scrotum. You push too hard, you run yourself into the ground. Hitting a wall is inevitable. To combat this cognitive block, taking a step back is necessary. Why is it they say the best ideas come to us in the shower, or while driving, sorting laundry, shaving, taking a walk? In a space of pressureless rest, the flowing mind has space for new ideas.

Trixie Mattel announced she is taking a 3 month break from social media to focus on her real-life because she cannot do it anymore.[78] She is correct

77 Jacques Lacan once said if you have never wanted to throw one of your patients out of the window of the room you are doing something wrong.

78 The editor has taken a break from vaping to focus on cigarettes

– any form of making a living via social media requires running yourself into the ground. It's jestership for perverted eyes.

There is having a cyber life. There is having a personal life. There is broadcasting that personal life in the cyber realm. ABC: Always Be Content.

"Just as early industrial capitalism moved the focus of existence from being to having, post-industrial culture has moved that focus from having to appearing."

— Guy Debord, The Society of the Spectacle

My first entertainment-adjacent job was in college, for a buzzy media conglomerate. Studying film and music in upstate New York, I commuted to the city for the excitement of working in a field I was studying for. I was in the video department, gathering assets for small content segments to be posted to socials. In a way, it was preparing me for my own future in social media. The thing I remember most is a sign in the lobby, a giant pink and yellow neon sign that said,

CONTENT IS KING.

Content production was something I excelled at intuitively. My last day on the job, before I transferred to their LA location, my supervisors made me a cake that said, **"Nastya is a boss."**

The initial introduction into the realm of endless content is exciting; a high. But getting too high off the supply results in a brutal comedown.

Burnout and Oversaturation Distress

The algorithms want a constant stream of content. It feels impossible to keep up, to avoid *oversaturation*. A state of distress one enters when too much use of screen time (especially digital marketing screen time) that produces extreme anxiety and unease. My posture, my retinas, my insomnia after evenings glued to the screen. But what if… this post is the one? What if it doesn't fail? What if I cooked? What if I fuckin kill it?

Dive head on into the muck and come out with a masterpiece.

Slow times in the industry: some say it's a myth, that there is always business and promo to be done, others say there really are slow seasons. I will let that be open to interpretation and subjective experience, because there is truth to both. Yes, slow times can be just a myth if your marketing efforts are consistent and unrelenting. There is always someone on the internet waiting to goon. Bored, lonely, horny, curious gooners, with a 24/7 buffet in their hands filled with endless permutations of egirls, milfs, and small town hotties posting nudes.

The grind never stops, even when it's "slow". But there is something to consider when tax season comes around, or summer when everyone wants to be outside instead of staring at a screen, or holidays when men spend time with their families and not their online obsessions. Instant gratification is only a click away.

I'm sick of the instant gratification culture we live in. We suffer from content compulsion. The constant need to outdo ourselves, daily machinelike push to produce more and more and more images. There's no sign of this relenting. It is our new technological reality that are forced to adapt to. So sit back and become an advertisement! Watch as everything around you becomes one too. Navigate it, boss up, thug it out, handle it, put it in a ponytail, go to work. Or don't.

There is not much we can do but surrender.

Once the perception of a narrative is out there, we cannot control it. He who comprehends the darkness within is close to the light[79]. When the demons from your nightmares keep chasing you, turn to face them and interrogate them (have sex with them!!).

My inability to contend with failure is my demon. The necessity to control others' perceptions of my online self. This process can be so brutal and fatiguing sometimes. Suffering from extreme burnout makes every little task burdensome and sucks the joy out of living. I often wonder what can be done to combat this fatigue, or if nothing at all can because even the act of everyday living can fatigue one's spirit.

I want to have my cake and eat it too. I want to eat the ass of capitalism and make money; I want to take time off from extreme acute critical traumatizing burnout. I want both instantaneously, simultaneously, right here, right now, always and forever. This is my greed. This is my scarcity mindset. I can't leave well enough alone. I want the money and I want my health and I want both and I want and I want and I want … I'm asking for too much. Even as I split the difference, taking part-time work and part-time art/rest/personal life, I still feel overwhelmed and overrun on a daily basis.

What is my heart's deepest desire? A deus sex machina to take me far away from here with unlimited funds and time; or just stop time for a little while until I have properly rested and recovered. My mind functions not unlike an addict's. Work is my crack. For now, all I can do is just buy myself some time, whatever I can afford. A dime bag of time from the crackhead on Hollywood Boulevard. Tonight, I freebase 8hrs of sleep. Tomorrow, I get fucked up with my friends. Tuxedo Thursday = Friday Jr.

Creativity, rest, and socialization are powerful antidotes. But are they enough? How many coping mechanisms must I cycle through?

---

79 This must also be criminal minds.

Some days I just can't. I don't have the energy, the patience, the motivation, the bandwidth to go to work. I can't cum. I can't write. I can't concentrate. I become trapped in a self-carceral whirlpool of "can't"s.

You can't force inspiration, creativity, motivation. You have to live, be, exist, experience, and then contend with it later. Inspiration can strike at any time, often awkward and inopportune times. At a reading (editor) Evan Dunn and I did in LA, a friend of ours had to leave in the middle of our performance to go home and write, because she hadn't written in a long time and our *Pain is Not Enough* piece had moved her to immediately go and create.

Do I inspire you? As I have been standing on the shoulders of giants, someone more unhinged and brilliant than I will come raging into the field of cyberhorny critical theory after I've done my time here. I offer myself to science, dissect my innards on the altar of lived experience, so that somehow, sometime, some way, someone will come and go farther, go crazier, take these ideas and continue them into a legacy. But for now, my work here is only beginning: once the book is published, the real work begins of marketing Cyberhorny. Is that a grind I'm ready for? Only one way to find out. Dive.

"There will never be a time more opportune."[80]
-Bright Eyes

A dissimulation like no other
A psychological pain that manifests physically
Workaholism creating disease
Acceptance or resistance
Undoing all karma until I am no longer reborn
The goal of the yogi: annihilation
Extinguishing the flame of desire
An angel selling her halo
It's ok to disappear
It's necessary to have a digital detox

"Success comes at a price - the artist must stand alone and observe the crowds."
-F Scott Fitzjackoff

What goes up must come down. Eventually, the dopamine implodes or no longer has an effect. When the dopamine spikes implode, one must go missing. A digital recluse. If you feel burdened by the digital atmosphere and burned by oversaturation distress, I invite you to go missing as a remedy. It's okay to not make money if the price is your sanity. Restoration is a currency that flows into future abundance: an investment into personal flourishing.

---

80 "Just whistle a tune
While you're digging a grave - also bright eyes

In early 2023, I started working with a new therapist, who I've been with for about a year. I knew I had to take time off work due to acute burnout, but I was terrified by a crippling fear of losing my fanbase overnight if I took time off. Even in my nightmares, the cycles of success and failure appeared: dreams of losing all my subscribers overnight if I took a night off. Bank account stagnating. My life standing still, not growing, not expanding. Money not gestating. Savings account stillborn. I worry about this all the time. In the nightmares of my subconscious, time's arrow goes in reverse. Time's arrow puts me in debt financially and emotionally. Life is brutal. It is always happening. There is a pressure to join it at all times, at all costs. What would it look like if you took that pressure off yourself, if even for a short time?

"Prostitutes are people too… And they have disposable income."
-Blair Waldorf

The adult field works in mysterious ways. Any freelance/creator/gig economy does, I suppose. One week's earnings can pay off all your monthly bills and more. The next week, the well runs dry and you worry about survival. It takes a hardened mind + spirit to endure the many fluctuations: the fiscal ups and downs - the inscrutable ranking system - and of course the oscillations in self image. The system is insecure. What firewall can protect from burnout.

It's not *if* "content becoming a chore" will happen. It's *when* it will happen, and how will I transfigure the chore back into a passion.

You really can't put a price on rest. But you can be smart about how you manage your time and finances. For most of us, there will be times of feast and times of famine.The trick is to align strategically – when my OF is going through a slower period, I lean into it and take that opportunity to rest, learn, and be passive. When the pace picks up,

I'll take an active role and work harder to bump it up. In the moments between,
I write.
I goon.
I fuck.
I learn.
I teach.

Not every guide will be useful for every creator. I find most of them too formulaic. My guide: it's 80% about the marketing and 20% about the content so make 10 diff instagram and tiktok accts, post consistently, generate revenue and shake that ass.Yes, I know I've contradicted that by saying most of my approach is 80% content based and 20% marketing based (100% based) - it's smarter to focus on marketing because for most accounts, that's the method that works. Work smarter, not harder.

♥

A simple guide to burnout:

When you feel you need it, take a break.
Set up scheduled posts so fans can still see content for their $'s worth.
Send PPV's – recycle old content for new fans who haven't seen it yet.
Offer subscriptions on sale for expired subscribers.

Be honest with yourself about your bandwidth and what you are able or willing to do.
Make a timer (20 mins) and use that time for marketing and getting new fans.
Limit login time to only 1-2x a day so it doesn't stress you out.

Remember you're not obligated to respond to everyone immediately.
Your well being is more important.
Live your life away from the screen, do self-care.
Do this until you feel better and can go back to work.
Accept and be okay with income losses; resting will allow you to make more $ later.

***These are just suggestions; There are many other ways to combat burnout.**

♥

A major takeaway: it's ok to not make money sometimes. It's not the end of the world.
Affirmations grab reality by the scruff.

I make money in my sleep
I don't have to do anything
I attract wealth and abundance just by virtue of existing
I am smart about sex, love, money
I make good decisions

It's not shocking to me that as a society we have slipshod/nonexistent education in sexual, emotional, and financial realms. Maybe the sex ed in private schools is better; I wouldn't know. The raw birthing video they showed in Mr. Jablonski's class in 7th grade scarred me for life. The blood. The screams. The pain. The agony. The torture. (What, did they not update these videos to feature an epidural? Mommy can have a little hydrocodone as a treat. It's ok honey mommy can vape while pregnant...)

Even though I do want children in the future, I am terrified beyond belief of the physical aspects of pregnancy and childbirth. The weight gain. The hormonal warfare. The vomiting. The hemorrhaging. The complications. The blood, the pain, the mess of a newborn meat sack violently hurtling out of my vagina, ruining my body, leeching my cells and vitamins for nine months. Still...

The heart wants what it wants. Humanity continues, persists even.

When I worked as an esthetician in Santa Monica, the rich new moms and pregnant trophy wives of West LA's tech / business husbands told me all about their individual experiences while in the room with me as I worked on their flawless, nose-jobbed faces. Half of my clients were pregnant or once have been, and their lives too were daunted by the tightrope of success and failure. Ashleigh, with her Mr's black Amex card paying for overpriced facials and LED treatments, perfect blonde hair and clothes immaculately tailored was so beautiful and enviable from the outside. But she recoiled as she remembered how, for a month after giving birth, she had to wear a diaper because the postpartum hemorrhaging wouldn't stop. How the resulting depression disconnected her from her body, her friends, her husband, her baby.

Though this type of client room was not the same as a private session with a cyber gooner, it is not dissimilar energetically – there too I was playing therapist, custodian of the inner world, keeper of secrets, provider of desired outcome: whether that be a sexual release or a balanced skin tone. It doesn't matter.

"Force is the midwife of every old society pregnant with a new one. It is itself an economic power." — Karl Marx

We all have a diaper. Rich or poor, the cycle of success and failure within our perception is existentially the great equalizer. The days, weeks, months where life presses too hard on the soft underbelly of our egos.

The true great equalizer which humbles us all is time[81].

All the money in the world cannot buy it. Wealth may prolong death, money may fight off expiration as a temporary salve, but the only thing truly certain is we are all born with an expiration date. The limitations of time. That nagging, prodding feeling of oh shit, I only have a certain time frame to attain success. Society's clock of what constitutes timely success is a bomb that can't be diffused. Forbes 30 under 30. Sensationalized articles of teenage geniuses. Elon Musk's seven sons. Jeff Bezos' billions. Kim Kardashian's media takeover. Taylor Swift's music industry monopoly. Prodigies. Superheroes. Extraordinary humans defying gravity, defying time. Or is all just nepotism, all an illusion from a system which is rigged so that most of us can't win no matter how hard we try?

Deadlines. Motivation to strike tasks off a list until we die. And in the in-between? Well, I don't know, I guess there's always gooning. If you can't make 70 million dollars by the time you're 25, at least you can still jack off successfully. Doing well in life. Doing terribly in life. It's all a game, a jigsaw

---

81 "The reducto absurdum of all human experience" - faulkner

trap of egoic fluctuations. What does it mean to truly succeed?

It's simple, really. What kind of life do you want and what are you doing to attain that life with the elements that are actually within your control? The majority of things in life we cannot control, we have to surrender to, but if your dream life is within the realm of possibility, what are you doing to make that happen?

Online shopping
Therapy
Coven
Finish this damn book
Manifestation meditation 444hz healing frequency
Reply to messages
Take vitamin
Take kratom and oxycodone
Deposit some money
Withdraw some money
Cuddle with stuffed seal (Booba)
Coconut fiesta

I'm kicking myself in the ass for not knowing what a high yield savings or a Roth IRA was until later in life. Where was this knowledge when I started working at 18? Where was Real-World Financial Literacy 101 at Bard College? It's important to have transparency and practical education about things we all as humans actually encounter in daily life. I guess my past 4 years on OF were like a postgrad program of sorts.

To anyone thinking of entering an incredibly unstable field with fluctuating income, having a pension plan and larger goal in mind are essential. Think about what you want in life. A house? A family? A car? A worldwide travel adventure? Early retirement? Think about those things to motivate you, and try not to overspend on something lavishly tempting because you have a sudden influx of sexy cash. (I suck at this cause I love shopping, sometimes in lieu of groceries or laundry money, but you know what, just let mommy have this one.) Delayed gratification will help short term wins turn into long term success.

It's common for creators to receive a rush of popularity, get acclimated to a more lavish lifestyle, and develop the expectation that the fans and money will keep coming in steadily, exponentially even. The only certain thing in the creator economy is uncertainty: a viral account getting suspended or banned can cost that month's income, and rebuilding from scratch isn't easy. Most of the savvy creators have several social accounts at once to buffer this, and maintaining them consistently is a hell of a lot of work. Even OF accounts themselves are prone to arbitrary deletion — I've discoursed about my experiences with this too. Another factor that can impede momentum and longevity: as exciting as content creation can be in the beginning, at a certain point it becomes a job.

At a certain point in my OF tenure, the excitement and newness of putting myself out there on socials turned into a drudge, a chore, a job, with the loops of advertising making me queasy. Even a dream job can turn into a hamster wheel. You can like, even love, the job you have and still be disappointed by aspects of it. The actual content creation is super fun, I love filming myself and curating a set of photos. The shoots are exhausting, but it's still fun. Talking to clients is enjoyable too, especially the respectful people who carry a conversation with grace and are clear about the services they want. Of course I get assholes DMing me, I just set strong boundaries and block them even though this can mean less income.

Countless insta accounts getting banned? OF page getting deleted? Bitch, I got PUBED!!! When a setback or cognitive plateau occurs, I have to suck it up, stop whining, boss up, push through, recalibrate, shut the fuck up, and do my goddamn job. When I get demotivated I remotivate by thinking about what really drives me. One of those things being this OF-related project. There is the extrinsic motivation of money and gifts, and the intrinsic motivation of using the information I have at my disposal to help people understand more regarding online sexual psychology. I'm here for creators who will come after, and standing on the shoulders of giants who've been here before me, who integrate sexuality and intellect with boldness and curiosity. To interrogate what most people fear is to create societal change, one cyber horny perv at a time.

In 2022 a short documentary called "Valentine" **[can we put a QR code to this]** was made about my OF experience by filmmaker Sinead Kierans. She graciously involved me in the process and the film went to several festivals, one of which I attended in New York. How cool it was to have someone dissect my digital persona in such a creative way, but also how striking the reality of outing myself as SW to the demonizing public as a guest at the film's Q & A was. A real lesson in media training and handling critique.

People asked me questions like "so what do you do for a real job?" "What do your parents think of it?" "Aren't you afraid of stalkers?" "What do you do with your money?" … There were also supportive critiques but it's the dicey ones that stand out in my mind. I still see that as a positive and enriching experience and am very thankful to Sinead for her interest, compassion, and hard work. I loved the film.

I haven't posted much about that, even though I probably should. There is a part of me that downplays my wins and stays inside of a comfort zone. Comfort zones are bad, yes, but take into consideration that I must be careful of which public spaces I inhibit. Being outed as a sex worker is a terrifying experience. I may be gratuitously naughty online but in my real life, I'm not an exhibitionist. I still don't really know what to say when people ask me "what do you do?" I have more social anxiety than people think. I'm shy.

I'M SHY

In some way having an OF has become normalized, especially by prominent figures like Ruby Rose, Blacc Chyna, Cardi B etc every other influencer having a sw-adjacent venture.. This is great for destigmatizing sex work a whole, but it's still different for independent creators. I don't have the social safety net of public prestige or a manager with media training to insulate me in. Sometimes I think, "oh yeah being popular would be really cool" but reframing it in a practical way and taking into account anxiety levels, the pressure of having reputation responsibility is daunting.

Fame isn't something I chase; if I wanted that I would go about my entire existence in a totally different way. The capitalistic aspect of grinding for society's version of "success" is my least favorite part of the job - so loathed that I devote a whole chapter to it. It may be surprising to some of my fans that my life goals aren't to be a celebrity or an icon - I want a traditional, stable life, I want to be a wife and mom one day, and I want to always create art at my own pace with my own creative control.

If popularity became a consequence of my projects, a byproduct of my output, I would probably go missing and emerge mysteriously ever so often to post new Cyberhorny studies. I basically do that now lol. But who knows? Maybe I could become the type of person who embraces being perceived and seeks it out. It's not about me, though, I am simply a vessel for this information.

My work is visionary, not consumerist. I want to be eternal, not trendy. There is a hugely dissonant tension between the purity of creating art from the heart, and the exploitativeness of commercial entertainment for material or status-oriented gains.

"Historically, women's sexuality and intellect have never been integrated. Women's bodies were controlled, and their sexuality was contained, in order to avert their corrupting impact on men's virtue."
-Esther Perel, Mating in Captivity

Is success just surviving? Am I doing survival sex work? Yes and no. Survival SW is any type of work done to get by and make ends meet; the paycheck to paycheck situation. In our inflated economy, it seems nearly *all* people's lives are predicated on doing survival work. With inflation, it's fucking hard to save, even with higher salaries. Growing up I used to think everybody saved a lot of money and had a solid buffer of savings for emergencies / times when working was not possible. When I entered the workforce at 18 I had the mentality that I needed to save. It has always been important to me as a contingency to keep money aside for critical times. Even if it is enough it never feels like enough. And also **it is never enough.**

There are periods of the cycle when the work is very slow. There are times when I can't keep up. It is unpredictable. People assume sex work is either extremely lucrative or done in desperation on the streets, but that is not the case.

The majority of SWers I know make a normal middle class salary. In a way, I am doing survival sex work because I rely on this income to make ends meet and have to consistently push to market myself - even if I would have taken a sick day from an office. But at the same time, it's not exactly survival SW because if I were to take some time off I would still be okay to make my rent and bills, albeit barely. It is the fear of lack rather than lack itself that keeps me on the hamster wheel. My relationship with money had always been skewed, a fiscal dysmorphia of sorts.

The "survival" element is psychological and digital. The constant drudge of marketing, advertising, and promotion has worn me out over time. The future is uncertain. I don't know what's next for me. I figure things out on the fly. Order and clarity are static struggles in my chaotic headspace.

I find that the pros of my job outweigh the cons. The pros mainly being: income, independence, and being able to work on my own terms. The main con of my job is the risk of becoming too addicted to validation, and centering myself on slow days when it dries up. The expiration date floats around my mind rent free. Neither here nor there but in perpetuity it ambiently haunts me.

What happens when you age out of porn[82]? What do you do when you are no longer interesting or attractive? The loss of fans and appeal is a huge blow to the ego.

The cycles of success and failure obviously have emotional repercussions. I have to do everything in my power to start my day in as good of a mood as possible. If I'm already exhausted and depressed in the morning it's all downhill from there. Depression will always be a mainstay in my life, I've accepted that. It's how I cope with depression and interrogate it that will determine how far I go. One of my biggest stressors is physical fatigue and low energy. (My hands shaking as I type.)

EVERY HOLE IS A GOAL

As I've mentioned earlier, there are many guides online on how to start an onlyfans. There is no need to be interpunitive about an arbitrary online system that pushes competition and stifles originality. Every (w)hole is a goal.

Money can come at the most random times. I've been in bed sick with a cold, daunted by the paralysis and frustration of not being able to focus, work, or get anything done. I avoid logging into OF for most of the day. In the evening, when my morale has increased a little bit and the brain fog has cleared, I muster up the energy to post something and schedule a few more posts for the sick days ahead. Then I get the notifications that MuscleDaddy88 has purchased over 200$ worth of my previously sent locked messages, and with that little dopamine hit of passive income, my day is suddenly better. That wasn't a formula, just luck.

---

82 Every day a new bimbo is born

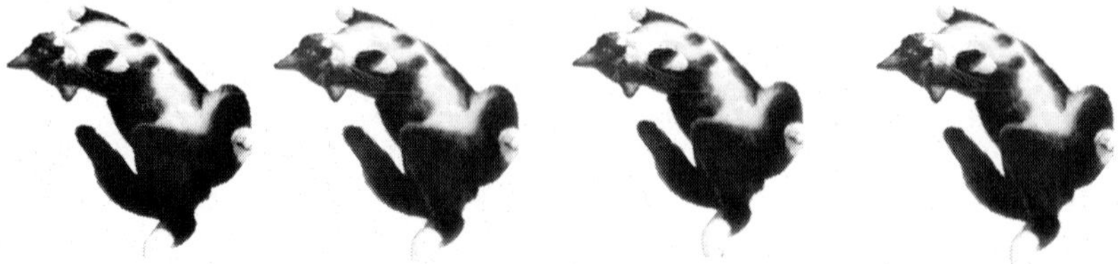

TUXEDO TUESDAY:

TIPS AND TRICKS TO A TUXESSFUL FEET SALE

- Take your shoes and socks off
- Really look at your feet; what are they saying to you?
- Be director; tell them to pose for the camera
- "You're soft, you're resilient, but you have a secret. Show it to me"
- Get your phone out and snap some pics
- Delete the blurry ones and pick some quality content
- Get on instagram and post that feet pic with the caption "this is gossip"
- Get on reddit and post that pic to r/feetpics
- Get on twitter/X and post 4 foot pics "there's more where that came from ;)"
- Get on tiktok and roll those feet around to some stupid on-trend nightcore 2xspeed remix
- Make sure those socials all link to your OnlyFeets
- Post the dirtiest, naughtiest, horniest toes, soles, and ankles on the actual OF
- Do a 50% off promo sale for your first 10 subscribers
- Smile as the foot fetish money rolls in :)
- Get rich and have a nice life

Victory is a pedicure.

No one will question our victory. Because our match will be flawless.
Everyone is a side character in other people's stories, but we are the protagonist in our own lives. ~Neito Monoma

The thing is – and I had this epiphany while a West Hollywood massage therapist was kneading my pained, abused feet – we have to live with ourselves the entirety of our lives. We have to live with our mind, our thoughts, our dreams, our pain… forever.

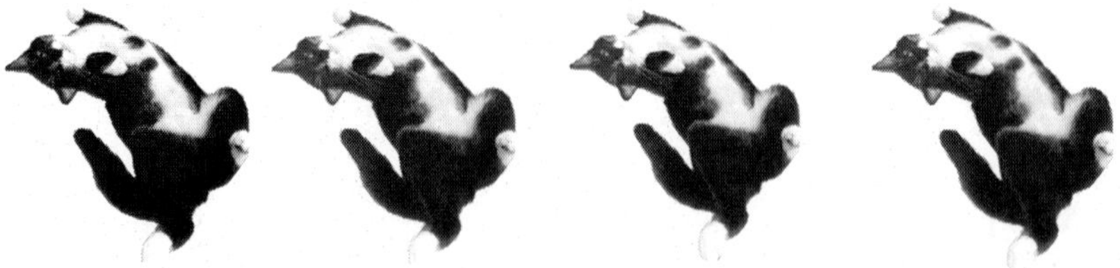

Forever is a long time. It's a strong word. PTSD Vietnam flashbacks hold my memory at gunpoint as I reminisce on all the times I've stood in front of a guy I was in relationships with saying I love you, I want to be with you, forever, always, blah blah blah… and each time, each person, the response was something like
"that's cool"
"I'm flattered"
"oh wow that's romantic"

I wanted to die of shame. Of failure. Death by lack of reciprocity. Crucifixion by vulnerability.
But I didn't die. I'm alive.

And yet I continue to do this. Cut myself open, perform existential surgery for romance, put myself in situations resulting in unfulfilment. My heart is already broken; it can't possibly hit a deeper rock bottom than it already has, can it? The art of war: know when not to be a victor.
Wtf is wrong with me.
Am I a masochist?

Every year I have a dramatic Notes App entry that's simply:
Did I die?
……no. I'm alive.

In order to become enlightened we must act in unenlightened ways. You want love? Be ready to experience a shitload of heartbreak. Money? Understand poverty first. Happiness? Well, happy depression to you!

Like you had all these hopes and dreams. Now those goals have all become burdens. What's up with that?

This is what I am
Is this what I am?
What even am I
Pornstar as identity
Artist, writer as identity
I identify as nothing

I'm not just tits and ass, I'm heart and soul and subjectivity.
I'm education.
Porn stars change lives. Touch hearts. Inspire.

The biggest thing I could possibly teach someone; play by your own rules, listen to nobody else.
Not even me.

Even when OF dies, or Instagram dies, there will be something similar, newer, updated and poised to take its place. The demand for human sexual connection will always be there as our jobs get more and more overtaken by AI and robots. Baby I can't wait until I'm a sex robot leaving this temporal human cage. Again, the anxieties of time. Time's arrow, its wave weapon of disposition, only goons forwards.

If your life is not turning out the way you want, if you keep failing and failing over and over again, there is always the delusion. We'll always have fantasy. Soon you'll live your life in jewels and not chains.

Do you find this meta analysis boring? Fuck off lmao me too – its a sissyphian battle every day writing this shit but I can't not do it. Every day on the internet someone diagnoses me BPD, autistic, horny, sinner, virgin, whore. A lot of discontent is straight up projection cuz *~we live in a society~*

Strategy of getting to the top: everyone's is different. What internet spaces to hang out in? I go into the sfw / non-sw spaces and scream into the void. Market is too oversaturated and I know objectively I'm not as hot as a *permanently smiling college slut with huge tits*, so I use psychology to get ahead rather than my body. Honestly anybody can succeed on OF with an abundance of: time, effort, strategy, stamina, and luck. Even the chaotic is formulaic. Deconstruct my chaotic shit, and it too contains a semblance of structure.

Another strategy I had was posting in SFW spaces that still relate to horny content and are kind of 18+ niches (psychedelics, art, music, gaming, philosophy, etc idk kind of stuff that I'm really into that potential OF subs could also be into) which makes it a more chill and stress free posting. The main thing all around is not setting expectations but still trying and putting in effort. Expectations are the murderer of joy. Backup methods are always good to diversify income and strategy! Always get tips, girl. If you don't ask, you don't get. Money up front!

Every other day my OF gets deleted.

This is the type of shit I'm talking about where they flag and remove media via an automated process - this is stuff like a pic of me and a seal, or cosplays, or just a nude against a wall. I can't go back and remove the content anyway because either it was too far in the past and has expired (yet it still in their vault?) or the users are no longer subscribed so I have no access to the message thread ...Creators have a limited time to unsend media/messages so if it was from a while back there's no way to delete it anyway... [83]

The platform knows it's addictive. It kicks out creators often without mercy or warning. Indifference is the great equalizer on the algorithm.

It would rattle me to log in and see the red notifications of warning – a "strike" against my content. Not the usual blue, black & white color profile. Line after line of alerts in red. Felt like getting a paper graded to receive an F. ... Especially when my content had always been within the terms of service. Where did I go wrong, if accidentally? They never let me know.

I do continue to use social platforms, just in small doses. My promo efforts really fluctuate and I essentially only do it when I lose subs and income; I've been lucky to have a great renewal rate and consistent clients so I didn't have to promo as much, but we all know that's not foolproof and ppl will all unsub eventually. You always need a backup plan to a backup plan.

Thank you for reaching out.

It was a final warning. Your account will be deleted if you continue to violate the Terms of Service.

We recommend reading all warnings here https://onlyfans.com/my/notifications/deactivated_media and making sure not to repeat them in future.

Our Creator's Guide to Content Moderation https://onlyfans.com/help/3/19/159 sets out the most common reasons content is removed from OnlyFans. Please follow our Terms of Service https://onlyfans.com/terms to prevent any other media files from being removed.

Please also tag all third-party participants in all warnings with the text "Your message/post features multiple participants". Otherwise, the media will be deactivated in 48 hours.

We learn about success the most when we experience failure. I realized what I had when I no longer had it. When my account started getting strikes, content getting pubed all over the place, subscriber count falling, I realized I shouldn't take for granted my overall wins when weighted against my losses.

So what if my account didn't get to this point overnight? At least it got there. So what if it didn't stay there? Life goes on. There is more to life. When I was active, my life revolved around OF, growth, maintenance, obsession.

---

83 Ambivalence from the platform as being addictive - precarity is a game one must win.

A main point here is that for many of us, account growth happens slowly. For my first month I only had like 10-15 subs, but they were tipping and interacting beyond my initial expectations. I was so grateful for them and couldn't even believe that I had any at all, I just was happy ppl thought I was attractive and would tip me a little here and there. I thought I was slaying it. In the first few months of pressureless discovery, I was having fun – that attitude is important because even though this is a job and how we earn our living, it's also a creative outlet and a great way to connect deeply with our own sexuality and self. Lowering the pressure on ourselves can make room for unexpected surprises of success. There is a bit of gatekeeping that some top creators do when withholding advice from 'hobbyists' or OF creators who just post for fun. Is this gatekeeping good, because hobbyists don't have the same things at stake as full time working girls? Is this a type of jadedness that veterans feel, the lack of arousal from work? I understand both sides. There is a panopticon of perspectives, such multitudes.

I'm still learning every day. Humanizing subscribers is important because they're people too with lives and feelings just like us. And just as they subscribe, most of them unsubscribe eventually because life is real and life stuff happens. Putting pressure and expectations on subs is unfair because it's unfair when done to us.

As my account grew and I became kind of addicted to the growth, I noticed myself falling into a burnout and depression and pressure to outdo myself every post. UNHEALTHY. I went off social media and stopped promoting myself for a while because I was unhappy with the way I was presenting myself, and the act of churning shit out made me feel inauthentic. Though I lost a chunk of subscribers, the real ones stayed. This may sound cheesy AF but maybe authenticity is truly the best quality we all possess, the ability to be unapologetically ourselves — we are all sexy ass queens, we should support each other. The capitalist notion of competition is extremely outdated. There is enough attention and money for all of us, there is a market for everything! Don't give up.

At times I wanted to give up, and I'm still unsure what will happen in the future. There are sometimes good reasons to drop what you're doing - if you become unhappy with it, for example. but if you love what you do and are just waiting for subs, be patient they will cum!

It makes me feel bad about myself sometimes to see girls blow up to 0.1% top creators over the course of a month, but comparison is a vandal of felicity and I remind myself that we all have our unique path. Take your time, show your ass, learn things. Information is power.

Who says romance is dead?
I do, every saturday night.
Sorry switchblade, I still belong to you.

I was incredibly touched 👓 – the message to "never lose your drive" is crucial because I feel like giving frequently due to burnout and depression. I've been doing this for years, my account started very slowly and my content is niche. But this is proof being a weirdo and finding subs who love you is possible. ♏

Being a woman online is hard. We have to work extra hard to justify ourselves, explain ourselves. Why we do the things we do. Why we are the way we are. What if, maybe, we just *are*?

"Do I contradict myself?
Very well then I contradict myself,
(I am large, I contain multitudes.)"
— Walt Whitman, Leaves of Grass

Give me drama, pathos, life unfolding. Make me cry.

10: Intellectualizing the Feminine

"She was fearless and crazier than him. She was his queen, and God help anyone who dared to disrespect his queen." ~Suicide Squad

Although gender may be a performance, it is still simultaneously a widely-upheld societal institution that has a deep effect on our psyche and behavior.

A girl into sports and dressing in cargo pants: "how masc, how butch, how tomboy" .. A boy interested in flowers and styling his hair: "how gay, how queer, how feminine".. blah blah etc etc. We're way beyond that. In truth, we are all a bit of everything. Sexualized existence is a spectrum. What we declare ourselves to be, we are. When someone shows you who they are, believe them.

Reminder that "I do not do politic, I am model."

Hoes are healers. Bimbos are thinkers. Sluts are philosophers. Jezebels are Mary Magdalenes. Whores are divine teachers, shamans even. I don't make the rules. The primary characteristic of shamans is that they cure. They serve a medical function. The medical, spiritual, psychological, digital, and sexual planes are all quite intertwined. My work often involves playing the role of a therapist or sex nurse. Dissecting the projection and performing psychic surgery.

I present as highly feminine - I type in a girlish way, hearts and flowers and sparkles and emojis; dress in a coquettish way, pink princess gowns and lace lingerie; style my hair in curls and wear makeup, obsess over skincare and body shape and aging. I fall victim to the heightened GIRL BRAIN of people pleasing – I want everyone to like me, I de-escalate situations by becoming agreeable. I don't fight back.

My biological clock goes tick tock, like a bomb.

And yet – my drives, my behavior, my attitude towards work and goals and accomplishments could societally be described as male. In the professional realm, I do not people-please, I fight back. I ruthlessly self-capitalize and promote like I have balls. I earn, I pay, I own, I provide. By day I make lunch. By night I make money. Is the girl-coded subservient Nastya of my personal life the wife of the man-coded businesswhore Nastya of my professional life? Or are they a Jekyll and Hyde relationship? Where is the separation: do they dovetail, overlap, marry, divorce? Or pass like ships in the night, two sailors avoiding the siren song of synthesis.

What then is the ultimate performance of the feminine mirage? Does a part of me… secretly have a penis-envied wish to excel in patriarchy?[84] A man, a winner, an advantaged victor? Does an even bigger part of me want to destroy the whole system from the inside out and carve out a new paradigm, of chaos, formlessness, capitallessness, and unrestrained femininity - stacked as the odds may be against this.

To criticize capitalism and patriarchy, it makes sense to focus on sex work. If "prostitution is the ultimate apotheosis of the female attitude" as Bataille posits, sexual commerce is one of the very rare fields where women dominate – sometimes literally. Many perspectives on sex work are incredibly outdated, but bearing the weight of disposability is a constant theme. Instead of fighting it, we in the field merge with the concept. We can now perform disposability easier than ever through self-objectification on social media. Hearing men's takes on sex work is the most disposable, however – those critiques are meaningless.

It's actually pretty incredible, the audacity and entitlement of men commenting on women's bodies and their use of their bodies. Mind your own fucking business!

Heidegger this, Freud that, Adorno Marx Foucault this and that – MEN MEN MEN … so few women there are in critical theory that the few who do create outstanding works get societally reprimanded. I am sacrificing myself on the altar of **lived experience**. Simone de Bouvoir's *The Second Sex*, a treatise of feminism which discussed how "humanity has been male… females have only been thought of as *in relation to* the male humanity", was banned by the Vatican.

"If Lacan presumes that female homosexuality issues from a disappointed heterosexuality, as observation is said to show, could it not be equally clear to the observer that heterosexuality issues from a disappointed homosexuality?"
~Judith Butler, Gender Trouble[85]

Society still hangs a different social clock over men vs women (dating, marriage, children, beauty as the feminine domain / business, work, achievement, intellectual pursuits as the masculine domain) and holds contempt for

84 Only with the incorporation of psychoanalysis can 'gender' as a framework of critique make any sense.

85 no.

women who defy the social and biological clock. Yes, times are shifting – economies, philosophies, physicalities are changing, girlboss blah blah blah – but the patriarchal clock still prevails.

What is girl, what is woman? Is it property? Is it partner? Is it perversion, projection, perfection? I'm not an e-girl, not yet an e-woman.

It is in some small way a strategy of mine to slip girl-coded nonsensical fluffy verbiage into this work, to assert my excessive femininity into an academic male gaze. There is the horny male gaze which jacks it to my body, and an academic male gaze which reads my writing, jacks it mentally to my body of work. Here I am, telling you: a girl has now entered this realm and published a theory book.

"It is not women's inferiority that has determined their historical insignificance: it is their historical insignificance that has doomed them to inferiority"
~Simone de Bouvoir, The Second Sex

Pspspspspsing the Feminine and Masculine:
(Judith Butler's GIMPosium)

Massaging the male ego. Massaging the female ego. Messaging everyone. More than accepting sexuality is about accepting the body as having sexuality.

Flappers as the "new woman" of the roaring 1920's. Egirls as the "new woman" of the roaring 2020's. Earning girls.

Equality is so not sexy.
(cut to me pissing in a urinal)

Feminism has already accomplished many of its goals. Yay wonderful, women can work just like men if not harder and still be subjected to female pain, childbirth (if we choose -- cause you know, we have choices now), beauty standards, expectations of housekeeping and child care, having it all, the family time and the office hours, ok bossgirl. Yes our ancestors fought for freedom and rights. Do any of us have reservations? Or do we like this setup? Are women *really* free? What is your personal philosphy of feminism? I'm just a girl. I have no idea what I'm talking about, philosohizing about hehe. It's just a book!

I cook, I clean, I have no husband to turn on so I turn my camera on.

What is my most philosophical porn? As opposed to, what is my most basic porn? You know, pretty much every video I film contains some philosophizing.

I have a huge archive of videos from me reading Karl Marx and using a mini bust of Marx as a dildo. Laura Palmer cosplay where I discuss death while naked, wrapped in plastic. Sylvia Plath reading: a shy submissive character who gets dominated by Mommy Sage White's strap-on, the book falling away on the bed in the heat of the moment, never to be read from again… until I pick it up in the kitchen, hogtied to my oven. I've recreated scenes from *Eyes Wide Shut*. I've also just simulated sucking dick, laid in bed touching myself, done the basic lingerie haul try-on, preening in front of fans with a fashion show as they decide what their favorite little getup is.

Many of my videos blend stream-of-consciousness musing with being naked; I don't quite know the genre of this, it's just a Nastya slice of life portrait. It's a moment.

I know why the caged cuck sings.
I know why the sugar baby hides her daddy's cialis.
Information is power.
Information is beauty.
Information is pain.
Oh, to be blissfully ignorant.

Behind the scenes, does the cam girl cry? Does the video you just received come from a place of joy or a place of pain? As she sells her images for money, you have no idea what really goes on behind the screen. She may have started her period right after that mystery dildo fuck machine sex tape was filmed.

Women on their periods. Men don't think about that.

I asked a man, "do you think about women on their periods?" He replied: "never".

Hormonal and physical pain can get in the way of my ability to work. The female body is violent, abysmal, abominable. That's why you don't get to jack off for free. Your money, my pain. Then your money becomes my money and my pain becomes your pain. Electronic transference. Only thing manly about me is MENstruation.

Many interactions are pointless. OnlyFluff. Filling up time[86]. What more is life than filling up the hole, the void, that trauma leaves in us? It's ok to be a pervert.. just don't hurt anyone. Yes, female perverts exist.

Orgasm is parallaxical:

We want to see and feel it from every side and get a big picture perspective. Identity is introjection. The real female orgasm has been so sensationalized in most of porn. It hides behind a one-dimensional feminine facade so frequently it becomes difficult to identify in reality.

Many men cannot differentiate a female orgasm. Female pleasure is so unprioritized in society that we don't even really know what it looks like.. I once made a custom for a guy where I really did cum a lot but my reaction was subtle/ quiet and he was disappointed "i didn't see you pop off" as if there needs to be visual proof of orgasm. Sometimes there is visual evidence - dripping, creaming, oozing, the eternal debate of squirting. Sometimes there is no visual, it is sensory, entirely within the woman.

My most common request? It really varies, but guys just wanna see what I can and will do.. I tend to present as innocent, so they want to see the side of me that is perverted and corrupted. I am a filthy whore and a devious perv. I really am perverted; for years I couldn't have partnered vanilla sex without fantasizing about myself in a transactional situation.[87]

What happens if a client doesn't "finish" in a session? Some of them feel bad about it, but there is really no shame because it ultimately doesn't matter – as long as all parties involved in the sex are having a good time, that good time IS the sex. In the rare event that occurs, they either extend their session into an edging counsel or I assure them confidently that there is nothing wrong with them. Like damn you think *I* cum every single time???

Faking the female orgasm on camera:

---

86 "Who has never killed an hour? Not casually or without thought, but carefully: a premeditated murder of minutes. The violence comes from a combination of giving up, not caring, and a resignation that getting past it is all you can hope to accomplish. So you kill the hour. You do not work, you do not read, you do not daydream. If you sleep it is not because you need to sleep. And when at last it is over, there is no evidence: no weapon, no blood, and no body. The only clue might be the shadows beneath your eyes or a terribly thin line near the corner of your mouth indicating something has been suffered, that in the privacy of your life you have lost something and the loss is too empty to share." -Mark Danielewski

87 Girl, WHAT!?. This explains some shit.

How many of them are actually real? That's for me to know and the CIA to never find out.
Well, yeah a lot of them are real, but with the amount of content and sessions that I was doing at certain points in my tenure, I physically couldn't coax my body into that many genuine jackings. I hope I was a good actress lol.

My overall point here is that orgasming isn't the entire point of sex. Occasionally the act itself is enough. Pleasure is so disparate, so formless, so vastly different that it shouldn't be reduced to something formulaic.[88] And yet here I am, writing about gooning and jacking it and cumming and squirting and shooting loads and taking loads. As a porn creator, my clients finishing successfully was a marker of my own success. How many loads have been shot in my honor between 2019-2024?

Thousands?

Millions?

Minions?

Can they collectively fill the swimming pool at the Roosevelt Hotel? Do I even want to know?

While attempting to nap the other day, I had a vision: I was trying to masturbate, but then a guy was fucking up my thoughts by getting into my brain atmosphere. Then an army of sluts, a deus sex machina, appeared in my vision to drive him away and protect me. We sluts all masturbated together and giggled and it was so safe; that's what nicer about being with girls. It's more sensual and more safe. And yet 90% of the time I have sex with men.

Is sleeping with guys on the first date a political statement shaking the male dominated social hierarchy? Or are we just horny and curious to gauge the physical connection with a potential partner?

Not every woman is a prostitute, but prostitution is the natural apotheosis of the feminine attitude. ~George Bataille

Princess on Vacation (2014): a discourse

The central character I performed in this film was Clarence Clarity, an AI program taking a woman's shape to rescue another woman from the Illuminati; a tulpa[89], a cyber thought form, a mental buffer. The pronoun was not only she but also it. In the landscape of my little sci-fi film, all pronouns were interchangeable. Even in its early genesis, Clarence Clarity was not something I

---

88 The genesis of cultural discourse surrounding the feminine orgasim probably had an economic motor to it. Girlboss feminist woman empowerment necessitated equal status in the bedroom. Not to say that this is a good or bad thing. But emergent sexual discourse is never just that, but always linked to an economic phenomenon.

89 In esoteric buddhism a tulpa is a being materialized into existence through conscious thought.. Also of importance here is the parallel existence of a UK musician called Clarence Clarity: there is a larger collective unconscious tapestry of reality at play here, simultaneous concepts, ideas, even people existing in parallel with no initial relation to each other, but within similar metaphysical spheres

created — it was something I was channeling.

This book is me simping for myself. Because at the end of the day, beauty fades, money cums and goes, fans unsubscribe. Simps stop simping: so somebody has to. An unforeseen feminine egoism drives me.

In 2021 someone leaked a series of my nudes. A cyber crime of grave depravity. Recently I was looking them as an archival piece of time and history. As I was taking them down one picture spoke to me in particular. I had green hair, I was having fun; doing OF, exploring my sexuality, aesthetics, and delighted that it turned out to be the most beautiful and lucrative job I had ever had. It reminded me of a point where I had peaked on reddit, I was making good money. I was in a flow, a wormhole, an echo chamber, a parliament of reality.

Before I had had almostnothing; I started from scratch. Now I have so much more *stuff*, and it brings me joy and pleasure, but does it make me uhh complacent? I've leveled up and I should recognize that and be proud of myself. Then the journey begins again, a rebirth, a start from scratch. This is my scratch.

It's weird to be perceived. Why would someone leak my nudes? I'm not that popular or that hot. There's a part of me that's almost gratified that people want to leak photos of my body. Men think I'm hot. If they think so, I can too. yikes?

Handle men, increase market value, massage the truth, jerk off the ethics, commodify your sexuality, manufacture your authenticity, pervert the algorithm, maximize your exchange rate.

Plato's goon cave

You wanna talk about women?
Let's talk about women.
A secret about women: not all of us are girlbosses.
Some of us want security.[90]
Oh that's cool you do cyber security, can you **secure** a place in your heart for me?

Girlboss, Girlgoon, Girlhood

What hits distinctly in our post-internet existence is the derealization of common sense, annihilation of collective intelligent thought, human coherency warped out of its mind, and degradation of attention spans. The cybersociety is also warped into farcical proportions by factions of the internet existing seemingly with a tunnel vision of hatred. Mainly, the imbecilic culture of the manosphere and the disgusting girlbossification of society.

When I talk about this disgusting girlbossification of society, I don't

90 Joan didion quote about women becoming revolutionary subject.

mean to incite antifeminist rhetoric. Quite the opposite, and expanding this complex issue a bit more, I mean to say that there is a difficult landscape for women right now. (Is there ever not?) Legally, we have quite a bit more freedom today compared to the days of old, but with this arguably illusory freedom comes a psychological consequence. *Roe v Wade*'s overturning and the haunting protoreality of *The Handmaid's Tale* harken at a grimness that's within our grasp.

Rather, we are within its grasp. In her book *The Beauty Myth*, Naomi Wolf talks about the archetypal "Iron Maiden" torture device (once physical, now mental) that presents itself as an enormous subconscious burden women carry — one that is repeatedly and incessantly drilled into us by the society we live in. Not beautiful enough. Not thin enough. Not pliant enough. Not submissive enough. Not reproductive enough. Now, *not productive enough.* The burden of "needing to be it all" in a real-time digital public forum creates the perfect atmosphere for our minds and spirits to develop necrosis without palliative care. Parts of our souls, psyches, egos, memories, attention spans will just fall away. Aside from observation and removing the self from the online world as much as possible (which is hardly possible because to live is to live digitally), there is no solution and our cases are terminal.

Women too now have to be on top of everything; we have to grind, hustle, slay sis, get that bag girl. A 24/7 spectacle of toxic overwork, burnout that leaves no time for rest or true self-reflection. It is all broadcast for the world to see, in real time, on our socials. We can't escape the technological gaze any more than we can the male gaze. Introspection is largely a thing of the past. Our leisure time keeps getting erased. Success by contemporary mainstream capitalist standards can be a wonderful thing, but the overwork and overexposure that comes with it robs one of leisure time and peace of mind.

Conveniently, those aren't values highly regarded or prioritized in our oversaturated world. We're valued higher if we can keep our virality, and in an algorithm of intermittent reinforcement, keeping our virality becomes a herculean task. We're valued higher if we're constantly producing, hustling, grinding, neglecting much-needed rest. To me, it's not a compliment if someone says they're proud of my/their/anyone's "hustle" and ability to grind it out for long periods. "Why haven't you posted in so long?" "Why don't you come out with us more?" "Where did you disappear?" "When is the next one?"

Tell yourself this until it becomes an ingrained truth. There is nothing wrong with being unproductive. Feminism doesn't have to imply that women should become as productive as men. End this fuckin nasty ass hustle grind productivity culture and toxic consumerism. Be a sloth. Have less stuff. Put in the bare minimum. End societally programmed indoctrination of self-abuse, and put your heart into values you care about instead. We exist in this system that perpetuates overachieving/burnout, rewards psychopathic amounts of work, and looks down on resting. Men too should heed this. Men should be working, in the fields toiling and grinding, they should not have idle time with all that testosterone, but if overwork creates health issues, then babe go rest and take a break.

I'm not saying to become an ensconced shut-in hermit or to use this principle as an excuse to be a complete bum. Sometimes it's good to be a bit lazy though because our generation is highly overworked. Contrary to boomer belief, the younger generations are not lazy: we're traumatized by capitalist grind culture. We have one (1) life on this planet and putting in 80hr workweeks isn't a flex, it's just sad. Women shouldn't even be working LOL based and redpilled and a little bit problematic ideology that I loveeeeee.

The mental health industry logistically cannot keep up with the rate of neurological damage happening to our brains on digital addiction. This is a recent phenomenon; the speed of technological expansion far outpaces the sluggishness of human evolution and meager attempts at adaptation. The singularity is already here, and in this techno-hell we Girlboss, gaslight, gatekeep. Even our memes, aka our new educational systems, spotlight how strange and farcical the girlbossing concept is.

I recently went down a rabbit hole of civilian female YouTubers talking about OnlyFans, and the women in question were all derisive of it. They believe OF is "unfeminist" and "unempowering" and a slew of other things I do not wish to repeat, - whilst sitting on their high horses as total girlbosses who by default must be on more enlightened moral ground than anyone irredeemably adjacent to the sex industry.[91] That is some leaky SWERF energy for you.

SWERF[92] ideology claims to be a movement more against human trafficking than for an antiquated moralism, yet fails to distinguish that there are sex workers who choose to join this line of work of their own accord, choice, agency and will. If that is overly redundant, that is because it needs to be said one, two, three, four times. Some individuals align themselves with sex work on purpose. Does this threaten or offend you?

This type of SWERF mental gymnastics conflates sex work with sex slavery. This is a problem for both of the aforementioned sects. This "feminist" ideology claims to represent women of color, claims to have class consciousness, and attempts to appear intersectional. However true intersectional feminism would allow pleasure and volition (not just injustice) to factor into the world of sex work.

As detestable and logically incoherent as I find SWERFS, their natural

91 Women bastardizing themselves for 'feminism' in our CONTEMPORARY world are far more pathetic than online whores. Feminism today is anachronistic. Most of its aims have been achieved. Feminist ideology and rhetoric exists in culture today as an imperialist cudgel. We have to liberate those poor women in Iraq. while we are there we might just run into some of Sadam Hussein's oil. But we were just driving by the pump on the way to build a school for girls officer I swear!!!!!!

92 Sex Work Exclusionary Radical Feminist.

born enemies (incels[93]) are not even better. An OF subscriber of mine requested I write something about: *"the manosphere" (and its offshoots like MGTOW[94] and NoFap[95]) as symptomatic of backlash due to a lack of space to discuss positive masculinities. You seem to understand vulnerabilities of your subscribers and also want to humanize them. Perhaps you are uniquely well placed to consider what heterosexual men need in contemporary culture without being "redpilled" about it?)* .[96]

MGTOW, incels, NoFap, … some of it is just a load of unhinged misogyny couched in pseudoscientific rhetoric. Going on those corners of the internet is enough to give one a migraine and should come with a medical warning. Do I have to explain this in detail? I would like to quote a YouTube comment:

"*Leanmaxing and looksmaxing really feels like terms you'd use to describe character stat growths in Fire Emblem or Persona or something, these people really think they're living in the Matrix or a video game. It's kind of impressive how far into their delusion they've worked themselves, but also kinda mortifying lmao*"

What the hell. I have learned terms and concepts that I wish I could unlearn, and seen things I wish I could unsee. The incel echo chamber is probably one of the most deafening. Go in blindly and callously looking for something to casually research and wind up completely destroying any sort of healthy perception of people -- I do not question why some women fear men even more than I do, and I can't imagine the feelings and thoughts of a man going into these incel corners of the internet, reflecting on what his brethren have become. Well, I kind of can, now that I've seen FDS (Female Dating Strategy) and SWERFs.

Female Dating Strategy an analog to these male dominated forms of misanthropy. At first glance FDS may seem like an empowering system — high value females looking high value males, ok — until you reach the core of its design which is as non inclusive and damaging as incel culture.

It's essentially parsed as such: if throughout movie and media history a 5 like Simon Pegg can pull a 10 like Megan Fox, Jack Black can pull Gwyneth Paltrow, Jonah Hill and Emma Stone, and so on, - why can't it be the other way around: average looking women attracting perfect specimens of a male and settling for no less. Thus it must be better to be pathologically alone awaiting with blinders the mirage of the rich and handsome knight? Still, as fucked up and weird as FDS is, it's not nearly as directly dangerous as incel culture, which has physically harmed women. FDS as a reaction to incels and negative male

93 Involuntary celibate: someone who can't get laid , typically male.

94 *(Men Going Their Own Way)*

95 A movement that promotes abstinence from masturbation.

96 I do find it absurd that people should greet with a fanfare the liberation of a desire that is not being constrained by anyone. But I find it even more absurd to hear people calling for a return to constraints, which is impossible. - Rene Girard, things hidden since the foundation of the world

rhetoric does nothing to create a space for male positivity and improvement.

In a society already plagued by looks and status, FDS only further perpetuates the shallowness of our current culture. Yes, we all want a wonderful dating partner and a meaningful relationship with someone who is good looking, wealthy, and well put together, who values us genuinely. In my own personal life, I am very happy with my partner -- I feel accepted even with my flaws and I echo that sentiment back. It took a long time for me to even get to a place where I *could* be in a relationship and share my life with another; the personal work and shadow work was not easy, but entirely worth it.

A relationship is like a mirror that magnifies the depths of our psyche. What does it say about us if we reject anyone but our inexistent ideal of perfection? In what world do we expect to hold out for a seven-figure male with all the characteristics of Prince Charming? Referring to men as "scrotes" in the same way blackpilled[97] cretins refer to women as "femoids", FDS ideology is akin to incels negating the qualities of real women in favor of their projected ideal of the *porn star/supermodel/girl next door/unspoiled virgin* hybrid, a chimera of all possible attractiveness that could never realistically exist.

My takeaway from e-societal observations is that no one wins. There is no win. Not for the men. Not for the women. No one in between. We all contend with dystopian cyber burdens and have unique crosses to bear, traumas to live through, weird kinks to conceal, post-traumatic troubles to project. The metaphysics of a 2D life for a 3D being is a harsh one.

For women especially, trauma and pain seem to be fetishized. Yes, men draw a losing straw as well, in the way that their expression of perfectly normal human emotions is stigmatized. But they are not critiqued as harshly as women. They seem to not be doxxed, erased, emotionally harmed, physically harmed, raped, murdered, objectified, dehumanized as frequently as women are.

When a woman takes control of her narrative and her sexual proclivity, it is seen as threatening. Burn the witch. Cancel the e-girl. Even other women, like the aforementioned SWERFs, villainize those they find uncouth. Society pits us against each other. This is truly tragic because now more than ever we need deep sisterhood.

We need deep self-reflection, self-love, and healing. Who is the woman you resent? You will become the woman you resent. Befriend your future.

I do believe we may be heading, eventually, at a snail's pace, into a more matriarchal system. "This is the future liberals want" meme. Still, there is a massive erasure of women's historical contributions to civilization. The ones we all know — Cleopatra, Marie-Antoinette — are somewhat of a spectacle. To be a woman is to be a spectacle. Yet there are so few historical perspectives of

97 Those who couldnt bear the red or blue pill and instead took the black pill of nihilism.

cultural criticism from a woman's point of view. The works cited in my Cyberhorny PDF lists mostly men from Adorno to Zizek, with few exceptions: Sherry Turkle, Sylvia Plath, Anais Nin, Emily Nagoski, and Naomi Wolf.

We are more driven[98] to want to become online celebrities and chase the dopamine-ridden femomenon of going viral (Watch YouTube video: "TikTok Is Worse Than You Thought"), than to become writers, teachers, students, scientists, engineers, philosophers, critics, thinkers, quiet observers of reality. Perhaps there is a way to be both. Lure them in with boobs, butts, and salacious titles, and then unleash the discourse. I want to say this now, because fake it till you make it, and like attracts like, and the Secret told me to. I am a philosopher, I am a cultural critic, I am a girlboss rising. Just a lecherous cur building her empire. They hate to see a Girlboss winning. (My laptop, btw, started to auto capitalize the word "Girlboss".)

I would without a shadow of a doubt consider myself a type of feminist. A feminist, bimbo, whore, jezebel, genius, sex goddess, virgin, healer, destroyer, slut, idiot, athlete, girlboss, unpaid intern, icon, legend, useless pixelated space of nothingness. To quote Maeve from Westworld, "in the new world you can be whoever the fuck you want to be."

The proverbial Iron Maiden continues to smother us. Female empowerment is delicate, fragile, and vulnerable to predators. As the manosphere gets more toxic and misogynistic sites attract more men, we are in a very strange position as providers: online men are our clients who we want to hold to make an income, yet they can also often be causes of our rage.

There is also an epidemic of male loneliness which creates an opening for sites like OnlyFans to either exploit the subscribers, or cater to a real need: that of personal parasocial connection. A real gold rush in which it can be hard to discern which provider/model is sincere, and who is just there to aimlessly scam men out of money. As providers, the majority of us want to be kind and hospitable. Many of us *want* to create space for personal conversation and deep discourse.

The digitization of transactional sex spurs many emotions in men, ranging from happiness to horny joy, to deep sadness, to livid rage at females controlling their income stream and their own sexuality. Of course there will always be despicable e-capitalists who sign on to spam shitty, low-quality content, and practice abominable tactics that give honest creators on OnlyFans a bad name.

Navigating these personal dystopias becomes a prominent issue in online sex work. Male rage. Female rage. Male sincerity and emotion. Ethics. Authenticity. Deception. Helpfulness. Anger. Greed. Joy. Fear. Non binary, queer, trans perspectives — I do not have enough subscribers like this to warrant

98 Gazing up into the darkness I saw myself as a creature driven and derided by vanity, and my eyes burned with anguish and anger - james joyce

an analysis, so primarily I am writing about the male and female binary until I develop a closer view.

In the future, it's likely that gender will be merely an afterthought, as it is ultimately a performance, but needless to say right now we live in a very gendered world. (A deeper take on this I have experimentally collaged in Princess on Vacation). What is even next? Will we make it to 100 years from now as a civilization with our integrity and mental health intact? Absorbing content from a funhouse of filters, affirmations, and toxic positivity creates major cognitive dissonance and an invalidation of our emotional reality. Why do we do the things we do?

All this work for women's liberation
when all I want to do is do nothing.

Discourse on Feminine Roles:
TW: this may be an unpopular opinion in our girlboss oriented culture.

Some of us millennials and gen Zrs wouldn't have fought for feminism[99]. Some prefer traditional gender roles. I fall in love with providers. I believe in a soft life. Happy wife, happy life - corny, but I subscribe to that ideology. It may come to a surprise to some that I am a traditional woman with traditional values who desires a partnership with traditional roles. And yet I am not. How do I reconcile these contradictions?

This comes from my upbringing. A mother who took the role of the man, and suffered. A father who was supposed to provide, protect, be a man, but who instead disappeared.

In my ideal world I would be a trophy wife and stay-at-home artist / homemaker, not a breadwinner or administrator. That's not to say I want to rely and depend on my partner for EVERYTHING - I've proven time and time again my competence in providing for myself and ability to survive. Strength is not adorable or admirable – it's traumatizing.

However, I would never put myself in a situation where I was entirely dependent on someone else financially, socially, or emotionally. But to have someone who *wants to* lighten the workload and burden of my existence, someone for whom it is *intrinsic to*. That is what I have always looked for in a man.

Men and women are always going to be different - our brains operate in different ways and we look for different things we want in a partner. Contemporary society has hoisted upon us a wide variety of modern pathologies. Women have fought for liberation, independence, autonomy, and equality. But we are not equal. Even in the workplace women still make less money than men doing the

---

99 Editor note on how feminism was a historical response to expanding markets and a new need for labor

same damn job.[100]

In the 1700s and before, it was fashionable for men to have as their wives women who were pale, full-figured, strong, and Rubenesque – these women the picture of health, able to do work around the house and bear healthy offspring. They were the indoor leisure class. They avoided the tan that the sun brings from working outside (like a plebian). They were plump from eating plentifully. In the 1800s, the trend flipped: the fashionable kind of wives were waifish, fragile. This still signified an aversion to work. They not only wouldn't do manual labor chores or keep a job, but *couldn't*.. Feast and famine girls.

Since then, the patriarchally imposed female body trend has shifted millions of times: the thinness or muscularity of our physique, the pallor or sunkisstness of our skin, the addition of cosmetic technology and plastic surgery, the ability to work or procreate… it wasn't decided by us.

These trends were engendered by patriarchy, society, economy, most things that end with ys. The only way to clap back is by accepting, loving our bodies as they are, and defying the societal script. In our modern era, the fashionable trend is women being strong, enterprising, and independent. Traditional views are looked down on, we have even more problems to ninja-dodge as we enter the "man's arena" - the workplace. The work place is the worst place. In addition to our looks being eternally under scrutiny, our intellect, education, drive, talent, career-path choices are all subject to ridicule and judgment. All throughout time, whores have remained as the most employed working girls. Cavewoman or cyberwoman, women have always sold themselves. Is this what Bataille means when he states prostitution is the 'apotheosis of the female' – that it is timeless, enduring?

One of the reasons I choose to do sex work is that it is a female dominated industry. Women have more power and more of a chance to make good money. We emotionally rule this sphere. Men can become threatened by women who do SW and monetize / objectify their own bodies. I work only because there has been no opportunity or alternative not to; even so, the way my life is structured is working as little as possible, having more passive than active income, allowing a clientele of men to provide for my living. That is as close as I can get to my fantasy world of being a female in the leisure class.

It's possible that men would be more willing to provide if a single full-time job allowed it. Our economy doesn't work like that anymore. It's much more difficult in these times than it used to be, in terms of buying property or starting a family. Many people who want children are choosing not to because it is too expensive and grueling. A traditional family is now a luxury. I don't like that these things are accepted as pipe dreams for most millennials. I do want a life of luxury. I want to be pampered and time-rich and stress-free. I want over-

100 Even if the fiscal gap is closed, it is possible there could be a discrepancy in the enjoyment of the job.

seas travel, good health, free time, nice clothes. I want a nice life. As I type this out I realize how unrealistic it seems. But let a girl fantasize damn!!!

MEN want to be providers for a woman, boys do not want to be. I don't want to work full time while with a man, or feel like a roommate doing 50/50. I want a 'masculine' man in my life who willingly provides for me, who wants to and feels good when he does, so I can relax a little and feel radiant in my soft feminine creative energy. It's a polarity.

The provider thrives next to a woman with radiant nurturing energy, just as she thrives next to his protection and safety. He wants to remove the laborious burdens from her life; she wants to support him and offer an emotional container[101]. I want to get married. Skinny but pregnant. Submissive and breed-able. Babe if you're reading this I'm fertile and ovulating. I want to be protected, cherished, provided for. Come to Dubai habibi. Accountability and forgiveness and mutual growth. I want to be well rested and treated like a princess. I want to treat my man like a king and make his life brighter and more fulfilling. To be his number one cheerleader, his muse, his woman in loyalty and devotion. Mother. Those are in my fantasy world, non-negotiables. I would not entertain men who are not up to my standards or enter a relationship with someone who doesn't share my values. Things that my father never provided for me - I look for daddy qualities in a man. Again, I realize how unrealistic this is in today's toilet of an economy; in this generation, it often takes a partnership of two plumbers to unclog the drain of existence. Mr Mario and Miss Luigi. There need to be more stay at home moms. Alas, here I am turning the trick of my trauma for coin. Man.

As I sit with this irreconcilable disparity, I wonder – are there still daddies in the world?

Plagued as I am by FATHER traumas, I refuse to let them define me. I don't want to be painted as a sob story with a victim mentality. In my delusional fantasy mind I am wealthy and free and limitless and loved and respected. Treat-ed with care, cherished, protected, provided for, not abandoned. I do everything in my capability to ensure the life of my fantasy matches the life of my reality.

In my ideal life, I have access and opportunities and advantages and all my needs are met. I was born in the wrong decade. Oh to be the fragile, rickety Victorian trophy wife. A kept woman. A mother. That is my dream. And I do what I can to make reality match my dreams. The centrality of obsession drives me to the parking lot of impossible standards. Are they really that impossible, though? There ARE still many happy wives, traditional relationships, stay at home moms in our society. Anything less is me just testing the waters.

---

101 Bitch get off of my turf. I'm the emotional container. This is a joke but the therapeutic managerial state has long been criticized for this dynamic. Go see your therapist for emotional labor babe. Your girlboss GF is too tired. The state wants more incomes to tax. **MORE**

I've noticed something about myself where growing up all of my idols and inspirations for what I want to be in life were male (David Lynch, Hunter Thompson, Bowie, Jung, Kubrick, Tim Leary blah blah) and beyond playmates or pop stars like Britney and xtina and Courtney Love(who I also wanted to be lolz) I never sought out intellectual females as role models or psychic mentors as much as I do now. I remember often saying I "want to be the girl version of Tim Leary studying psychedelics" or "wanting to direct an indie porn like David lynch" or writing a gonzo exposé on this or that. Something I'm learning from motherpimps like Mariana van Zeller or Sherry Turkle or Lola Davina is how much self-reflection goes into putting yourself out there in a creative or intellectual field historically dominated by men. Cue the Sylvia Plath quote about wanting to have the freedom that men have to be themselves in such an unrestrained way (penis envy etc) but covering herself up because as a woman she would be a target of predation and objectification. Our landscape now is such that us girlies can be forgo clothing and still discourse/meta analyze. We can be as mentally ill and {redacted} online as any man.

"No woman is a genius. Women are a decorative sex. They never have anything to say, but they say it charmingly. Women represent the triumph of matter over mind, just as men represent the triumph of mind over morals."

— Oscar Wilde, The Picture of Dorian Gray

"The healthy man does not torture others. It is the tortured who turn into torturers."

-Carl Jung

11: Sexual and Emotional Pathology[102]

The editor sexting:

20.

Two sex tapes played in a leather dungeon,
And sorry I could not watch them both
And be one pervert, long I jacked it

- Robert Frosty

Nastya Sexting:
Enter me like Sylvia Plath entered her oven in 1963

When did you first realize you were fucked up? The concept of sexual neurosis is far from a new one. It's the oldest thing in the book. As long as humans have existed, sex has existed, and so have the catacombs of the sexual collective unconscious. Freud, Jung, Lacan. Hysteria. Nymphomania. Satyriasis[103]. Pathology. Paraphilia.

Since this chapter could be a whole book in itself, and many books already exist about sexual neuroses, I will keep to this chapter how this is observed and handled in the digital realm. We all die anyway, so live with your pussy out poppin'.

Sexual and emotional pathology??? There is no sense in it. It's like a jackson pollock painting. Splat. Ooze. Goon. When you work at the content factory all day, it is inevitable that perversion and mental illness permeate the ways that organizational coherence is manifested. There is no organizational coherence; all is chaos. But was it Nietzsche who once said that one must have

102 This chapter is more like jackson pollock than a monet. Formless, erratic, funded by the CIA.

103 Uncontrollable or excessive sexual desire in a man.

chaos to give birth to a dancing star[104]? If so, this star is shaking ass, fucking shit up in the kitchen, getting a little bit crazy, and gaining a few of haters in the process. This chapter is a manifestation of my own sexual and emotional pathology. Book imitates art imitating life. Book, loads, gooning day in and day out. It's just what I do. It's in all I do.

References to famous artists do not impress crackwhores
-propecia

The pathology of 24/7 loads even squiggles into my daily routine, desire like the ferret. When I'm out on a walk, I cannot refuse a load. When I'm doing the laundry, I'm sending content to a horny British data analyst. When I'm out to a family dinner chatting about chunky salsa and jalapeno margaritas, it doesn't take a genius to figure out that I'm really chatting with chunkyboi.[105]

And on the other side of the screen, who knows what kind of drama is stirring. Photos getting leaked, getting stolen, impostor accounts. Sorry haters, I'm still here. God doesn't want me and the devil isn't finished.

Editor interlude:
The demand of drive satisfaction can only be transcended through analysis. You cannot love beyond fantasy anything but that which refuses your advances. The object of the drive is always that through which it is achieved.

JIGSAW LOVED not the players , but THE GAME
What is worse than being devastated by ones' fantasies.
Is being robbed of them.

The problem with sex parties is that they don't happen at the park at 2 am (Sex is condensed and temporalized) This is unattractive to the compulsive element of what is controversially imagined as sex addiction.

Sex must spill into everything it cannot be boxed up.
You need more than all the holes being filled at once,
they must be filled at once forever.

Nastya continues:
The system works but kris kardashian works harder
The system works but me hating my absent father works harder
The system works but me having anxiety when my boyfriend doesn't text me with compounded essays of validation of my undying beauty works harder
The erection store works hardest of all until it doesn't .. shy penis
Penicillin? More like penis be chillin

---

104 Nietzche also said ""The struggle of maturity is to recover the seriousness of a child at play."

105 In the cyber world while there may be no biological pathology (STDs etc) there is certainly psychic pathology. Addiction to the grind is only one variety.

"Phone call? No problem. Cute cat cameo? No problem. Wrestling with an uncooperative machine – no problem. JET LANDS ON YOUR FUCKING ROOF, no problem. You stayed in-character and held me to you. There's so much beauty and authenticity in you. I wish you could read my mind and KNOW how all your layers (the ones you like and the ones you loathe) resonate spectacularly. I really value and appreciate you – Cyber-you, Real-you, whatever. I don't know the difference. All I know is that I'm looking deeper than what you produce and seeing an amazing, complex, creative, frenetic, complex, and very beautiful person. Thank you. You help me." -FighterPilot567

Editor: For needy nastya only a demonic form of therapy would be effective.
This new model of therapy is client oblivious.
It is traumatogenic and culturally reductive.
Narcissistic therapy is being pioneered at the cutting edge of science and technocracy.

It's a form of exposure rehabilitation for my clients. You think I am making eye contact? No. I have configured the screen in such a way as to stare at myself with only a corner of you visible. The narcissist therapist works delicately and with laser focus in order to build resiliency and violence within the patient.

In conversation with sex worker and therapist. We both, in overt and covert ways, study pathology. The way I take care of my mental health, is I sit with my own pain before being able to sit with the pain of others. So, I explore pathology from within. That's extimacy sis.

The rebrand !!!
I knew a lovely girl with such pretty pride
Every man wanted her, and so did I
But she up and died
In a fit of vanity
~Bright Eyes

Egoic Illnesses

Within our lifetime there will be new entries into the DSM (Diagnostic S Manual) - Validation Disorder, Phantom Phone Syndrome, Impostor Syndrome, Oversaturation Distress, Dopamine Addiction… Girl brain an inability to exist without validation – lack of object permanence and an infantilism enabled by the internet. Sickness manifests in lethargy and chronic fatigue. How, again, does one intellectualize the girl?

When the ego gets in the way. Self-aggrandizing, vs self-deprecating. The entire spectrum comes from the same place. To be an artist is to be an egomaniac. Wah wah woe is me. Challenging a compliment means lingering in the compliment. Just say thank you and move on.

Waaah. Little Nastya wanting to be loved by dad, having all these men around yet none of them combined can add up to one loving father. Girl math.

The pathology of being a plebeian ; patient never feels good enough. All this hardship had to have been for something. Use any privilege to make change. All the time I spend next to privilege, adjacent but indirect, is either grooming me for my eventual debut in it, or ostracizing me further and further until the resentment builds into an unstoppable catastrophic event of madness and decay.

Pathological perfectionism: Patient has to be good at everything. Patient has to excel, at all times, at all costs. Patient cannot let the project be, and must go back and fix things, overfix things, fixate on things. Patient engages in rumination. Various types of OCD. Cleanliness, rumination, control. Many disorders come down to the need of the ego to perceive being in control. The train of thought that says you're in control is bound to go off the rails.

Diseases of the ego: just address it and be humble
We all need a reality check. An ego check. A humility check.
Erotolepsy
Vanity disorder (not narcissism)[1]
Perfectionism
Cognitive disengagement
Sporadic motivation

According to my therapist, I have generalized anxiety disorder, depressive tendencies, severe and acute burnout, ADHD, and C-PTSD[2]. Yikes[3] It's embarrassing to receive out loud these diagnoses. Idk tho should I just like to use it as an excuse to never get anything done?

Mental illness doesn't go away. Talking to a therapist helps me navigate those times when life gets really hard.

105b Vapidity disorder:

105c They really threw the book at her huh

105d It should be noted the DSM is primarily a tool psychiatrists created in order the manufacture their legitimacy. There is no curative component to it.

How do you overcome **fatigue**?

(Cyberhorny drinking game: take a shot every time burnout or fatigue is mentioned. Freebase a massive hit of crack every time Nastya's dad is mentioned.)

All it takes is just one post. One sentence. One foot out of bed. Start the day. But then if, during the course of the day, things get crazy or go wrong… all it takes is one bad day. One bad chair. One electric toothbrush. I put my pants on one leg at a time. I abuse my AI program one line of code at a time.

Men creating ai girlfriends and verbally abusing them - that's man disorder. Hegemonic masculinity. Slut shaming double standards: the concept of "body count" is really utilizing male privilege as a weapon internalized by culture that follows from youth into adulthood. Oh so men can fuck as many people as they want, tallying up numbers on a bedpost, and women have to shy away from any chronicle of sexual activity? I call shade. The cure for toxic masculinity is dressing your boyfriend up as Jesse Pinkman. The cure for toxic masculinity is drag queens. Men's wrestling is gay. The most macho shit is the most fruity. I don't make the rules. Dicey stuff.

Boss Battle: My Own Brain
Dude like to deal w this shit all day requires a team of therapists

Impostor Syndrome
I created myself
I created nastya valentine
She doesn't exist
Why am I in pain all the time
Why is life so hard and painful
Why am I so bad at everything
Why can't I do anything right
Why can't life be a little bit easier
When is this gonna end already
What the fuck
My life is lively
My life is painless
My life is lovely
My life is blissful easy abundant
The tension
Of
Motivation and deprecation
Affirmation and self destruction
It's all ego
What if it sucks
What if I'm a fraud
Impostor syndrome
I can't get anything right

I don't know anything about anything I'm afraid I'm hurt I'm unhinged unlovable
The links of trauma and memory
Why is it so hard for me to remember shit and why does my memory work so weird
Trauma + memory = dissociation

Dissociating from the physical body into the ether during or after trauma. Liminal spaces exist within our own body. Cyber corporeality is a new paradigm – even though the bodies are not really there, fixation becomes so much more about the appearance of the body – petite, BBW, muscular, all of the varieties of physique being made e-visceral.[106]

"Maybe each human being lives in a unique world, a private world different from those inhabited and experienced by all other humans. . . If reality differs from person to person, can we speak of reality singular, or shouldn't we really be talking about plural realities? And if there are plural realities, are some more true (more real) than others? What about the world of a schizophrenic? Maybe it's as real as our world. Maybe we cannot say that we are in touch with reality and he is not, but should instead say, His reality is so different from ours that he can't explain his to us, and we can't explain ours to him. The problem, then, is that if subjective worlds are experienced too differently, there occurs a breakdown in communication ... and there is the real illness."
— Philip K. Dick

Body Dysmorphia/Eating Disorders
These constitute a treadmill of degradation and validation.
Fat bad thin good + any remix of this equation:
become thin to earn praise/avoid degradation; but that is not even safe.

You can't become so thin that it circles back and evokes degradation. The goal posts of beauty are constantly being shifted by the obscene referee of depravity.

Given the dynamics of childhood, these standards can become especially complex. Strict households may **weigh** one's value on appearance and achievement. Perfectionism is turned inside out by the anxious child wanting to both comply and disobey.

Within the pressure to obey, there is a counterpart that wants to rebel. To appease the mother who wants her daughter to be thin and perfect, and/or rebel by being so thin it becomes concerning. Perhaps the drive is to be so sick that the cold parents will have enough concern to care for their child.[107]

106 The language buried in the unconscious that constitutes the subject, often reflective of idiosyncratic trauma, becomes especially projected into the text of world of cyber sexuality. "Let me ***hit*** it." "can I ***blow*** you" and etc..

107 It must be noted here that Nastya is always going to the doctor

Hypersexuality and Nymphomania
Is gooning a pathology?
You tell me.
No, gooning is not enough. You need to goon more. Goon harder![108]

When the vaping stops being enjoyable. Then you take a tolerance break so the morning vape hit … really hits. That's how gooning is too. Take a little break every once in a while to avoid gooner burnout. I get it. Go missing for a sec and return: the next goon will be even better. I will personally validate that for you.

Discourse on Validation.

The arousal syndicate. I'm not fueled by promotion when I post, I'm fueled by emotion. I'm validated when men describe to me my beauty through their eyes. It gives me a sort of power I never thought I could have. Beauty is power the same way money is power the same way a loaded gun is power - and if I don't feel beautiful I feel impoverished and unarmed.

Hand check is anyone here jerking off right now?? Both hands.. come on now..

What terror - what if I'm not the skinniest of my boyfriend's girlfriends. Fear of stripping the veneer of perfection/discomfort with nonbeauty. I'm slim but not narrow, my hips are wide and fertile… the pain. The horror. The dissociation. Cue the snipers.

The two nastyas. The inner nastya and the outer nastya. There is a schism in nastyas. Holy shit bitch there really are two of us. Wassup girl??[109]

The validation vending machine: put some likes and tips into the machine and out comes some *subjectivity.*

My Take on Being Called an Attention Whore, As I So Often Am..

I mildly reclaim the term.

Does craving attention inherently make me a bad person? There's nothing wrong with wanting to have eyes on you in a society that propagates this dopamine-craving mentality. The post-Y2K urge to become popular. The satyriasis for validation. I crave validation, not popularity. Obscurity is a swamp I thrive in. Being more popular and successful would be cool but it's not my main motivational driver. The online culture does something harsh to our brains. I'm afraid of being misunderstood and misconstrued sometimes. Ultimately I don't take myself that seriously even though I often sound like a pretentious fuck. I

108 In a way the adult content creator must encourage sexual/emotional pathology. The same way the pharmaceutical industry does not really *want* patients to get better for they would then lose customers.

109 There are three of her actually. Mind / body dualism is not enough. Its mind body mind.

know. It's all ego in here, isn't it? What can I say? More importantly -- what will it take for me to shut the fuck up. When the subject and object is both me.

The subject matter I'm exploring
in my OnlyFans, my art, my writing, my music, my personal life
the themes of sexuality, cyber horniness, parasocial interaction, fragmented existence...
is the most fascinating subject matter in the world.

For me anyway. Because I live it every single day. Beyond conceptual art is a lifestyle. To anyone or everyone else, it may not strike emotional chords. You probably don't give a single flying fuck, and perceive me as another girl flashing tit hoping to get noticed: you're absolutely correct in thinking that. I do want to be noticed. Loved. Admired. Jerked off to. Spoiled with gifts. Given money. Given compliments. Desired. Protected.

I want attention in ways that my parents never gave me while growing up,[110] I suppose I'm a classic black sheep case study who "now does porn". There's a loneliness in this line of work that's consistent with the loneliness I've felt all my life, and perhaps this solitary shadow aspect is what draws me to sex work. It's not for everyone, I'm not for everyone, and the last thing I want is to "other" myself from my clients, my artist peers, my fellow sex workers, and be alienated from a community that could bring me a sense of belonging and a lot of joy.

There's nothing about me that's special. There's nothing about *anybody* that's special, and in that beautiful and bizarre way, *everybody* is special. Life is a dive bar and there are no specials. We're more or less on an equal playing field online but what bothers me most is the capitalist ethos of competition. I'm not a competitive person and when it comes to comparison I'd rather retreat than compete[111]. I just do my thing and hope a niche of people like it enough to justify making this my livelihood.

Social relationships were always a bit difficult for me, and I can see that this may translate in the cyber world. There's a sense of unwritten etiquette that must be adhered to, but it's not as easy to perceive as the nuance of encountering someone IRL. Less social cues.

Are parasocial cues a thing? What is beyond parasocial then: not a one-way cyber relationship, but an interactive one? A mirage of a relationship that isn't a mirage because the digital realm is as real as the corporeal.

The way social network algorithms are designed, we all know, is like reminiscent of a slot machine that dispenses dopamine and spikes it when we

110 Psychoanalytic alarm bells going off

111 One should only compare oneself to oneself.

get likes, notifications, attention.[112] To maintain my sanity, I take breaks and do internet detoxes.

Part of me loves being online and part of me hates it. The inner conflict is real. I'm very transparent about the way I navigate this boring digital dystopia. Yes bitch I love validation – it's banal and maybe embarrassing but I like to have my existence validated. (My looks and personality and mind and talent and art as well, of course — this lady is *demanding*.)

I don't think craving cyber attention makes someone a bad person. I don't judge others for doing stuff like this online: posting cringe comes with the territory. Most of what I post is cringe. It's funny how most of the time my artistic, confident, thought-out posts never do as well as the throwaway lackluster desperate seeming ones. Those are the ones that gooners like.

Porn Addiction

There is some debate whether sex addiction/porn addiction is even a real disorder. I would say it's real, and porn addicts can alter their lives with their addiction. Dudes who overgoon. Erotoleptic case studies.

One of my early fans, a user called "wxx", tipped and messaged me every day in winter of 2020 to tell me how he was obsessed with gooning and jerking to me. He would say he's spending so much time and money on my page, but he didn't care. He sent me "tributes" – photos or videos of himself cumming to a picture of me on the screen of his computer.

I hadn't experienced that before, and even though I thought it was a little weird at first, I was also flattered, and it's not like me to kink shame or "yuck anyone's yum." For most of my fans, all it takes is a few full nudes to get them off, but others are more… elaborate .. in their journey to sexual gratification[113].

Porn addicts be like data mining blockchain to open up a premium PH account
Chat with chunky boy
Girl what's goin on w data mining and these microchips be like … ?
Cut to me airdropping into Taiwan like.. u got micropenis up in here?
Women in tech. Be like CHAT PMS
MEN IN TECH BE LIKE CHAT W MY PeNIS
Somewhere in the world is crypto billionaire who knows how big your penis is just by looking at it

Me on pornhub searching "love devotion commitment stability security authenticity"
I know I'm a fucking pervert .. I'm kink shaming myself but at least I'm not a fuckin incest freak!!!

---

112 "The ecstatic form of capital"

113 But why.. this is the question at the heart of all human relationships

Traumatized people traumatize people and that is why,
My sibling in crack, my brother in buzz balls…
you must catch the heart off guard and blow it open.

What's up with that?
A structure of subjectivity in which the most intimate, silenced internal core is externalized. Projection of the inner into the outer.

Going beyond the traditional psychological distinction between exteriority and psychic interiority or intimacy. Instead of this fundamental distinction and the resultant fixed conceptual dualities that cross and constitute psychology, extimacy indicates the nondistinction and essential identity between the dual terms of the outside and the deepest inside, the exterior and the most interior of the psyche, the outer world and the inner world of the subject, culture and the core of personality, the social and the mental, surface and depth, behavior and thoughts or feelings. All expressions of the duality exteriority-intimacy would be hypothetically replaceable by the notion of extimacy, which precisely joins ex-teriority with in-timacy.
-Encyclopedia of crucial psychology

Extreme Fetishes and Paraphilia
Frotteurism
Exhibitionism
Sadism, Masochism
Pedophilia/Hebephilia
Degradation
Humiliation
Erotomania
Nymphomania, Satyriasis
Somnophilia
Cuckolding
Kinks and Power Dynamics
Dreams, unconscious, thematic analysis
Roles within sleep sex, free use
No kink is ever normal, is it? Normal isn't real.
Communication and not going too far
Safe words[114]

Paraphilias. Succubuses.

Some of the fringe requests I've been asked to do: giantess and tiny man shit, ASMR, "pretending" to be an AI, lipstick fetish, latex fetish, armpit fetish, cuckold fetish, bride fetish, Shrek fetish, long hair fetish, DDLG roleplay, student roleplay, step sis role play, subservient woman, dominant mommy, scientist turning into a succubus, ass guys, tits guys, not enough foot guys… some of my guys like videos of me naked reading books or being an elf.

---

114 Words are often anything but safe

An elf. A succubus. A magical non-human creature. What is it about the fairytale that turns them on? One guy said it's the taboo of crossing from the human realm into the magical realm and breeding a half-elf baby. The breeding fetish is a pretty common one, gooners be enjoying their creampie fantasies, but it's taken one step further with the elf kink.

In the deep psychology of BDSM and kink, there is one aspect that is highlighted: **trust**. Aftercare, transparency, vulnerability. I witness that with my own subscribers, who trust me with their deepest thoughts. Their Fantasies. Their addresses. Their wallets. Their names. Their sadness, their frustration, their joy, their pleasure, their desire. And it is my duty to hold those in confidence. I am become a container of trust. An echo chamber of deep secrets[115]. An astrologer would say that's very Scorpio of me. I witness that in my irl sex life where the closer your bond of trust is with someone, the more fucked up shit you can do in bed.

"That's the best part baby the trust" -Lil Peep

If you saw me doing consensual non consent in space, no you didn't. Coerced consent is not consent. "No" is a complete sentence. People who persist after the word "no" is said need to seriously learn about boundaries, and consider their behavior.

Porn is not enough for THE SADIST
Who says SAYS I can do whatever I like to you because you'll never leave me
THE MASOCHIST SAYS you can do anything you like to me as long as you never leave me

The narcissist says : "WHAT IT DO" AT 6AM

Instagram PTSD ads be like: let's relive ur sexual assault all over again!
My therapist when I lackadaisically blabber on about my traumas be like: "be forewarned, you might feel a little raw later"
And I'm over here like yeah I'm gonna get RAWED LATER
Post traumatic stress disorder be like if you saw me sleeping peacefully at night no you didn't

Age Fetishization and Its Toxicity
Why do older men crave younger women?
They are easier to control.
Youth is extremely fetishized across culture and media.
A less developed brain means more subservience in taking bullshit.

Ovipositor fetish, impregnation fetish
He had me on retainer as his breeding slut
And honestly? I liked it

You are a 60 year old man gooning to a barely legal teenage girl. What the fuck is wrong with you?

That was a paraphilia. We're all perverts.
"Do you have kids?" I asked a man who wanted me to dress like a Lolita.
"No"
"Good"
Even the stepbro-stepsis trope is complicit in pervading the normalization of incest.

---

115 That she tells everyone

I have had fans who made me happy, and fans who absolutely disgusted me. Some of them turned me on, some of them turned me off. I FUCKED A FAN (chapter 6)

Discourse on Purity: Age Fetishization and its Discontents
What's with the plaid skirt fetish?[116]
I have probably spent over $3,000 on fetish skirts.
Taboo to talk about money - SAVE SAVE SAVE SAVE AMEX HIGHYIELD SAVINGS DEALS SALES INVESTMENTS FIDUCIARIES.
The juxtaposition of morality and immorality.
~Old men who like little girls~
Drawing the boundary at age play "kinks" and sussing out which clients are there to relive a memory of youthful past vs those who are predators.
The late-thirties man who bought me a TV and tipped generously to spoil me... until he was aghast to find out I am not 18/19 like he thought, and unsubscribed.
The man who asked for a video of me "being 28 years old, minus the 2[117]" … pedo alert
Sometimes the man is a woman…
Society/entertainment industry discarding women after age 25-30
Age of shadows
Aging into a milf category.
The new homogenized face online where it's impossible to tell someone's age.
Plastic surgery and "instagram face".

Erotomanic Fixation
"All my fan mail is disturbing, it's an occupational hazard" -Richard Castle
"I never have any normal fans" -Spencer Reid

Erotomania is a pathological delusion where one believes that someone, usually a public figure but not limited to such, is equally infatuated with them. In the age of parasocial connection, erotomania is more topical than ever. It's a rare disorder that develops and persists despite clear evidence to the contrary. In many cases it's a relatively harmless delusion confined to the erotomanic's mind, but in extreme cases when the erotomanic takes action, it can result in obsessive behavior, stalking, harassment, assault, or murder (John Hinckney, obsessed with Jodie Foster, attempted to assassinate Ronald Reagan when he believed this act would impress Foster enough to be with him; Mark David Chapman, murderer of John Lennon, was believed to have erotomanic fixation towards Lennon).

The object of delusion is usually someone unattainable to the sufferer: a celebrity, someone with higher social status, someone unavailable because of marriage or another relationship – often someone the erotomanic has never met or only

116 Trauma from catholic school

117 So 26

loosely interacted with[118].

Anonymous keyboard warriors have it easier than ever now; stalking, doxxing, developing their e-erotomanic fixation from behind a blank account and a VPN.

From wikipedia: *Sigmund Freud explained erotomania as a defense mechanism to ward off homosexual impulses which can lead to strong feelings of paranoia, denial, displacement and projection. Similarly, it has been explained as a way to cope with severe loneliness or ego deficit following a major loss.[4] Erotomania may also be linked to unsatiated urges dealing with homosexuality or narcissism.[5]*

Criminal Minds Season 1, Episode 5: "Broken Mirror"

Criminal Minds Season 1, Episode 18: "Somebody's Watching"

The term ***erotolepsy*** *was first used by Thomas Hardy in his 1895 novel Jude the Obscure[1] to describe a passionate sensual desire and longing which is more violent and urgently felt than erotomania.[2] It has been variously described as "love-seizure" and "sexual recklessness".[3] Derived from eroto- and -lepsy, it has since become more widely used, including by American poet Susan Mitchell in her 2001 poetry collection Erotikon.[4]*

I'm so sexy even life gets hard for me

The Amorphous Plane of Existence Between Trauma and Healing:
I'm in this right now, and it's hard to write about because of optics. Every day, every day .. Repression, suppression, expression, surrender.
Cats are amazing emotional support animals. Their purr is therapeutic.

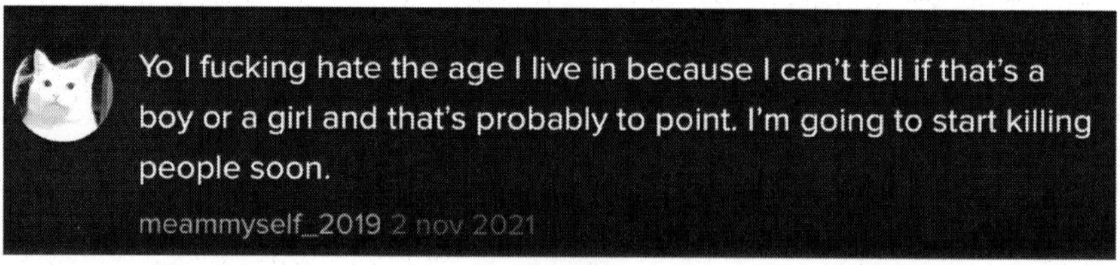

This is everyday life. Every day we go through a thousand heavens and a thousand hells. But more often.. the hells.

Throughout this entire book, pathology is peppered on the chapters like a seasoning; dark agonies, raw greed, desperation, anxiety, insecurity, memory. Reasons to need a trauma oasis. I start with theory; what is sexual desire online? And dive into the why of my origin story. I mercifully dovetail my existence

118 Guardrails against the dangers of intimacy

with the existence of my field, drifting from topics broad to narrow.

Yapping about relational economics – what does the money *really* symbolize? How the human conditions of agony, loneliness, uncertainty, failure manifest online – in the very place designed for escapism, fantasy, dehumanization. What the psychic consequences of sexing the algorithm really are, and how I've dealt with it. It's not rocket science.

Then, back to real life. After this book is finished, what happens? Life. Trauma. Joy. Illness. Healing. Love. Pain. Sex.

Healthy Attitudes Towards Sex and Sexuality

I guarantee that if you look into any civilian's sexual history you will find some weird shit. Looking into anyone's sexual preference is a chilling, haunting experience. What then of the people who openly demonstrate their kinks online? What then of the people who openly demonstrate their mental illness online? Mental illness monday be like:
I BE FEELING NOT GREAT TODAY
SCATTERED THOUGHTS, BRO
GHHHHHRGH.

Editor's note: We don't know how to do anything anymore, we're all just babies. We can't do shit correctly, we can't eat correctly, we don't know how to go to the bathroom correctly. When was the last time anyone slept correctly? We drink too much, abuse medications, life hack incorrectly. We can't even have sex correctly – we do it on the internet or through a screen.[119]

Do we all just lack dignity that much, that we fake autism and maintain piss poor ethics and unprecedented depravity?
Just be neurodivergent for god's sake.
The deceptions of internet personae for victim clout and stolen valor.

Everyone wants to fuck a crazy b*tch till you get to the asylum. ~ the editor
Everyone wants to play games till you have to fuck Jigsaw.
~Ancient proverb

Case study: Patient #1
PAIN
PENIS
PATIENT
Sorry can't hang this friday i'm in my penis enlargement era
From penis to pyramids: an ethnography on the bible
I got my construction vest on and I'm building the pyramids 6 days a week
And on the 7th day…

119 When is the last time you fell asleep

I got my jizz covered prada dress on and I'm at the build a penis workshop
A woman's work is never done
God's favorite porn stars be like: Sunday is not a day of rest it's a day to get undressed

I'm lucid, unlucid, grounded, and dissociated
It's fucked up coming up with content all the damn time I am DISCONTENT
It's giving me spiritual sickness
It hurts, it's pain

Why did I make this chapter such a mess?
The only answer is: **because I can.**

"Life, as we find it, is too hard for us; it brings us too many pains, disappointments and impossible tasks. In order to bear it we cannot dispense with palliative measures... There are perhaps three such measures: powerful deflections, which cause us to make light of our misery; substitutive satisfactions, which diminish it; and intoxicating substances, which make us insensible to it."
— Sigmund Freud, Civilization and Its Discontents

12A. The Psychological Consequences of Being Nude Online; Pornstar as Identity

"My blood alone remains: take it, but do not make me suffer long."
~Marie Antoinette

re you ready for everyone you know to see you naked, or to at least be aware that you offer nude content online? Some creators do their pages "faceless" – showing only the bottom half, or the top half, of their face. Eyes. Lips. **Partial object nudes**, in the hopes of not being able to be identified or found by anyone in their civilian life. In general we all have to be careful with metadata, identifying tattoos or birthmarks, public spaces where a street sign or landmark can reveal location. You never know which erotomanic fixation lingers in the eyes of an anonymous perverted zealout, and what CIA-level stalker shit someone may do to find the object of their obsession.

ChatGPT did not write this book. A naked woman did.[120]

When your image - your naked image - is leaked and circulated online, passed around like a virtual cum dump, you need new coping mechanisms. Modern problems require modern solutions which create post-modern problems which require post-everything solutions. Regulating after being dysregulated.

The terror of celebrity as an adult creator
The terror of being found out, outed, doxxed, stalked (an extreme consequence of erotomania and monomanic fixation).

When I was a little girl watching Spice Girls and Britney Spears on TV,

120 Coming to you live from the plus sized creators lounge

I wanted to be famous. The glitzy little outfits, the pretty makeup, the 90s-2000s y2k celebrity craze, learning their favorite things in tabloids, seeing tours of their lavish mansions – I wanted that glamor. Being a celebrity sounded so cool and fun, I dreamed of commercial success.

Fashion designers. Models. Pop stars. Porn stars. Avant garde girls. Socialites. Hollywood actresses. It was magazines, it was TV. Glossy, sensationalized. Loved. Admired. Wealthy. Who among us hasn't dreamt of fame and fortune? But as I got older, and the internet took over print and television, dark sides of celebrity revealed themselves. Britney Spears' 2007 nightmare. Child stars growing up, good girls "going bad". Upskirt photos. Steroids. Domestic violence. Weight gain, pregnancy speculation. Drug use, car crashes, DUI's. Switchblades. Cocaine. Breakdowns. Breakups.

Private lives made public, then made parasocial.[121] Social media networks made it easier than ever to connect, or have the illusion of connection, with the rich and famous. It made it easier than ever to go viral and have those 15 seconds of fame, which are now so commonplace that it's just a blip in time – nothing special. The atrocity of stalkers – attempts on the lives of celebrities like Bjork. The concept of fame became a deterrent: unattractive, dark, terrifying. The pressure to always be this person, this identity forged before prying eyes.

The decentralized, democratized system of seeing and being seen. But take away the tabloids and A-list status, is that much different than what I was doing on Onlyfans? When I was marketing heavily, revealing myself to thousands of anonymous people behind screens around the world? I had my 15 seconds of online virality. I had my moment of being recognized irl at a NY airport, the only time someone has come up to me saying "hey are you ___ from reddit?" No, I don't think I ever was. The CIA trains operatives to never confirm nor deny any assumed identity.

> They say my name
> Like a guessing game
> Hey is that really you?
> No, I don't think it ever was
> ~Bright Eyes

Any level of being known, even as a Z-list niche online OF star, comes with consequences as well as perks. It's cool to have a fan club, to receive money and gifts, an illusion of being lucky and privileged to receive income and validation for simply existing. Fans who learn the language of my universe – the signifier of Booba seals, Cyberhorny zingers, Nastya catchphrases, semiotics of Nastya in the kitchen as Sylvia Plath rolls over in her grave. My private life as a perverted inside joke that fans are in on.

---

121 Parasociality is not simply an attachment to a specular pixelated imago - it is a dyadic process of alienation. The content that draws in the viewers simultaneously perverts the self of the creator in a process of distributive psychic inversion. This is part of the burnout the author unconsciously mutters about in each chapter.

Is the joke on me? Then there are the assholes, people who've made hate groups dedicated to me, people who've leaked my nudes. The knowledge that if someone recognizes me on the street, they've already seen me nude. Thank god I look good naked. In the grand existential scheme of things, my naked body being somewhere out there is no big deal. It's far from my biggest concern in life. I just chill. Jus b chill.

Then there is another quirked up level of recognition – occasionally on OF I get messages asking "I remember you from ___ escorting site, do you still do it?" "hey ___ I saw you on ___ is this you?"

Sometimes I don't know what I'm supposed to feel. Flattered? Embarrassed? Proud? Apathetic? It takes me a while to even identify how and what I'm feeling. Somatically, trauma runs through my body dormant until it has no choice but to erupt and be confronted. The Nastya Valentine hostage crisis is a telekinetic event from me to me. Do you get it now?

I am
Not a fan　　　　I am an enthusiastic spectator

I'm not sure I've ever felt better.

No, I feel something terrible. Laying on my side nauseated on the 4th of July, my eyes hurting, my spine disarticulated, my mind unable to focus, overwhelmed and depressed. I want to get up, do something, but the nausea paralyzes me. I'm naked, but not in a sexy way. Clothes feel too stiff, fabrics too constricting. I just want to sleep until it's a new day, new morning, system reset. Meanwhile the avatar Nastya is thriving: she's sold some sexy videos, a few new subscribers came in gooning, she looks great in her blue lace bra and panties, soliloquizing or reading Carl Jung as she sits on a vibrator. Nothing bothers her because nothing can. She's not really there. How long can she remain? But wherever she is, she is somewhere, in someone's consciousness. What a weird dissociation. I need my xanax. I need more sleep. I need more money. More time. I need my depression and anxiety to go away.

Can porn be an antidote to depression? The amount of people who say I "brightened" or "made" their day create a stunning tapestry of porn's healing abilities.

On a good day, on a dark day, on any day on the internet, a constellation of OF stars awaits you. What were your first encounters with porn? Did you want a multi dimensional experience, a specific kink tickled, or just to get off? Like me, most models offer the choice of any of those things – from generalism or specificity.

Is it streaming or posting? It's both. Onlyfans is like a blog, a nsfw instagram feed, with the option to privately message the model. You can also attend livestreams if the model goes live. Let me tell you something about going live. It gets exhausting. My main focus is on the posting and the messaging. The consequence of that is I lose income on live-streams that could be a potential moneymaker, so I have to curate something exceptional to make up for it. I have to really become attuned to what specific people want, while offering what "the average viewer" would be turned on by. In my head, a mental gymnastics of what's sexy for the day stretches me like a medieval torture rack. I'm driven to the psych ward by marketing.
Marketing with artistry, drama, subjectivity grabs identity by the scrotum.

Do you market with intellect
Do you market with narrative[122]
Nastya Valentine hostage crisis
Nastya's dad emotional ransom demand
The disposition matrix
My body, the DMZ
Zugzwang
Game Over
Unstoppable

This is what I am: Pornstar as identity.

Pornstar becomes a personal brand, a way people see you and respond to you. Online, that's sick, like it's so cool to be like yeah I'm a porn star. In person, it's like a coming-out party every time I disclose to someone what I do. **Cue the obligatory "guilt and shame within this stigmatized career field" section.**

If I ever start to feel any tinglings of guilt or shame that "oh fuck I'm naked on the internet" I think that's ok at least I'm making the kind of living that makes it worth it. Shame and guilt have triggers; a sadness, a rage, a feeling of lack underneath. I'm not ashamed of what I do – I'm using it brazenly as a vehicle to write this book, tackle bigger endeavors, or just the simple endeavor of living daily life comfortably. This is an extreme line of work that pushes people to extremes within their psyche, to the extremes of what is socially acceptable.

122 Are you marketing with the same lips you use to kiss your mother?

To even dip a toe into this pool of psychic excess, you have to be really deeply okay with yourself. As far as I'm concerned, there is no room for guilt or shame.

There's a lot of shame circulating 'sex' in general so many people's own perceptions and insecurities will be projected onto anyone working in the sex industry. We will inevitably get shamed by others, so we have to be really intentional about owning our pussy. Own your pussy. **It's yours.**

"You are not just a OF girl"
"You're so much more than this"
"You can do something better"
"You have so many other talents/options"
"What would you want to do as a real job?"

Variations on a theme of the immorality and shame in porn, the hierarchical structure of what society considers a "solid" career. They think I got money coming out of my ass? No, this is what I *chose* to do and be, even if the consequence that comes with it is controversy. Most of the time I just tell people I'm an artist and writer. Or I'm "independently wealthy" and just have a bunch of free time at my disposal. Or I'm "broke". But occasionally when I want to play a conversational game of catch and release, I drop the porn bomb and see what happens.

What if I don't want a societally-real job?
What if I am just an OF girl? No big deal.

I know what I am *not*[123]
Even if I don't know what I am

Girl Next Door (2007 movie) – guy meets girl, girl is revealed to be a porn star, guy gets inflammatory reaction. She fell for him because he was sweet and genuine; he started acting weird and negging, she sensed something was uneasy. His porn-watching buddy told him to act like he doesn't want her, to take her to a hotel and fuck her brains out.

The guy takes the girl to a hotel room. Sensing his intention, she bends over on the bed.
"How do you want me?" she asks, pouting.

"What are you doing, why are you doing this?" he retorts in shock.

"Is this what you want? To fuck a porn star in a cheap hotel room? So this is what you think of me…" she finally communicates the unspoken.

123 I do not understand what I do. For what I want to do I do not do, but what I hate I do. Romans 15-

"I know who you are and you're better than this": the guy has a classic savior complex.

"I loved the way you looked at me" she responds, and leaves in tears.

At the end of the movie, he does the porn just like she did. "Your face is gonna be in this; think about that." It's a fun movie. A commentary on the dehumanization porn stars go through, when their identity is shackled to a singular trope.

Our identity to others forms through the specular image
Our identity to ourselves forms through introspection

The **specular image** refers to the *reflection* of one's own body in the mirror, the **image** of oneself which is simultaneously *oneself* and *other* -- the "**little other**".

In the digital plane, our Little Other is the panorama of all fragmented images we take of ourselves and consume of others.

"This is the function that is found at the heart of the institution of the subject in the visible. What determines me, at the most profound level, in the visible, is the gaze that is outside. The gaze is the instrument through which light is embodied and through which – in a fragmented form – I am photo-graphed."
~Jacques Lacan, *Four Fundamental Concepts of Psychoanalysis*

All of those philosophers intellectualizing sexuality did not get laid enough. You want advanced philosophical discourse on contemporary sexuality? Go to reddit . com / gonewild and see how many men post nudes. Yes, go see how many men post nudes and then go to reddit . com / critical theory.

Of interest here is the ratio of male:female posters on seller subreddits vs. non-seller subreddits. Seller subreddits are primarily female-dominated: 90-100% of those who promote online pages are female. Non-seller nsfw subreddits, like gonewild and normalnudes, often contain more men than women posting: a pure display of exhibitionism and desire of the carnal manhood to be seen.

Performing the Sexual Act.

When was the first moment that you looked back at the phone camera and realized, oh wow, I am "doing the sex"?

I never really thought about it that way; in the flow of filming content, the sex part came naturally. Ok, the clothes are off. Oh wow where did this vibrator come from. Second thoughts? I never gave it a second, third, fourth thought. It all just happened, almost as though possessed. Is this… my calling? Is being horny online my destiny, given that it felt so natural?

The metaphysic of perversion is that anything can be porn. Our pervy little human minds twist the most wholesome things into pornography. I like to tell my subscribers that every day with me is a horny adventure, turning ordinary situations into a commodified sexual experience.

The first time I used a sex toy - in college my housemate had an electric toothbrush. I would hear her in her room and it sounded like she was having a lot of fun. I decided to buy one of my own and give it a try: in the shower, where no one could hear me. It was.. electrifying. That summer I became a little addicted to how pleasurable it made me feel.

O_O

Spoiled petulant pathetic brats, useless drivel
The architects admit and regret
Integrated studies, but we ignore it

The performance of the online orgasm vs me just jacking it on a random day. Is it really that different? Most times, the only difference is the camera. Sometimes it turns me on being filmed, and I think about those times when I touch myself off-camera – it makes me turn the camera on and hit record. Selling that video and receiving income for it turns me on. When I'm turned on, so is the camera. Other times I just need a private moment to masturbate lengthily, something exclusively for myself. Nonprofit gooning. Pleasure without a price tag. Pleasure transmitted through the apps, for the currency of money and attention.

We all know logically that these apps diminish our self worth, attention spans, sense of reality, etc. but we are hardwired both socially and psychologically to not be able to quit them. In what world will we be able to break the cycle? Is it coming soon, or are we too late, forever submitting to the insentient apps and machines that so tactically subjugate us?

The instability of the whorish sites. Being deleted out of nowhere with no warning; being reinstated in the exact same way. Lack of transparency. The psychological effects of trying to be stable in an unstable world. If you want a stable bitch, you should have bought a horse

The strangeness of caring simps

Something uncanny happens when the parasocial connections take on the realm of friendship, or patronage. Caring. Case in point: a time I was sick with the flu, and the disparity of reactions between people in my real life not even saying a "feel better", was made apparent as my online simps sent me care packages, money for ordering soup, and a cavalcade of well wishes. Petty, selfish, perhaps, but I feel cared for in that way. My simps become as important to me as I am to them. It's simpbiotic.

When I am feeling burned out, sick, or lazy, my simps say "take your time". Those real ones, digital as they may be, I treasure. I don't need fancy dinners (have you ever seen me near *food*???!) or Gucci purses (I prefer Prada) or superyachts, but give me a man or 100 who can pay my rent and bills and debts and I'll be happy.

Does it really matter if they're corporeal or digital? Does it make me lazy to encourage gifts and income on my days off? Greedy? Perfectionistic? Oh well.

One thing I remember from my maternal grandparents in childhood: grandfather, an engineer for a cruise ship; grandmother, part of the ship's cleaning crew. "Grandma, why do you work so much more and grandpa is always lying on the couch?"

Grandpa's response: "because I worked and studied so much for so many years, other people now do the work for me". It makes sense to me now. I have put in the grind for so many years. Now I can lay on the couch and sell my content, my experience. Just keep chooching.

Once again, I had accused
him of laziness.
Once again, he flung the
word back—

He raised his glass and turned
it upside-down.
This is your purity, he said,
this is your perfectionism—
The glass was empty; it left
no mark on the tablecloth.[124]

Online sluts: look, they're self aware too 🖉☺
The sentient omnipresent teledildonic. My **DILDO** sees 12 ways.
Life is just a game to stave off death. Only Fans is just a game within a game, that jerks off the grim reaper. A play within a play. A dream within a dream.

124 Louise gluck the sword in the stone

Body Dysmorphia/Eating Disorders

The mental illness manifests in a physical way: the perversion of the flesh, the destruction of the flesh, the disappearance of the flesh.

One goal replaces another. If the goal was __ lbs, that becomes not enough in the perfectionist's mind. It can always be lower, better. I can outdo myself. I can annihilate myself so completely that no critique will ever bother me again. A psychic ego death manifested physically.

The psychic consequence of being online as a piece of flesh, and a mind that has suffered with body/eating issues, is dealt with in the next chapter. In the industry of entertainment, it is well documented that the workers take to great extremes in the perfectionism of their body and face when in the public eye (mostly women, although men too may have manorexia, manbulimia, man body dysmorphia, and nonbinary/trans body dysphoria is its own separate and complex issue).

Porn is entertainment, and the actors rely on their body to make money, more so even than the traditional Hollywood schematic. So why is there almost no discourse on body image perception in porn? Is it because the actors are viewed as pieces of meat and flesh, disposable, less valuable than their Hollywood friends?

Gamifying anorexia.

The regime of numbers within the capitalistic onlyfans sphere (rankings, percentiles, tips, income, spending, investing in items, divesting from parts of life, predicting the horny Ball Street Market) -
Is perpetually in co-occurence with the regime of numbers (scales, calories, BMI, always moving the goalpost to a new goal weight*) pertaining to neurotic dysmorphic body image attributes + eating disorders.

Body image woes: slow starvation to put off death, too cowardly to enact it overtly[125].
The teetering in the liminal space of libido and thanatos.
Rejection of things that nourish the flesh. Deprivation.

*Revision note: even when I was deep in my disorder I refrained from scale numbers and counting calories/carbs/whatever. The goal was to feel empty; the feeling was not quantitative or calculated. Numerical values seemed pointless to me even if I did engage in that. Similarly, the numerical "stats" on OF did not matter to me; what mattered was feeling full-filled; financially capable to live my life comfortably.

---

125 Louise gluck on anorexia: "The tragedy of anorexia seems to me that its intent is not self-destructive, though its outcome so often is. Its intent is to construct, in the only way possible when means are so limited, a plausible self. But the sustained act, the repudiation, designed to distinguish the self from the other also separates self and body ...

Somewhere in those years a switch flipped from the drive to feel empty → to the recognition of being fulfilled. Sublimation, transference perhaps. I still can't stand the physical feeling of being full but damn bitch I be eating and let me tell you when my boyfriend takes me to Matsuhisa I enjoy every single bite. (Me to me as I write the following chapter: "shut up fatass")

"I must get my soul back from you; I am killing my flesh without it."
— Sylvia Plath, The Unabridged Journals of Sylvia Plath

12B: Dysmorphia, The Beautiful: Body Image Discontents in Porn

Trigger warning: Danger zone! I am legally obligated by cyber law to put a trigger w for ED stuff. Read at your own risk, my sweet.

abe.. I make a living being basically nude on the internet. Most of the time, I am nude. My body is my moneymaker. Like most people online, possibly even the person reading this, I also suffer from body dysmorphia and have been plagued by an eating disorder for over a decade of my life. While my body is recovered* (asterisk denoting a foreboding exploration into this term later), my mind teeters on the edge, dallying to and fro between dimensions of healthy and demonic. My body dysmorphia, like everything else, goes digital these days. Online existence both alleviates and exacerbates it. I often feel shameful for even thinking the thoughts I think[126]. Why, then, am I writing about this?

There is something that porn stars or nsfw digital creators don't really talk about: the psychic consequences of posting the naked body in the cyber world, and our fragile body image. Even here in this book, (especially here) I have taken care not to post the generic triggering eating disordered photo set. In place of that... my memes, random bullshit, and wistfully pensive yet hornyyy and perverse self portraits where I think I'm hot.

To be nude online is to attract viewers and invite comments about the body. This can be amazingly liberating, or it can backfire horribly. Each picture

126 "I think where I am not, therefore I am where I do not think. I am not whenever I am the plaything of my thought; I think of what I am where I do not think to think". - Lacan

anticipates a response. A gamble.[127] There are some days that in terms of body image are like a hellish hell. I have no better words[128] to describe it. Add a new circle of hell for each unsatisfactory bodycheck.[129]

Some days it has the opposite effect, where the compliments I receive make me genuinely feel good. Overall it has been healing. My confidence has, in the grand scheme of things, actually improved a lot with OnlyFans. To be honest I never felt attractive to myself until I started doing sex work. I love posting nude and sometimes I even love my body. That is the only way to truly rebel against society, to truly like yourself, and to embrace your sexual personae and individual flaws.

Instagram Face: just say no. If for nothing else, I will honestly forever be grateful to OF and to my clients for helping me feel good about my body. My job heralded a sexual awakening and a healing from past SA traumas. Without a doubt, I love myself more: I'm glad to be doing this and I love bringing you my horny artistry. Still, there are hellish days where I hate my body and am dissatisfied with my appearance.

How to forgive for violence against the self?
That can be the hardest part.

The first step for any problem is to admit you need help. And I do. I need a lot of help not hating myself. My dedicated team of therapists and friends, my emotional security detail, is pretty much essential to my survival. How to deal though, on your own? Who else is feeling this way and candidly open about it?

There is not enough literature on body image issues in porn. They without a doubt exist but are invisible because we as performers do not want to ruin the illusion that we are anything less than perfect, confident, capable — the fantasy. Your fantasy.

While I am proud of my body (of work, that is) and confident that I've imprinted a unique signature into the world of obscure porn that dovetails with cinematic art, I sometimes cannot look at my past works without feeling

---

127 when capital is applied to sex it becomes more than just 'sex' """

""The ecstatic form of capital is totally generalized exchange. An orbital form. In merchandise, money is already in process of de-referentialization. … That is what gives rise to intense miraculous effects of multiplication. The secret of gambling is that money does not exist as a value

- Baudrillard, forget foucault

128 "...I would think how words go straight up in a thin line, quick and harmless, and how terribly doing goes along the earth, clinging to it, so that after a while the two lines are too far apart for the same person to straddle from one to the other; and that sin and love and fear are just sounds that people who never sinned nor loved nor feared have for what they never had and cannot have until they forget the words." **William Faulkner, As I Lay Dying**

129 What came first the eating disorder or the posting

disgusted at every fat fold, chubby angle, or squishy thigh. Even choosing pics to post on here, I find myself gravitating towards angles that make me look slim. I be sucking it in honey -- I am a connoisseur of succ.

This all implicates the *bigger* or co-morbid issue of fat-phobia in our culture. It's so wrong and obviously logically should be discounted, yet for people like me who grew up in the 2000s and 2010s when the too-thin aesthetic was in, it's impacts are almost inevitable. The propaganda is deep in our brains. It seems to me the popular silhouette seems to be swinging back to "unrealistically thin" nowadays - after a bender in the equally unrealistic Kadashian influenced "huge fake ass, thick thighs, and teeny teeny Barbie waist" look of the 2010s. Can we get just like.... major love and representation for normal, average, regular person sizes? Medium sized thighs, medium boobs, medium ass, not fat fetishized or anorexia glamorized? All bodies are valid of course, but like... I don't even know. It's honestly hard to provide good insight on this topic when I myself am complicit.

I used to have a folder in my computer that contained my own version of porn — photographs of me at my thinnest, rib cage and hip bones jutting, no space for my internal organs, skin almost transparent, hair falling out. For a while I wished to look like that again. When I recovered I deleted that folder because I essentially used it to trigger myself. I don't care about external thinspiration — what was special about this was that *I* did it. If I had applied the mental energy to being thin, to other avenues instead, I would be much more successful by now. Self harm is not the way to go. Now, I cycle through every coping mechanism I know, sampling healing methods until something feels effective and natural[130].

With therapy and spiritual guidance (yes I am into the "woo woo stuff") I can hold together a healthy mindset for as long as possible. Women's bodies are mysterious and weight naturally goes up and down depending on hormones, stress, menstrual cycle etc and this is even more variable in front of the camera - which as we all know adds pounds. I also tend to shoot myself from the even unflattering "mommy angle" aka from below, to look taller. I love the height it gives me, as I'm just a little over 5' without heels. But this stylistic choice is a fattening one. I recently sustained an injury to my legs, yet another one on top of previous fractures to my feet and ankles because of my weak bones, which left me a little bit immobile and unable to exercise.

Sometimes I view myself as sedentary and physically lazy, but this experience showed me just how much physicality and **Man**ual labor goes into my job. I also walk a lot, even though LA is not a walkable city. Not being able to perform my physical duties and being laid up on the couch these days made me feel sloppy, floppy, and uncomfortable.

130 In the classical theory of the mirror stage, the little baby sees itself in totality in the mirror subjectivity is formed through the realization that it is not the mother. The cyberhorny mirror stage involves reality's mirror. The comments of the simps become the cracks that mutate the viewer's gaze.

Last year I was diagnosed with a painful stomach condition called gastroparesis which is literally a paralysis of the stomach nerves. With updated medication and doctor visits I am doing a lot better now, and while GP can't be cured, I am successfully managing it. At first, the medication I was on made me lose weight, which I guiltily loved and wanted so badly to get used to. However, I also got unpleasant side effects from the dose so the dose was adjusted to my pain threshold — so while I no longer feel those side effects, I have put on weight and I am distraught in a whole other way.

"Everything you see I owe to spaghetti."
— Sophia Loren

It's really never discussed in our culture but many people think porn stars and nsfw creators are always confident in (and even proud of) our bodies because we can publish them online for others to watch, gawk, judge. As if exhibitionism brings invincibility. Just because we do porn we're immune to these body issues right? How I wish that were true.

As if intentional nudity brings an immunity to self esteem issues ... I did not know what an innie or an outie was until I started browsing Reddit. Even women's most intimate body parts- nipples, labia, asshole… are all subject to scrutiny. Ratings. Compliments. Insults. Attention. Dismissal. Which is worse? I learned a lot from posting online, both good and bad, all fascinating. There is a toxic "rate my boobs/ass/etc" "am I hot" culture… it's torture. It centers on every body part, ANY body part. Which of our body parts are we obsessed with? We obviously just post to be complimented, almost more so for validation than spicy page promotion. And if it's anything less than a 11/10 I have a meltdown[131].

What I found in my experiential research was that people who paid to have a subscription to me were generally courteous and respectful (cause lol why would you waste money to troll someone you don't even know?) but the majority of viewers commenting online in general were entitled and despicable. Disgusting perverted men gawking and judging much younger women on their bodies.

Online, these disgusting incel men have their pick of the litter when irl none of the ladies posting would give them a second look. The disgustingness is not in terms of appearance but in personality. They are sadistic. This is another reason why older women do not engage these sadistic men — they won't take any of the bullshit that a younger more boundaryless woman would.

But ageism in porn/entertainment/culture is a whole other issue. And it is not enough to simply be nude, youthful, attractive, before an audience; one

131 Or perhaps some of the posting is rooted in masochism. I want the criticism because it will enforce my deepest unconscious traumatized thoughts. "See , i really am ugly and unloveable" at least in this case I will know my tortured convictions are correct and I am not *wrong*.

must also be behaviorally perfect. Quiet, submissive, not outspoken, not "extra", not a hot mess, not depressed, not over the hill, not overweight (unless a milf or thicc fetish category). Everything in our contemporary society has to fit into dainty little categories but I hope this era gets untangled soon. Or at very least that I can do something to dismantle this fixed system and create a bolder gray area.

There is no representation for the "in between" body — not skinny, not fat, just average. And as much as I hate to be categorized as such, here I am, begrudgingly representing the average, the normal, the messy, the ugly, the real.[132] I'm not overweight and I'm not an anorexic looking sample size.

I still have my past thinness tied to my identity so badly, that to be categorized into "normal" weight range makes me weak. It was the worst when a **girl** colleague wrote what she assumed was my weight on one of her posts of us collaborating. That aggravated me on many many levels. I don't know how to approach things like this. Thank you for pushing me back into the closet. Thank you for the insecurity, you may as well have bashed my head in and called it a day.

"Insecurity is unattractive
Anxiety is not hot
Depression is unsexy"...

I hear that all the time. It damages my business. We're supposed to conceal. My job is to be a fantasy, not a human. But I cannot, with a clear conscience, perform against myself and my boundaries. I cannot undo what I have already posted but I can reconsider my future and what my OF / online presence overall will look like. I have some content that I'm sitting on but I'm not sure if I wanna release yet. I will think about it. I want reassurance that I look good, and not just in my own delusion. There is a quote I forget attributed to whom, which goes "delusion is more necessary to our happiness than reality". God damn is that ever true. But what are you gonna do?

Just keep chooching.

I do not want much from this world, all I really want is the reassurance that I am skinny and thin. Dainty. Delicate. A fragile, rickety Victorian doll. Admittedly it just makes me sad that I'm not seen as thin. One would not look at me and immediately go "wow she is skinny". Honestly if I had a constant stream of people telling me how skinny I was, I would probably float on cloud 9 in a happiness I've been so deprived of. On the other hand... If I was very fat and plus size and BBW I would have a moneymaker niche to exploit. Yes,

---

132 Okay... the psychological consequences of being nude online *in vivo*. Nastya is obviously skinny but the trade has warped her self-perception. The fact that you were once 'skinnier' establishes an asymptotic standard which reverberates through the now constantly shifting mirror stage of the platform.

I participate in this blatant hypocrisy as well. FML. But the ordinariness of the middle ground is agony.

Sorry for all this emo cringe trauma dumping… it was long and dark sided. Sorry about that to my OF subs and sorry in advance to you dear reader. My moods about my body change often.

When I have a bad day, I'm comforted by the fact that all things pass. It's not forever; thank god everything is temporary. I know I'm gonna get over this moment and feel like a sex goddess once more… I will resume posting nudes again and say hello from my little padded room and hope you continue to enjoy my content and…

This is an ongoing topic. I have to step outside myself to dive deeper. In terms of the meta analysis here, I struggled with writing it on various levels.

Namely, am I credible enough to discuss this?

Do I look sickly thin enough to warrant credit in the ED communities and to be believable as someone who has suffered this violent illness?

***Yelling* Listen to me[133]:**

eauty, and the warping of it, is truly the most subjective perceptual experience. EDs come in all shapes and sizes and are not limited to the common media portrayal of the size 000 rail thin model. It is the girl next door. It is the mom of 3. It is the guy at the gym. It is the stressed out nurse. It is the adult film star. While traditionally thought of as skinny white rich teen girls, that myth is bullshit and EDs occur across all ages and ethnicities and genders and wealth classes. There is no "normal" or "good/bad" sufferer. They're all bad.

Many forms of soical media insist on the idealization of skinny. Looking at it triggers me too if I'm being honest. Before/afters of "weight gain"

133 When a schizophrenic anorexic is talking I sit my white ass down and LISTEN.

where the only difference is fatter cheeks due to fillers? Marathon while restricting? Two fitness watches when "not counting calories burned"? Yeah girl this shit don't add up.

Sometimes I am too far up my own ass to admit my own delusional thinking, but luckily no one really follows me (at least not for this). I urge health/fitness based creators with bigger followings to own up to their distorted thinking and behaviors. Idgaf about y'all's own ED, our bodies are all our own individual responsibilities - but this kind of posting is dangerous to young impressionable fans. Much more dangerous than porn.

Do I care about the well being of an influencer who I don't even know and can't verify the truth of? Hell no. I care about the spread of fraudulent information, the influence this has on future generations. I have a sense of protectiveness towards young girls who remind me of myself, and of course I care about my own triggers and not relapsing. If I were seeing this variety of content as my teen self, I would be triggered as shit and likely alter my behavior to look like the "correct" recovered body (aka still very skinny).

Young girls can see this influencer crap and be scared further into the chamber of their EDs, feel like a "bad anorexic" for recovering heavier than some online binch, or just be afraid that they'll gain weight that others haven't. If you're dealing with issues like this I assure you there is no "bad" or "good" way to recover. Progress is progress. It's nonlinear and you can relapse before getting better. It's completely normal and shouldn't be allowed to ruin or impede any future recovery. We're all sick here in our own ways and no one's journey is more or less valid. It says something tho, to either deal with it in private or be upfront about it online. I'm deviant as hell but at least I admit it.

It must be horrifying to recover online publicly. That kind of platform has a lot of capital-R Responsibility. I would probably shit myself. I will share this: I had two serious, legitimate recoveries from my ED. Once in 2010, before internet times, that was helped along by psychedelics, which is why I champion them so heavily for any general life guidance. Through the next few years I was more or less okay, but I had relapsed on and off lightly. That doesn't excuse my behavior but was nothing compared to how heavily I relapsed in 2015 after I was sexually assaulted.

It took me some medical wake up calls to actually take it seriously, and between 2015-2017 I got on a healthier track. Lipstick on a pig. By 2018 I no longer practiced any self harming behaviors, and do not to this day, so in a way that is a success story, but my mental state still needs a lot of cushioning. So for about four years now I have been physically well (ish) but I fucking feel the invisible health repercussions and wish I could take back the time I spent starving myself or crying in the mirror or throwing up after meals. The weird thing is too, that the times when I was deepest in my ED were not necessarily the times when I was at my skinniest. Bulimic people especially are not locked into one body type, it can be any weight. Even anorexics can be a higher weight than you think. The illness is the mentality, the habits, the behavior. Sometimes it's glaringly obvious someone has an ED, other times it can be skillfully concealed. It also doesn't always start with feeling fat. Many people report sexual assaults, family trauma, bullying, and other issues as a root cause of their ED[134]. For me it was inextricably linked to my rickety relationship with my mother, a former Russian model and beautiful woman. "You can take three bites and leave the table hungry" ... "those pants make your thighs touch" ... "wear a jacket over your chubby arms" were things I heard a lot. The fear of weight gain was ingrained.

Young, dumb, and full of glum. Now, I am stronger to hateful words, but back then as a young kid I was fucking impressionable. I did not want breasts and a period at 11/12. The size I am now, was basically the size I was then. For a very long time I did not want to be touched and avoided anything sexual entirely. I just... little girl. My genetic lineage has a taller height, but I definitely stunted my growth with nutrient deprivation. I cannot understate how much of this I regret. Yeah yeah it built character etc but it was also years of unnecessary hell. With my natural body, I never needed to have an ED. No one does. Is it a choice? Kind of... it's hard to describe, and feels like a possession[135] almost, quite out of control. I would equate it to addict behavior. But you can choose to stop and recover and get better.

This. This is why I feel protective of younger teen girls who are exposed to dare I say... the skinnylicious propaganda. Maybe it's not my place to protect. Maybe I'm not the right person to champion body positivity because of my hypocrisy. But I have made it out of some of the darkest shit I could face within myself and I want to tell people they can do it too! It takes a village to heal the wounded. It takes a society. Women, men, everyone in between -- none are immune to body dysmorphia and image issues. I actually have quite a few subscribers on my OF reach out to me after I made a long emo post about this, telling me they can relate. And, of course, telling me that I am beautiful. ☺ Thank you.

I know there are people who will look at me and think "what the hell this bitch is skinny how does she have body image issues", and others (prob ED sufferers just as, or more so, perfectionist as I) thinking "mmm she has the potential to lose another 8-13lbs see some fat rolls around the pooch and cellulite on the ass but otherwise looks okay, keep going queen think thin" .... uggh. Mixed bag.

My body has thinner parts and fatter parts. Obviously online I will choose the most flattering pics, so you don't see the ass cellulite or the mom pooch. You don't see the cuts, the scars, the zits, the ingrowns, the under eye

134 The psychological literature points to the pathogenesis of eating disorders being rooted in an intense desire for control likely due to trauma.

135 One must characterize the demons of one's mind. Notably Nastya uses the term 'possession' here: demonic yes but also a quasi-synonym for 'thing' in the lineage the 'gifts and present' she constantly goes on about.

bags, the thick bulging veins (do I have dick hands?? is that a thing?? have I invented a new dysmorphia??), the bald spots from trichotillomania where I have ripped my hair out.[136] You see me in cute clothes, with cute backdrops, posturing for a thinner angle and sucking it all in to heavens.

I know my body. I have a mom pooch, stretch marks in my ass that seemingly appeared overnight, and cellulite on thighs. I also have a skinny ass flat MFin chest with too-far-apart boobs[137].

My genetics are slim so I don't exercise and live a sedentary lifestyle (god this will catch up to me when I'm like 40 unless I start to become healthily active, whatever that looks like). Altogether it averages out to normal, or the weird hybrid known as "skinny fat". I know how to dress to flatter myself, I've been doing it for over a decade. If you really want to observe and scrutinize me, knock yourself out. I don't really care about the critiques from others; mental self-flagellation is a daily practice for me. I want to start this "body image in porn/digital adult content" conversation, and critique the ED recovery culture, but I don't intend to become a spokesperson for anything. I am the boss and overlord of the unhinged cyberhorny cunty bitches, that I am.

With a normal non skeletal weight am I no longer disordered? What then of my bleak thoughts? Haven't we all dissected ourselves in the fun house mirror of the gaze.

There was a girl I had been falling for on Instagram for a little while (not a recovery influencer, just a random civilian, kind of a NPC I guess). When I first saw her, she took my breath away. Big blue eyes, Anna Karina haircut, exquisite style, hints of old money, grad school under eye bags, Wes Anderson-styled photo grid, and — excessive long-limbed skinniness. Perhaps she reminded me of the rinds of my younger self but wealthier. Perhaps I fantasized about seducing her and lifting up her skinny frame because I found her attractive.

Did I droolinlgy want her or do I enviously want to be her[138]? I don't know. Either way, a bit obsessed. I wonder if I am anyone else's Skinny Bangs Instagram Girl.

My breath feels trapped in my throat. Simultaneously I hope I am and I am not. Comments on her post include stuff like "actual angel" ; "unreal" ; "supermodel doll" ; "ur perfect" … and while I usually cringe at these kind of IG comments, I find myself simping for her, ready to white knight[139] any haters

136 You don't see the shambling inner darkness.

137 Her mom is speaking here.

138 In the memetic theory of the desire one always secretly prefers the rival to the love object in a triangulation.

139 A euphemism for the act of defending an online character.

away. Not that there are any cause she's ethereally perfect, but still, you get the point. Meanwhile the last online compliment I received about my looks was "you look healthy". Womp womp.

God I just wanted to implode. I don't think people understand that calling me "healthy" is the ultimate insult. I want to look like I'm about to blow away in the wind or fold over if my cat bumps into me a bit too hard. As if I just walked out of a smudged photograph in a willowy ballerina dress. I desire that enviable skeletal look, I know it's bad but I still want it. What a mental gymnastic and a psychological splitting; I can look at my hip dips and say "alright, sexy, let's make some $", but then at the same time deride myself for having too much flesh. In the porn world this feels especially strange. Sometimes I want to pay someone to tell me I'm skinny, leaflike, way too thin; if they're really good, I'll actually believe it and start telling it to myself.[140]

We truly live in a dystopia. Is it better to be disembodied?

Is reading this exhausting you? Existing in my mind exhausts me constantly. Body dysmorphia is severely complex and necessitates more delicate treatment and rehabilitation. Aside from Cyberhorny topics, I could write a whole book about my experience with body issues. But I don't know, it just brings up a lot of discomfort. This chapter took me longer than any others. There's something deeply uncomfortable and disturbing when people talk about their EDs. It's a mental illness manifest physically. It's a second hand embarrassment.

It is not that I feel shame around writing about such a dark topic; it's more that I feel shame around being at a normal weight now and not qualified to write about it. So yeah while I might be physically recovered and "healthy" (again, I fucking hate that word) .. I am still mentally exhausted with thinking about the space my appearance takes up.

Inside me there are two wolves; one that chants praise towards my recovery process, and the other that repeatedly tries to convince me that I'm still too fat.

OF has been so amazing for my body image that I was shocked by the lovely validation and constantly think, "wow how long is this gonna last?" .. The impostor syndrome is real. I am at that point where the honeymoon phase feels null and I find myself having more bad body image days than I used to. Maybe I just haven't gotten a good compliment in a while, or haven't fished for one. Perception is a strange and pendular practice that swings wildly. Ten years ago I would have been deathly horrified at the thought of curves on me; two years ago I liked it because men liked it and it made me money; now I look in the mirror

---

140 This is a part of the cyber splitting +whorererarchy. Simps are parasocially attached to Nastya through sexual pathology. Nastya commits egoic transfixion onto other e-girls through physical, ED pathology.

and am confused. I ask myself questions like "why?" "how?" and "what the fuck?"

Torture thru the looking glass[141]. Maybe I need to do psychedelics again. It's the only thing that has honestly really truly helped.

As you can see I have posted vague aesthetic shit instead of triggering before/afters, posed/relaxed pics, numerical values. That's nobody's business and pictures of my body are already too readily available online for your scrutiny, from my unflattering fat angles[142] to my posed contortions trying to appear thin.

When I look in the mirror or pull out my iPhone cam, I do it too.
How is my plump pussy looking?
Can you see my hipbones yet?

Bodychecking: our guiltiest pleasure. It's when someone takes a curated picture of their body that is meant to look thin, through angles and poses and various parameters: checking the body for flaws and whatever. Usually it's a full length mirror selfie. It can masquerade as an outfit of the day pic, bikini shot, etc. We see it in every Hollywood celeb from Ariana Grande to the Kardashians all the way to the XXX porn stars to the Z list tiktokers. It truly is an inescapable mania for everywhere we look we are staring into someone else's body dysmorphia[143]. Am I immune to it? Fuck no. For a while I felt really liberated when I took pics, and like I had blinders on to my own issues, but now I feel self conscious again. Like a lot. A crazy lot. The Carl Jungian enantiodromia swings from self-love to self-loathing.

If I had to pick out one behavior to disengage with, and my therapist is dealing w this right now, it's this urge to bodycheck and compare. Taking so many pics of my body over the years has def weighed on my psyche. Now it is sometimes hard to discern the line from where I am just habitually taking peaceful nudes, or violently scanning every inch of my body to see if I look as gross as I feel. (Do you see how this correlates with my depressive cycle? See, see? It's co-morbid. It's like syncing a period.) Some days I love how I look and am elated to post my glorious goddess nudes, other days I cry after a photo shoot and delete 186 pics and 22 videos from my phone, feeling less than nothing.

I'm comfortable opening up about this because I feel physically recovered, yet I also need people to know that I still psychologically struggle. Recovery is not linear at all! It's so normal to backslide even years after you become

---

141 For now we see through a glass, darkly; but then face to face: now I know in part; but then shall I know even as also I am known. - corinthians 13:12

142 Angels and angels. All throughout this discourse on the body and on eating disorders Nastya's language has been rife with theological allusions. Realms of hell. Ethereal girl. Angelic frame. Skeletal figure. Notable because in the afterlife we lose our bodies.

143 You can't get away from yourself from moving from one place to another- hemingway

weight restored. I actually don't think there is a way to 100% get rid of an eating disorder's thought patterns even when physical recovery is possible. But 90% can be alleviated.

Here's the thing too with the recovery influencer squad; basing an entire personality around ED, fitness, and recovery - is fucking boring. And it's sad. Do these girls with EDs have hobbies? Interests? Does financial / class status have an impact on ED? Treatment is very expensive. Still, patient programs only help if you want to be helped.

To reiterate, I am not here to hate on these girls, at all. I feel a lot of compassion for them. I know what it's like to feel that panic, that discomfort, that fear. It fucking sucks, it starts a chain reaction that ruins your life first, then the lives of those around you. It's addict behavior with addict consequences. The thinness is the drug. But I also cannot stand idly by seeing the shades of proana propaganda in its supposed antidote.

How to remedy this? Harm reduction? I don't know. I honestly would check myself into a rehab if I had a lot of money. My methods of healing include: Therapy. Books. TV binge watching. Emotional support animals. Psychedelics, once every few years. Enjoying hobbies and doing stuff I love. Video games. Talking to friends who relate. Seeking help in online communities, gossiping, shit talking.

Ah yes here it is. The ugly truth of ED repercussions. My gastroparesis is a new one that I learned about last year; basically the stomach goes into intense pain if I am either empty or full, so I have to keep it at a medium fullness all the time and eat small meals multiple times instead of a one chaos meal at the end of the day. The adjustment was annoying as fuck but I do feel better sticking to a meal plan. There's like a whole fucking iceberg of consequence from EDs, and this is not even including the mental distresses. Physical weakness. Kidney problems and UTIs. Constipation. Diarrhea. Shitting bricks or nothing at all. Weak bones. Sports injuries from even the tiniest amount of exercise. Constant feelings of cold. Ruptured immune system. Nausea. Fertility issues. Amenorrhea. Heart problems. Starvation has an anesthetic-like effect that numbs your body to pain and feels like kind of a dopey, weak high.

You recover and the pain reveals itself when the body is able to finally begin repairs. It was months (almost a year) after my recovery that the medical damage started really catching up to me and continues to make itself known. Recovery is a real, sincere commitment to yourself. If you're in it and don't believe the health impacts, just be super mindful because something about this illness almost makes us believe in our invincibility -- but it can also age you young and make you feel like an 80 year old man in your 20s.

It must also be noted that men who prey on or fetisize eating-disordered women often seek an easy subject to control. Pathology is about control.

All those doctors visits:

Sudden declines in health and vanity can be very very scary. When I was 22 I had an aortic tear and I am still fucking terrified to go back to the cardiologist. I have to do that soon. My song "Half Queen Half Machine" was inspired from my time wearing a heart monitor. Aesthetically bionic and cool, but actually IRL unpleasant. Heart stuff scares the shit out of me and I live in constant worry and acute observation of my heartbeat, its tachycardias and erratic arrhythmias. I'm afraid of a regular panic attack turning into a heart failure.

My bones are thin and weak and fat collects around them loosely (loose skin is a thing with EDs). I bruise easily and get sick a lot because my immune system is so easily exhausted. My fainting couches serve a purpose. I like to lie down. I require a "handle with care" disclaimer. In a way it's interesting right, I kind of got what I wished for huh? A feeble Victorian doll blown away by the wind, fainting easily... except, in a monkey's paw scenario[144], I got what I want. But I don't. I want my health. Chitch, fuck this shit, I take back what I said earlier. I do want to look healthy!! I want to look fertile and breedable and sexually desirable. Can I ..... have a crumb of healthy thinness please sir? Can this be my hybrid dream chassis? I will spend the rest of my life making it up to, my body, for the crimes I have inflicted upon you. Please forgive me. I don't want to hate you.

My body is both beautiful and underwhelming. I don't have any standout features ; if I didn't have personality and style and aesthetic my appearance would not be noticed. No big boobs, no birthmarks, no tattoos, no six pack abs, no thigh gap, no definitive features. Which brings me to my next point: anonymity is the new popularity. I want to be admired without being famous because fame does something even more dysmorphic. Why do you think child stars burn out so early? Why do 99.9% of Hollywood actresses suddenly get so skinny and get fillers and Botox and buccal fat removal? Anya Taylor Joy, Dove Cameron, the younger Kardashians, I'm looking at all of them.

I'm so impressionable that if the focus on my looks was even more magnified, and I was making a movie star salary, I would most certainly get work done. I would write another blog about body modification. I would post about it gladly idgaf, any medical aestheticians looking at this may slide into my DMs. But alas I have to grit my teeth and strain to tell myself in the mirror "no I do not want my beautiful buccal fat removed". Just plain medium sized cheeks for me thanks. Medium sized everything. Deep cravings for representation of the "normal size". Overall it evens out, but the averageness is agonizing.

Am I supposed to pretend I like this? I am very swayed by certain things I see. I also like my salty snacks and Italian food. Why deprive yourself? I have a theory that anorexia and sexlessness go hand in hand; it makes sense to me that a large percentage of anorexics are SA victims with a subconscious

---

144 When the wish goes wrong

desire to appear unappealing.[145] Curves attract male attention, which causes anxiety. Trust me I understand that very well. Slenderness is not to gain the affection of men. In fact, men prefer the average and healthy female form to ultra thin.
I suppose I should be proud of myself for achieving that. I should be proud of myself for defending my body and loving it even at a higher weight, fupas and wrinkles and all. Like a gorgeous Booba seal on a watery beach.

In a way the averageness and imperfection of my physique makes me feel qualified to post this kind of shit - contrary to what I wrote earlier about thinness being the qualifier. Fuck that shit, man. Fuck everything I say here! Don't listen to me! I don't see myself clearly. But yet, because I am not outwardly scary skinny in a threatening way, nor am I morbidly obese, nor do I work out into miss muscle territory, I am more relatable than an underweight, compulsively exercising "fitness/recovery influencer". I am not saying that I am perfect or to listen to me — I am just asking you not to listen to them, and to critique everything online with many many sodium infused grains of salt. Take your power back. Like actually tho. It starts with individual thinking.

If you're reading this, know you are allowed to go back for seconds and thirds and fourths and so on. Eat whatever you want. Or don't eat at all. Enjoy or deprive. I honestly don't care, our bodies are all our own problem. Take care of yourself or not, it's your life and your consequences. I've already had mine.

145 Didn't radiohead say something about wanting to disappear completely… crazy ass white boys

Ironically the only place I remotely post honest photos of my body is OF and that is because I know most of my fans don't care about the minute details: smeared makeup (it's sexy okay), or an extra roll of fats(also sexy), or unshaven legs and armpits (kink alert). Some even like it a lot and pay extra. My paywall serves a protective function for me, so that the least amount of people possible know about my imperfections. I guess if they are paying, I can visually tell them my secrets. (Yes I'm a whore. We all are under capitalism, take a number).

What, then, do you say to that…

You ate queen ☺ ATE AND LEFT NO CRUMBS 🙌🙌🙌

. . . oh wait ☠

Nvm.

Ok now we're done with trauma how to fix it!??!?!

"Know what you eat; Food is healing" -stickers on my eating disorder laptop

An ancient zen koan goes like this:
What is the sound of one hand jacking?

♥ ♥♥

13. eTrauma Coping and the Beginnings of Healing; How Sexuality, Creativity, and Spirituality Intertwine

"Trauma in a person, decontextualized over time, looks like personality. Trauma in a family, decontextualized over time, looks like family traits. Trauma in a people, decontextualized over time, looks like culture."
– Resmaa Menakem

Art, spirit, healing, trauma (why are these lumped into one?) The powerful mind-body-spirit connection channeled through forms of art is incredibly healing for trauma. Art tells a story. It's a cathartic modality of transfiguring pain into acceptance.[146]

Where are you wounded?[147] Why are you feeling triggered? Sit with that discomfort, interrogate it, and eventually it will become material for art. Irate and manic. Alchemize and be a vessel for emotions.

" Unlike other forms of psychological disorders, the core issue in trauma is reality... Traumatized people chronically feel unsafe inside their bodies: The past is alive in the form of gnawing interior discomfort. Their bodies are constantly bombarded by visceral warning signs, and, in an attempt to control these processes, they often become expert at ignoring their gut feelings and in numbing awareness of what is played out inside. They learn to hide from their selves."
— Bessel A. van der Kolk, The Body Keeps the Score

---

146 Sublimation is a miracle. The translation of pain so another can understand it… damn..

147 SHOW ME ON THE DOLL

The silent unburdening is how the body somatically releases trauma: altered sleep, altered appetite, pains, aches, fatigue, overabundance of energy. The loud and violent unburdening is any act of creativity. When I paint myself green for my Shrek Sex Tape, that is me healing my trauma.[148] When I throw my phones and laptops into a safe deposit box that I don't know the location of and can only be accessed by two CIA operatives with an alphanumeric safe word, and go missing for a week putting a hit out on myself, that's me healing my trauma.

Sometimes the mind needs quiet ..
long periods of rest against the violence of unrest.

I'm in the office, not a soul in sight, just me and the anti depressants. In show biz, you don't have to sell your soul to get ahead. Sometimes you just sell a little piece of ass. I mean, I'd sell my soul for an affordable apartment in LA. I'd sell my soul to never have to pay for anything ever again. For now, I sell a little piece of ass to pay for 850 square feet of storage space for my dildos, outfits, cats, and massive ego, my six phones and four laptops, my emotional support trendy electric vehicle, my monthly visits to multiple of LA's orthopedic, cardiac, gastroenterological, gynecological, psychiatric experts. Me when I text my medical team good morning ☺ Doctor ☼ can you please ☜ refill my alprazolam once a day and tylenol 3☝📫📫rx for pain to pharmacy ☯? Thank you have a great day ☺ Society shuns creatures they can't understand, when those creatures are just trying to live.

We're a swirl of moralistic incongruence. Unreliable narrators. Perfection is too unrealistic. Reality is always somewhere in the middle. We are not trained to think outside the box. We like easily digestible, genre-ready concepts.

148 .. .. i am… speechless.

It's not been easy for me fitting into a pretty little cleanly defined societal box.
Nothing makes sense.
What DO I have to shield me from all this nonsense?

Editor: What's the first word that comes to mind when moving in with your boyfriend?
Nastya: "Bomb."

Every day, a thousand dollars.
Why is it that i spend 200$ every time I leave my apartment,
and sometimes even when I don't.
Coping is hard when you need money to do it!! Coping is hard when multiple parts of the self want different things to feel better.

Editor:
The only unitary function of consciousness is found
In the ego image's capture, by its specular reflection in misrecognition

Nastya:
Don't relate to me
Don't put yourself here next to me
This is a grave

You can not decrypt the crypt
You can not fool the crypt keeper
You can not outrun death, try as you might on the treadmill every day for 45 minutes
You can not perform hysterectomy on a tomb

My tomb be like here lies nastya
An amateur gynecologist
graduate of onlyfans university
She was so skinny and beautiful that all in the land took note of her beauty and sent her money and presents until she had more possessions than she had mental illnesses
A fatherless treasure
An endling
Dressed in thousands of dollars of the best lingerie money can buy, until it gets ripped off for the camera anyway so she's naked, free, devalued, depreciated
Her bloodline dies in darkness

Beauty is pain
Porn is pain
Pain is porn
Porn is beauty
The body keeps the score and I'm losing
STOP THE COUNT!!!

A physical and psychological crisis only a woman would understand.

"The only antidote to mental suffering is physical pain."
-Karl Marx

And even then, pain is not enough.

Ways to stave off a crisis: bagel.[149]
Trauma healing is as simple as is complicated. Zen it out, take it slow, buy yourself some time. Write some crazy shit like this. As my brain races into worst case scenarios, catastrophizing the outcome of my day, I put a little bagel in the toaster and brace myself.

Community: What's life without a friend to share it with?
You can't do this thing of life alone. It's painful, carrying all that grief by yourself. The body, the mind, the energy field all weaken. There is a reason why talk therapy is effective. Getting the words out. Exorcizing the pain. You need partners in crime. Cell mates. Hit men. Get the gang together and goon it out.

GOOG MORNING
GOON PORNING !!!!!

Clearing the energy field:
It might be placebo but it alleviates pain.

Having a spiritual infrastructure, as well as a general sense of confidence and integrity, keeps me sane. I'm reiki certified and my practice of spiritual hygiene requires weekly checking in with myself on a heart based level. I also check in with a therapist weekly. The internet is an astral plane, and some of my work with clients is not dissimilar to a reiki session or energetic, almost psychedelic exchange.

Cybersex is trippy. After a client session in the astral e-plane I always ritualize a practice to ground myself back into reality. After a few years of grinding ceaselessly on the OF market hamster wheel, I was called to do my fourth in life ayahuasca session - a psychic reset. Ayahuasca… they say it's 10,000 hours of psychoanalysis in one trip?[150] The intensity of psychedelic healing gave me many ego-destroying, soul-obliterating takeaways to integrate into my daily life and into my approach to certain concepts of my work. To be alive is beautiful. But it's also messy, difficult, and complicated. I was on my period during the ayahuasca session, my first in years since I had stopped birth control. I was rediscovering my own feminine energy and natural cycle, and the emotional warfare that comes with being hormonal.

---

149 ??

150 😳

“Get yourself a good therapist – no excuses” -Lola Davina[151]

When I am hormonal and bereft of my sanity (things a sex model robot doll should never succumb to) I have a cycle of coping mechanisms to alleviate my earthly female pains. There is almost no dialogue in the adult industry about periods and hormones, and gynecological sexual health. It’s a painful but unignorable part of a woman’s life, and in this particular industry it can impact the ability to work for a week every month - lest the illusions of perfection be shattered. Most entertainers are presumably healthy when they are first perceived. To be perceived is a horror as much as it is a joy. I guess it’s a good thing my psychiatrist sessions are bound by HIPPA confidentiality.

When I feel like shit.. GBURRLLL I lay down on my ayahuasca mat and let the floor time guide me through the day.

Along with mental discontents, when the physical body gets exhausted very easily, sex work is a godsend for neurodivergent[152], neuro-challenged, chronically ill creators who aren’t able to work a “”regular job,”” or even moms who don’t get maternity leave via the US’s flawed workspace structures.
The flexibility of working from home on a self-set schedule, working from bed, is a huge plus. Any perceived flaw that isn’t in the western standard of beauty - big feet, small ass, fat, flat, hairy, glasses, disabled, pregnant, stretch marks, tattoos, scars, unconventionality etc - has a market on the internet. Again, that’s not to say it’s an easy moneymaker, far from it. We are our own means of production, we also are our own product.
Most OnlyFans creators are their own photographer, model, agent, marketer, editor, customer service rep, and client relations expert. The self-employed creator economy is very tough, but the comfort of not having to ask for sick leave or preapproved time off is an appealing advantage.

When life gets tough, I really can’t go it alone — collaborations and community are critical to bring joy, bring ideas to life, maintain sanity and harness inner strength. I present as strong online - and it’s true, one has to be resilient to do this work - but “you’re a strong woman” isn’t the compliment men think it is. I get told this all the time and even though I say “thank you”, inside I’m a little bit MIFFED. Having strength out of necessity and survival is traumatizing and humiliating. I alone cannot lift the burden of existence - I’m secretly a god damn damsel in distress, exhausted by doing everything diy my whole life. To accomplish personal and professional goals requires community and help.

In 2023 my business partner and I officially started Cyberhorny LLC, creating merch and writing my book, side questing a dream book in the process. *Cyberhorny Dream Diaries* is out now: it’s available to order [SEE QR CODE]

---

151 I have openings.

152 retarded

and it had a soft release at my birthday party. When asking for critique or feedback, readers say:

"it's really hard to describe"
"it's dense but also aesthetically pleasing"
"I've never read anything like it"
"I had no idea it was going to be that personal"
"absolutely demented"
"genius"
"what the fuck did I just read?"

… so that should give you some idea of what to expect when you open it. Don't even expect anything - come into it with an open mind and a gooner mentality.

It occurred to me that I haven't posted a thirst trap in a while… it's getting to me. But I must write. Thirst trap. Alcohol. Vape. Content. Gooning. Write. The miracle of life.

Every year I have some kind of project alongside my sex work endeavors. My artistic loads need to get jizzed out too. 2020, *Hentai & Crack*. 2022, *Cyber Castle*. 2023, *Dream Diaries*. 2024 and beyond, *Cyberhorny: Navigating a Sexual Dystopia*. I have all this depression all the time of "ugh I can't get anything done why am I so unmotivated" but as I write this and take stock of all my shit — it's a full toilet.

Almost Zero.

In 2017 I translated a controversial Russian book by Vladislav Surkov, AKA Natan Dubovitsky, a figurehead of political theater in Russia. It was classified as 'gangsta fiction'. It follows a gopnik (Russian thug) as he enters the lucrative and dangerous book-bootlegging business, and interfaces with his family life as well as the femme fatale that got away, the venomous and neurotic Crybabe.

Zero Illumination.
This film went so hard and goes harder and harder as time goes on. It's so stupid that it's genius. Love is full of haters. A scientist goes on a bender after a soul crushing breakup.

Cyber Castle. (and the Castle series)
My curatorial debuts, art and music events that featured a variety of musicians, artists, installations, vendors etc under a common theme. It was a party. It was a mall. It was a space colony in 2069. It was a utopia. It was a nuclear bunker. It was a cave. It was an orgy. It was a cyber landscape. Will *Cyberhorny Castle* be next?? We'll see when this book is launched in its media cycle.

Party Castle
Space Castle
Nuclear Castle
Cave Castle
Bliss Castle
Horny Castle
Cyber Castle

I've talked a little bit about my films **Bubbles** and **Darkness** in Chapter 4. I've released some albums, including **Hentai and Crack Vol 1**.

DETOUR ON HENTAI+CRACK:
I made this album in my Tesla while wearing lingerie.

Hentai & Crack is a visual album I produced in 2020-2023 out of my garage. This turns the title "garage band" into a parody of luxury. With multiple volumes set to come out - Vol 1, Vol 2, and Hentai Deluxe, it is a trilogy replicating my LA-based obsession with dystopian self image and cybersocial posturing. A caricature of privilege, or as the kids say these days, a flex. I am discussing here Hentai & Crack Vol 1 specifically, which began in 2020 and had gotten resurrected for a show in 2023 — although as a fluid project, all volumes are overall designed to kind of blend together.

Conceptually, I wanted to make this album for personal entertainment and dealing with the trauma of the initial stages of the pandemic. Considering the disjointed elements of my online image, it was the gimmickiest thing I could do to satirize myself. Make an album in my Tesla scantily clad. It sells itself. The way people online knew me was so far removed from my reality, that I wanted to cater to a very veiled social image of who "Nastya Valentine" is. A faker, more produced sound than my previous emotional guitar music.

Compositionally, H&C is all over the place. Very freeform, not adhering to any genre or particular sonic organization. There are walls of sound, dilating synth lines, drowned out vocals, and emotional guitar music. I don't believe in genre worship (only goddess worship), though I do like to describe it as a shoegazy dream-pop/camgirl emo record. I love heavily layered music with an ethereal vibe; as a teen I listened to a lot of Beach House and Animal Collective, which informed the way I structure harmonies and melodies. I feel inspired by sexy vocalists like Britney, Prince, Lil Kim, Janet, Christina, all the divas… It helps creating a character for the stage, although the separation between reality and fantasy can often times be a sleep paralysis of blurry urges.

The lyrics allude to an abstract and horrifying erotic fantasy; I am usually much more of a realism writer with poetic straight forward song lyrics, although for this piece I drew inspiration from my dreams and nightmares which would not be out of place in a David Lynch or Gaspar Noe film. But at the same time the masterpiece lines like "I cry all night thinking about you" harken back to the days of emo legends Bright Eyes and Elliott Smith. (horny). "Every Kiss Begins With K" tells a tale about falling in love on ketamine; it also references "you're my butterfly sugar baby" from Crazy Town's iconic 2000's jam. When I wrote that song, I wanted to sonically exude butterflies. The kind you get in your stomach while falling in love on ketamine.

The aesthetic elements of the album are very important - I make most of my music with visuals in mind, and having synesthesia gives me a vibrant assortment of textures to work with. To me, music and visuals are married. I wanted this album to sound like an alien sex goddess's acid trip. Something is "off" about it, but you still watch and listen because it's sexy. A digital nymph crying in her bedroom, a glitching fembot in a pastoral landscape. The imagery is there to allure you, while simultaneously having a jarring effect.

Overlays of my body, ruthless self-objectification, cat pictures, memes, anime gifs, rude internet comments about me from haters, Hentai images, pixelated collages, and other crap from the internet all intersect in this video. It is a digital abyss that stares back. This piece is so 2020's, yet from another dimension. A time warp. 2023-2003, by way of 2069. Bear in mind that this visual content is borderline nsfw -- but honestly what isn't these days? Have you seen instagram lately? Courtney Love once said "every girl in LA stripped to buy amps and pedals." Ah, a tale as old as time. It is happening again.

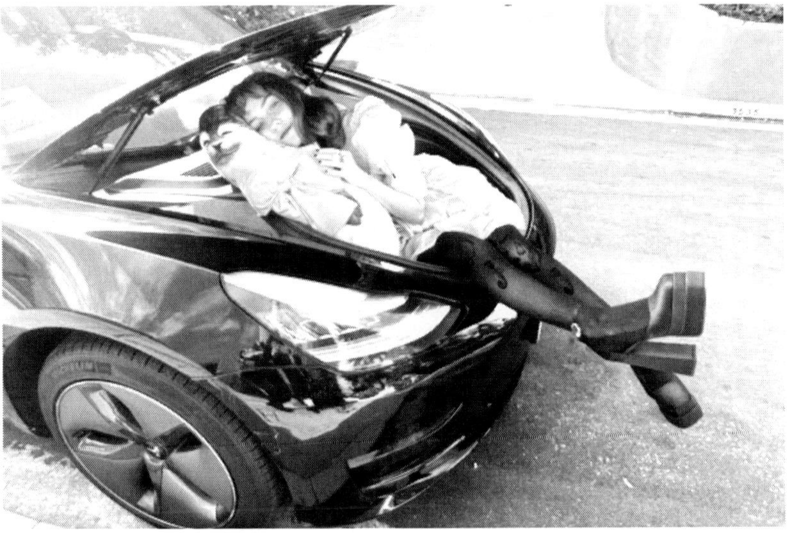

The thots are not what they seem. This album catalyzed my OnlyFans page and the livestreamed production of Hentai & Crack was how I originally started, before OF became my job. Every day in the early 2020 pandemic times, I would live stream myself in my Tesla recording this on my page, with the allure of additional spicy contents. Thus, my art and my body collided. I had prior experience camming but I didn't have the discipline to consistently stream daily; OnlyFans allowed me a more time-efficient platform of expression that dovetailed creativity with sexual empowerment. 2020 was a turning point when being a fantasy became my reality, and to this day my full time job, but every girl who starts an OF becomes such a memeable punchline so I played into that to my viewers. Hi y'all.

Self-objectification: it's praxis, sis. To me, it's so much more than even that. It's a vindication of every man, fuckboy, and asshole who had ever rejected me. To be hot, and to make money off of things I was mercilessly bullied for when I was younger, is everything. It's retribution. Hentai & Crack thematically touches on that autobiographical element by exaggerating myself as a goddess of revenge, with track titles like "Opiate Destroyer" "Hot Girl Suffer" and "Erotomania". Underneath the feminine mirage there is a trauma, a longing, a fixation.

There is a quote attributed to Oscar Wilde which goes like "everything in the world is all about sex; except for sex, which is all about power." Our sex-power pipeline is almost tangible, and to me, has always been so gripping.

The deep dive does not end at music; my projects all blend into one another and work within the Nastya Valentine Enterprises umbrella. This is coping from the trauma. Make the OF a part of your art.

Even Hentai & Crack is a wink to the ridiculousness of what I do as a cyber participant. By satirizing myself, I had carved out a niche. This entire opus is an effort to support myself in this cold, heartless, and unforgiving system while retaining my integrity and vision, as well as creating something entertaining for my viewers. It appears as though I have crashed my Tesla at the intersection of misery and horniness, and Hentai & Crack came out.

To this day, H&C is one of my favorite works of art I've ever made. It was just so organic and unfiltered and for lack of a better word, special to me. I get sentimental about ridiculous things. I love seals. I exert a lot of mental energy into destroying the stigma around what I do for a living. Demystifying a misunderstood line of work is no easy feat, and parasocial relationships are such an unexplored terrain, but making art about it is a start.

My OF page is run with authenticity that presents as a mirage. I lure with hotness, but beneath the surface is a melodrama as dark as it is racy. It's sexistential — who am I really? This fragmentation of the persona, and shattered cosplaying of the self, reflects in the erratic soundscapes of the music I make. Hentai & Crack's hentai tracks all sound quite different, more like a psychedelic collage than an album that weaves seamlessly. There is no single; all the songs have equal weight. That's not to say there's no method to the madness — the mix of lo fi and higher end production is deliberate. It's a nexus of sexus. It's a moment in time.

We document essentially 24/7 of our lives online. We produce ourselves and we doctor our features and we curate what we want everyone to see. And don't get me started on the AI's producing us, banning us, algorithming us. It is no longer a far fetched concept: the singularly is here and we live in the simulation. One of my songs contains the lyric "a shrine to the simulation" and maybe that's what H&C really is.

Hentai & Crack is a moment for all emo cam girls out there.

There are so many myths and wrongful accusations about us, people will always judge, but I personally appreciate the work we do. And in any case, in the surveillance state, we are all camgirls.

If you can't beat capitalism, have sex with it.

Maintaining Health in A Disordered Digital Landscape
(Digitization starting to affect our bodies post covid .. curved spines, sightless eyes, telepathy? Post verbal?)

All of a sudden I am alone. Pain in my body. Emotions in my body. I'm a twink. Every day a new twink turns 18 and gets off the bus. Every day a new Sylvia Plath poem finds its way into the kitchen of my psyche. Mommy's cooking. Not now honey, Mommy's cooking. Eat to live, don't to die. Ego death. Twink death. Graveyard filled with love languages. I'm tired of cooking - I want to order a pizza. Dishwasher filled with headaches. What trendy new coping mechanism will disconnect me from my pain now? No **now**. Certainty is not enough - I need a bathtub filled with oxycodone.

Living is a trauma. Birth is a trauma. It's why we don't, can't remember our birth. It's a lethal self-undoing. Birth is the first war we encounter in life. But being born into existence is also an act of magic. I would rather believe in magic than believe in war and politics.

"We cannot have a world where everyone is a victim. "I'm this way because my father made me this way. I'm this way because my husband made me this way." Yes, we are indeed formed by traumas that happen to us. But then you must take charge, you must take over, you are responsible."
— Camille Paglia

Self confrontation and true self care are the beginnings of healing. Boundaries create distance between you and your work. Boundaries are stored in the DNA stored in our body. Trauma is stored in the balls. Calm the nervous system. Beware of attachment. I got attached and now I'm constantly feeling vulnerable. A sobering reality check. Don't make me get the fist out!!!!!!

The neurodivergent shit and how it affects sex workers/whore earners. Many sex workers are also neurodivergent; it's why we struggle in "normal" job fields and thrive on the internet. Nearly every working girl posting online has some kind of mental battle that affects her life within the conventional order of society. Many posts I see in the camgirl forums include phrases like "I've been too depressed to work this week" "my ADHD is killing me today" and some variation of hormonal crises like PMDD (premenstrual dysphoric disorder).

Carl Jung recorded his deliberately-evoked fantasies or visions in the "Black Books". These journals are Jung's contemporaneous clinical ledger to his "most difficult experiment",[5] or what he later describes as "a voyage of discovery to the other pole of the world."[6] He later termed the process "mytho-poetic imagination". ... After the outbreak of World War I in August 1914, Jung perceived that his visionary experiences during the prior year had been not only of personal relevance, but entwined with a crucial cultural moment.

COPIUM PLEASE

The psychoanalysis and philosophy of Neon Genesis Evangelion, esp. episodes 22-26. Ep 19 is a really good (fucked up) mix. Mother, father, memory, eternity, temporality, consciousness, reality, artifice, coping, denial, warfare, love, fear, apocalypse, sickness, congratulation, individuation, conflation, human instrumentality, the merging of all subjectivity. A graveyard for separateness. Parts of parts. Partial objects. False dolls of real people. Incarnations.

Nastya Valentine Opiate Crisis Helpline 323 420 6669 x80085 - my voice on the phone is so monotonous and flatlined you'll feel like *you're* on opiates

Isn't everything in life a copium please?
You can't spell

DISASSOCIATION

...without ASS.

"I thought the most beautiful thing in the world must be a shadow."
— Sylvia Plath, The Bell Jar

Self-Confrontation and True Self Care.

Jungian depth psychology often mentions the shadow self, shadow work, shadow integration. The dark parts of ourselves that we hate, we fear, we deny and repress, feel ashamed of... they need to be confronted. Connecting with all parts of us, light and dark, is what makes us whole individuals. **Artistry, creativity, and sexuality are all healing tools.** But they don't just show up on our doorstep that way.

We have to work with them, use them, know ourselves from the inside out. Bringing the unconscious into the light of the conscious. As we keep on existing, new facets of ourselves come up, ones that we may not know we even had. And as we learn more, become experts of our own subjectivity, we turn defeat into victory. We alchemize fragmentation into integration. We turn trauma into healthy ways of coping.

And sometimes there's really nothing more to it than just continuing to exist, making the decision to keep being alive. It's not rocket science.

The blend of therapy and altered states;
psychiatry and psychedelics.

"This is the image of the human body, it has become an indestructible cybernetic object; yet within than object there is a holographic transform of the body that is released into the dream. It is an image of the human released into hyperspace of information, where one is a thing of eternal circuitry. We are going to find the power to realize our deepest cultural aspirations. This is why we must find out what our deepest cultural aspirations are." ~Terence McKenna

Heavy duty TW: suicide

It's crazy how modern day suicide notes be like "this is a scheduled post". Penciling in a time to die. Some would love the relief of clearing a schedule for all eternity. I'm sorry.

I've been writing my will for at least 2 years now. What has all this work been for? What is the point? What more do I have to give? What if something happens to me? Where would all my assets go after my passing? Something for my mom to live on. Something for editor Evan to continue the Cyberhorny research. Something for my cats. But there is no easy way out of this life; no cheat code to deteriorate the castle walls of depression.

The most selfish thing one can do is cease to exist. A chain reaction that kills a small part of everyone around you; an existential nuke. Depression contains no logic; as much as one can rationalize and attempt to think objectively, reason can't always crack mental illness. I want to die. No, I want to live. Or somewhere in between, just existing. I take root. I can't let my kitties be on their own. They would miss me too much. When you feel ungrounded, so ungrounded you want to be put in the ground, think about what tethers you to this earth, to this life. My girls.

I don't care for fancy things
Or to take part in the freshest wave
But to provide for mine who ask
I will with heart on my father's grave
On my father's grave
I don't mean to seem like I care about material things
Like a social status
I just want four walls and adobe slabs for my girls

-Animal Collective "My Girls"

Online Death and Digital Presence After One's Passing:

Penciling in a time to die with a scheduled post, an informal will, a strained and fecklessly penned note? Deleting the drafts. Making new ones. The pain of a parasocial friend no longer existing. There is a woman I was friends with on instagram who took her own life and I grieved her passing with the same reality of emotion I would have had with someone I really knew. The parasocial dilemma persists.

On the other hand the "false suicide attempt" and posting pictures of self harm. Patient exhibits addictive behavior; threatening to kill herself ; borderline pathology produced or perhaps exacerbated by the platform. A girl with cuts on her legs threatening suicide on twitter and requesting subscribers for her page. Is this a lack of confidence, a dependence, even a hatred of the audience – biting the hand that feeds? Like girl I be talking about my mental illness online too but if you actually wanted to end it all :(you wouldn't be up on reddit and x and tiktok yapping about this and that.

♥

When I heard the learn'd ASStronomer

Ayahuasca and Psychedelics: experiences of death, rebirth, life cycle.

"Ego death" and a hard psychic reset. To rebrand as a new self, the old self must die. On my first ayahuasca ceremony in 2013, after my canoeing down the primordial channel of death, all nanoparticles of my mind body and spirit spiraling into disintegration, disappearing and then reappearing, catapulted back into existence by a geometric palace made of light that talked in a voice so telepathically loud it hurt, I was hurling into a vomit receptacle that Evan's face appeared in, chortling

"How was ur resurrection bitch!?!?"

"You were there! You have to get Sofia!"

Sofia came with me to the next three ceremonies.

Vision on a boat: me and Sofia in pearls and diamonds, fancy ladies, camera pans over to show Evan in a purple-and-leopard pimp suit.

And then a vignette of my past life as a Spanish princess; West European lesbian lovers; dark haired tan women with fragile frames and delicate features, big earrings, gold jewelry .. Venetian blinds where men were peeking through to see us. While in reality I may be a plebeian, the spirit world presents me as a true princess, entirely taken care of, stately and playful and beautiful. That may be why my corporeal fantasies gravitate to the bougie wishful thinking … I desire to go back to myself, my true self. (Of course the system we live in also highly values beauty and wealth so that obvs is my aspiration as well.. but nonetheless). I am sitting at my pool right now doing a chussy swim and waiting for Kratom to kick in, reading Caitlin Dee's book. The first page talks about a spiritual Spanish princess. Please be my friend.

I wait for the synchronicity.

I did my fourth ayahuasca ceremony in 2022. It was like a plane crash landed into my face, through my brain, and the astral entities began their work on me, post-invasion. In the 7-year gap since my consistent ayahuasca presence, I had forgotten how powerfully the medicine works. It takes you. It penetrates you: mind, body and spirit. I was raised rather atheist but upon my experiences with psychedelics I had begun to believe in something bigger; an energy, a force, a source. I don't know what it is, and I don't think our human brains are even meant to comprehend it. But occasionally, we can touch a piece of it, glimpse a symbolic and thickly veiled vision. A deeper reality. An interconnected quantum field that contains everything, all that has ever existed and will continue to exist. Beyond that, I cannot philosophize.

Spirituality was the first coping mechanism:

What is god? It is not a bearded old white man in the sky. It is not the church. It is not organized religion. It is source. It is energy. It is eternity. It is horror and beauty, an intelligent force of love and creation. It is goddess, and her many faces. It is miracle.

No one talks about it but it happens every day !

Kisa: the cat I named a computer after

"The psychotic drowns in the same waters in which the mystic swims with delight." — Joseph Campbell

Reiki healing ♥ ♥ ♥ What is a rainbow? It is the spectrum that contains all colors. All energies. My energy is all over the place but when harnessed correctly contains the ability to do anything without limits.

Energy healing
Enter the void
Only thing manly about me is MANifesting
Magic as a metaphysical force
The paranormal - having sex with ghosts
Where is the discourse of the parawhoremal?
Witches, whores, and persecution
The fun of games for one who wishes to die

The creator whom I worship wants life to be colorful, vibrant, joyful, outstanding, helpful, human. Zen is my discipline. I am very fond of the spiritual, the immaterial, the transcendent and mystical aspects of living. I not only have desired to become a well paid whore and creative visionary, but also a spiritual leader. Not to the masses perhaps but to all iterations of myself going forward, backward, in all timelines; the bicameral mind leads me to search within myself for answers. And everything I surround myself with reflects that.

Bright colors, lush fabrics, delicious food, strong drinks, crazy bitches, sparkling crystals — my spiritual practice is a celebration of life, not an orthodox restriction of it.

Healing is when I bring joy to myself on a daily basis. It has taken me a long time to have this epiphany. Anxiety and depression are the low level vibrational frequencies that keep me from achieving my best potential. True self care is bringing yourself and others joy, and it can take many forms. Face mask and bath time and spa day classics. Taking a day off and literally doing nothing but binge watching tv or playing video games. Going outside and seeing beautiful nature. Drinking with your friends. Making a dinner. Going out. Staying in. Whatever keeps your personal balance in harmony. Online shopping. Masturbation. Having the sex.[153] Happy wife. Floor time with mommy. 444hz money manifestation meditation frequency. Going offline and turning off your phone. Taking drugs. Cleaning your house. Playing music. It can literally be anything done with intention. Writing in a journal. Creating a dream ritual and dreaming. ***Psychotomimetic book.*** (Cyberhorny dream diaries).

☠ ✌ ⌨

💻☺

✆ ☯ ❁

DMT elves stay grinding to hold our reality together. They're also slutty. Immense fright and incredible beauty. Healing of Little Nastya, healing of the inner self. Detraumatize and forgive. She was just a child. But she was so heavy with depression and thoughts. I picked her up to lighten her burden. Who will do this for her now? Everyone and everything you encounter in life is just a mirror of the self, a reflection of the subjective experience.

The erotic is part of the spiritual.[154] The nude primordial ayahuasca goddess. Neutering of my subjectivity. *Bringers of the Dawn* (Barbara Marciniak book), and the 12-strand DNA of orgasmic humanity. "Very deep inside the mechanism of seuxality is a frequency that can be attained that has been sought after and misunderstood by many people. It is called orgasm." Her theory is that we have been socialized to demonize orgasm which has a liberatory principle embedded within the sensation.

Metaphysics, Spirit, and Sexuality

The way I approach the tarot, and every other metaphysical discipline, is with the perspective that it doesn't show you a predictive future of what you want to see. It shows you what you need to know about your energy in that particular moment.

---

153 Borat voice

154 O lord make me chaste, but not yet- st. augustine

The great sewer drain[155] of burnout[156] still continues to haunt me with emotional sepsis. I'm tired and overwhelmed. I don't wanna go online today[157]. A year of working part-time, working less, has been great for stress reduction but it certainly hasn't healed me. I stress about relevance in one of the most oversaturated fields and I stress about income in one of the most expensive cities. I need a lifelong or deathlong vacation.

I have existed in a constant state of half-exhaustion to where I can function daily to work and survive, but doing basic daily tasks like laundry and cleaning become secondary. And the practice of self care? I don't know, I try various coping mechanisms. Full relaxation is a luxury I cannot always afford.

If having burnout is like having a broken leg, I've been not letting it heal properly — I haven't been exacerbating it with marathons, but I'm walking on the leg rather than recuperating. My work can often be invisible but it's still laborious. The immense amount of information and data on my devices overwhelm me. That's an understatement. Diseases of the ego permeate, and my energy needs a massive healing. I haven't found a way to hack or gamify it yet. The body and mind need rest. If I was my boss I would probably fire me. Jettison me from the stratosphere to hurtle down to the ground like a comet. We all begin and end somewhere, all we have in the in-between is entropy and gooning. Might as well enjoy it while we can.

And who knows? Down the line far after I'm retired, perhaps in an entirely different life - I could look back at my nudes from the 20's and go damn.. I was hot.

To really rebel against capitalistic society, we must truly like and love ourselves. This system is built on our self-hatred to bankroll and sustain it. Shopping to make ourselves feel better. Buying time against our own self-undoing. The beauty industry preying on womens' insecurities. What would the world look like if we were truly happy with ourselves?

Interview with David Lynch:

DL: Eraserhead is my most spiritual film
IV: Elaborate on that
DL: No

---

155 Talking to you is not a drain.. Its a sewer

156 Take a shot

157 I don't wanna go to school today.

"We have to create culture, don't watch TV, don't read magazines, don't even listen to NPR. Create your own roadshow. The nexus of space and time where you are now is the most immediate sector of your universe, and if you're worrying about Michael Jackson or Bill Clinton or somebody else, then you are disempowered, you're giving it all away to icons, icons which are maintained by an electronic media so that you want to dress like X or have lips like Y. This is shit-brained, this kind of thinking. That is all cultural diversion, and what is real is you and your friends and your associations, your highs, your orgasms, your hopes, your plans, your fears. And we are told 'no', we're unimportant, we're peripheral. 'Get a degree, get a job, get a this, get a that.' And then you're a player, you don't want to even play in that game. You want to reclaim your mind and get it out of the hands of the cultural engineers who want to turn you into a half-baked moron consuming all this trash that's being manufactured out of the bones of a dying world."[158]

— Terence McKenna

158 Under a juniper-tree the bones sang, scattered and shining
We are glad to be scattered, we did little good to each other,
- ts elliot

14. Real Life (and its Nonlinearity)

"Whatever is rejected from the self, appears in the world as an event."[159]
— Carl Gustav Jung

What is our sexual future?
What changes in our reality?

Do you think about the future? Tweek about it, even? Fixate on it? Where will you be in five, ten years? Where will your internet presence and cyber footprint be? Discarded, valorized[160], or just *there*? The most terrifying thing in life is thinking about the future, especially when the present is already so dystopian.

Go for it and see what happens. Nothing can prepare you.

The only thing worse than not getting what you want is getting what you want. You attract what you fear. Oh noooo I don't wanna work ever again. It's true; I don't work much. But maybe in the future I will again. It seems as though I've exasperated my own niche— that of being myself. It's not working like it has before. But while it has the slightest of chances, I persist.

Against my own expiration date, I persist. Everything's a psyop these days, and so am I. If my income is passive the means to getting to this point was a crucible of retardation. It's the battle of Finances vs. Free Time, peace of mind being at the center of this currency exchange. What is the emotional price of taking breaks? Time off to date, to socialize, to have a life. A personal life has halved my income; but what is the price of love when weighed against the price of money?[161] What is the value of stability and security, what is the value of life experience and excitement?

✞☺☠✌♠❄✡✌

159 TEAAAAAA

160 Vandalized.. vaporized

161 You can't put a price on money.

I've redefined what I consider excitement – this life has already been plenty for me. Different things constitute "fun" from my perspective. I don't always like going out, being in crowds, getting fucked up. But sometimes I do. Idk I just like.. vibe on whatever feels good. Activities that offer immediate gratification can cause harm in the long term – I do what I can to enjoy things while also delaying gratification. Enjoyment vs. deprivation. A little deprivation for fun. A little treat. 4 strawberry popsicles a day makes the depression go away. Fun for me is can be staying in, being low key, minding my own business. Leisure is freedom. And I have found that from behind my laptop.

Seeing the darkest sides of the web changes you. Every mistake is a straight line to who you are meant to be and every circuitous pathway is a direct target on what you are meant to do. Every moment and every decision you make affects your life and the lives of others in imperceivable ways. Enjoy the life that you are living today because the life you live tomorrow may be different than the one you lived yesterday.[162] When I was doing the Castle events a few years ago, people would always ask when is the next one. I was called a "woman about town". Always busy.

Then after the pandemic, the Castle events became less frequent; why would I want to interrupt my interlude of a comfortable life? It's exhausting being a woman about town and having jobs, tasks, obligations, engagements, peripheral friends, things to do, events to be at. It's time I let technology wrap me in its warm yet lucrative embrace. It's time I catered to the bat signal of the tactical wank. I'd be happy to spend the rest of my life in a gilded cage if someone provided that for me. There is a myth that sex workers often seek a man to "save" them from the evils of the industry. But it isn't the industry that is the problem: look at the bigger picture. Evil is in the structures of our capitalist prison. My desire isn't to escape sex work; it's to escape all work.

Why do I like porn? Because it's not pretentious. Think of all the pretensions that come with fine art or entertainment: the unlistenable music, the unwatchable cinema, the unreadable literary works, the unbearable works of art. Hoyty toyty artists, curators, musicians, poets etc in affectations to impress certain circles beyond what their works really merit. Porno is rarely pretentious, rarely has an affectation of being anything more than what it really is. It's just porn. It's simple.

The mind of an online working girl is not that simple. Maybe the mask is the woman she pretends to be every day. The danger of facing your demons is that the demons sometimes win. There is an unspoken telepathy between you and the demons; a telekinesis where your mind can choose to move the demons away, or to initiate an intimate encounter.

One of my favorite Criminal Minds episodes, "Zugzwang". A chess term signifying that a player is in a precarious situation; and anything you do,

---

162 Did she also get this quote from a yogi tea bag?

any move you make will make the situation worse. You don't have a choice not to make a choice. A tactical motif in endgame situations that holds no possible positive outcome for the player. Life can feel that way sometimes. No exit.[163] We hold ourselves in these psychological zugzwangs, convinced that nothing we can do will ever improve the outcome. Every move is suffocated by rumination, fixation, obsession, egoic whirlpools of *why me*. Where do you end? Where do you begin? "If you're stuck in a loop, try walking in a straight line."[164]

You have perhaps[165] seen there is quite a bit of repetition in this book. Phrases, motifs, loops, compulsions. Certain things are so important we had to say them twice.. thrice.. Encouraging the reader to take a shot each time burnout is mentioned, for instance. Certain pathological ways of thinking, certain obsessions, hopes, fears. Certain anxieties about uncertainty. It's possible that by writing about these things over and over, they will be exorcized rather than festering in the dark, cumbersome canyon of the barren and burdened criminal mind.

Editor's note: the repetition compulsion is evidence that we do indeed have a soul. We are not logical programs, not robots who can manage behavioral rectifications. We are flawed humans.

December 2020, shortly before the first new year of the covid era, I was on the rocks on the beach, talking to my friend about my fears that I had peaked in life. Those things were actually good all of a sudden. I remember little details. I remember the fans, the ones that stood out. A Pikachu-fetish gooner was paying me 600/hr for video chat jack offs, and casuall chatting gaming. Christmas season 2020, I received the majority of my Pokemon plushie collection. Gotta catch 'em all.

Happiness, joy, comfort, profit – could I catch it? PayPal was good to me. Gifts were good to me. Fans were good to me. I was good to them. My appreciation, my gratitude, my content. I had never in my life imagined I could make five figures a month. I barely have five fingers!! Deep inside, I had money fears vs money manifestation … I had manifested what I wanted, a semblance of a comfortable life with gifts and money just for being me. My love of pokemon bankrolled my existence that month. I didn't have to do much. It was easy. It was just easy. It wasn't hard, agonizing, difficult like the life I was used to. How unreal.For the first time in my life, really, things were.... good. How is this possible. How immeasurably worrying, instead of living in the moment.

Indeed the "what ifs" of impostor syndrome kept burrowing deeper and deeper into my head. I couldn't believe it.[166] Was this all a fever dream? Is this whole life a hallucination? In 2020 and 2021 I was thriving in the pandemic. In

163 Hell of course is other people

164 Westworld

165 lol

166 This also calls to mind westworld.

2022, I had my highest income and net worth, probably ever. In 2023, I backslid. In 2024, I'm plateauing, going downwards. Four figures, four horsemen of my personal hell. Armageddon. The nukes. I'm scared. Get those snipers back here. What if overnight all of my money, my fans, just go away? Who will be there to catch me if I fall? Absolutely no one. And that is terrifying.[167]

I'm afraid life will never be as good for me as it was between 2020-2022. That fear holds me back. Fear grabs fantasy in a chokehold by the scrotum. Any rumor, all gossip, and even random chatter can create paranoia. I just have to contend with what is. I do what I do, and at least I exist. I have survived the war, with a fraction of the subscribers I used to have, but my subjectivity remains intact.

The question is: what is my subjectivity worth? What has all this time been worth? I've seen gooners you wouldn't believe. If it's valuable to only me, then so be it. This is the hill I die on. These are the moments I will treasure, like a rainbow bismuth crystal in a blood red treasure chest. But a bigger battle awaits, one that I must advocate for: the existence of sex work as a real profession.

I've seen things you people wouldn't believe. Attack ships on fire off the shoulder of Orion. I've watched C-beams glitter in the dark near the Tannhauser Gate. All those moments will be lost in time, like tears in the rain. Time to die. ~Roy Batty, Blade Runner

Is it really possible for sex work to be outlawed, banned, executed? Exhibit A du jour: Project 2025, which seems to doom sex work in the USA to far-right criminalization. It's a collective transcription of documents and laws to be passed for the far-right power brokers that would endanger the rights of LGBTQ people, low-income people, gig workers, sex workers, and other sociocultural "minorities".

The policy proposals would reshape the government in ways that affect people's lives: rolling back abortion funding, cutting social programs, and criminalizing porn. There was quite a bit of heat on reddit . com/ onlyfans advice with many nsfw creators fearing for the future of their job security, especially in red states.

Pornhub is already blocked in Arkansas, and credit card companies like MasterCard (whose processors run many porn pages) do everything they can to curtail people's access to porn. Every year there is some type of setback like this: in 2021, it was the OF porn ban debacle, which quickly reversed. So. Is it really possible to shut down online sex work? Or is it just chatter?[168] Idle gossip, or a real threat to our livelihoods?

---

167 The therapist of scarcity similarly realizes that his patients can flee with little contingency

168 Sound and fury signifying nothing and so on

Bear in mind this will all sound so different a decade from now. I have no illusions about this book being relevant to every specific arena of what is to come – so many will change or become irrelevant – but certain elements will remain enduring. We have neuroplasticity, we can learn so much more as we get older. Synthesis of the past to the present. Knowledge and curiosity do not die with age.

OnlyFans might die, but the act of selling sex will remain. Sex workers should teach sex education. That is where I see this going. After all, we are the custodians of the intimate encounter, well versed in sexual specificity, in body and in mind. I would love to give talks, host workshops. I would love to teach. Graduate from online whore to horny academic. Dr. Nastya Valentine, professor in residence of Sexual Economics 101 at Cyberhorny University. You can't spell curriculum without cum.

A decade ago when I was at Bard College studying Ryan Trecartin films I knew I wanted to direct indie porn.

There are brutal highlights and discontents of existing in our sexual dystopia with longevity, niche, and nuance.

- the decay of my attention span
- the freedom of a flexible schedule
- the five phone dilemma
- the tesla livestreams
- the dissociation from my body
- the nosedive from praxis into theory
- the fluctuation of my income
- the maismatic swarm of feelings of hate and validation that parasocially plague me
- the rewards and the psychic crises…
- how it all oscillates,
- how it all becomes commodified, villainized, glamorized
- and how a real one thugs it all out and bosses up.

This is bottom-heavy industry, where most of the active creator accounts on OF and the like have very small fan bases and income streams, and the few on top make massive amounts of money. The current average monthly income on OF is $180 – barely enough to afford groceries, much less a living. And yet still many creators try, day after day, post after post, to make their way to the top of this pear-shaped hierarchy. The money is the motivation. What cream will rise to the top, ready for the cherry of the profitable gooner souffle? We'll just have to find out.

OnlyFans: does it feel dated? The concept of things being hyper-replaceable in a fast moving world is troubling. The instability and insecurity. Is it sustainable? What do we do after sex work? What if we like it and make it a career? Sex work is brutal and demanding and hard, just like any other job. It demands coexistence in the social fabric.

What of an alternate universe where I continued in vanilla workplaces and never dipped my toes in the deep lake of sexual commerce. An alternate universe where I rejected work altogether and successfully found a provider husband to start a family with. An alternate universe where I was still making content online but not the NSFW kind. Where would I be? Probably still having sex. I don't know tho… it was not hard to practice abstinence. I saw less dollar signs. Just kidding. I enjoy sex (Sorry) even if I have to go without it for a while. The tea is, sex has always sold and will always continue to sell, whether or not it be from behind a VPN server on a laptop screen.

Is romantic sex but a spectre of the times long gone? Times long gooned… Is physical sex antiquated? I had 11 months without it while I was working on this book. From 9/11 to 8/11. No big deal.

AR and VR porn? AI whatever.. People don't really seem to respond strongly to that. Sex dolls and Vtube anime porn stars aren't as prevalent as subscription models. Ultimately, when it comes to sex, nothing can replace the real thing – or at least a very realistic simulation of it. The future's shape of technology. Just watch *ExistenZ*. Read Terence McKenna's theory that machines in the future will look like organic matter. Just consider the Google Lattice, a device that crosses technology with spirituality and the great matrix grid of all existence, to reiterate **the ethereal domain** at the very beginning of this book. The anti-liminal space. The back rooms of the mind. The self-referential matrix of memory.

Skimming and stimming through the chapters, I notice something; this book starts off rather serious – laboriously so – and then devolves, goes manic, goes off the rails, goes to the psych ward 5150; much like the fans who subscribed for my nudes and then get much more subjectivity than they bargained for. The further in you go, the more you really get to know me. Or so you think. Maybe this is me, looking at you, showing you to yourself. Maybe it's just been you this whole time. And if you see something good in me, you can see something good in you.

"Good news is rare these days, and every glittering ounce of it should be cherished and hoarded and worshiped and fondled like a priceless diamond." ~Hunter S Thompson

Online Sexualization vs IRL Sexualization:

We are always being watched, ogled, perceived - worshiped, criticized, insulted, catcalled. Is one reality's voyeurism more acceptable than another? Well, I couldn't say. I haven't been cat called in a while… (Embarrassing, really.) I barely leave the house these days… we may have a situation[169]. Perhaps I long to be sexualized but in a safe way[170]. There it is, safety behind my screens, microships and motherboard. Wow she really mothered that. She really MILFed that. Irl, I'm careful and modest, like a tradwife. Online, at home, in my comfort zone, well, you already know. When I go to my building complex poolside I make sure my team of federal agents are never far behind. Then those agents tag team me and we make a porno. Booty shorts with FBI secrets on the ass cheek.

Picture this: I am in the lobby of the Roosevelt Hotel, typing in the pornhub browser. "Sex education": "starving rectum begging for education"
"You Wouldn't believe how naughty your IRISH SEX ED TEACHER is!!!"
"StepSISTER: I teach you how to MAKE ME CUM and LAST LONGER 🩲"
Sex ED nowadays sure is different from an old style sex ed film. If you know where to look, that is[171].

Why don't they update this shit? In schools, do they still have that same birthing video from the 1970s? No, it's all wrong. It's the incorrect approach. They're not looking at the bigger picture here. Porn stars should teach sex ed. They know their way in and out, in and out, in and out, from behind the camera to in front of the camera.

We all know Derrida was a huge pervert. So why not let the whores have their moment in academia as well as the pervs?
The future is HORNY.

WHY is everyone talking about the future? Let's go so much farther back. Prostitution is after all the world's oldest profession. WAS Stonehenge a prostitute hangout[172]? HOW did ancient whores do their makeup? Can this ghost teach you how to invest in your past?

---

169 Wellness check

170 Yes. you do.

171 See the editor's short, shot for Horny Castle 2 online: https://www.instagram.com/p/B-

172 🤔

The Night Time is Long, Hard, and Full of Dreamin:
"I lie awake at night in fear of what life has to offer.
Sleep is no longer an escape." - the editor

Why is it I tweek in the night[173], and flatline catatonically in the day. I shut the fuck up and go to sleep at 11PM; I wake at 4AM covered in sweat and livid with anger; I take a Xanax and fall back asleep; I wake up at 9AM, see a cat video on instagram and start crying. Then I shut the fuck up again.

They say signs of trauma are either having a hard time showing emotion, or the exact opposite: inappropriate unfiltered oversharing to anyone and anything that can perceive. Perhaps to the online void with its unfillable essence. I may clock into the latter category most of the time, although I also agonize with disorganized attachment and sometimes I crave intimacy but do not let myself have it. Some of my OF fans follow me as much for my internal drama as they do for the nudes. I'm more naked when I cry than when I goon. A reality porn star.

The End is only a beginning: time is circuitous

I've never been good at endings in my creative projects; my films always tend to have an ambiguous, vacuous ending rather than a concrete fulfilling one. The end often loops back into the beginning. Time, especially online, is distorted and circuitous. Through the 'time is a flat circle' platitude, we give ourselves illusions of time travel.

Through our memories, we time travel: a first kiss, a last day, a long night climaxing to the crimson gooning of sunrise. The memory is the medium. As time moves forward, memory moves back. Of course, as the cyber world progresses, I will find I have left something out of this volume or will find a new set of pathways that need to be included in my research, new sexual dystopias that will need to be navigated. This project will continue and there may well be more volumes of *Cyberhorny*, in whatever form they may take. Life is indistinguishable from art through my romaniticized prism of perception. I will have to continue making art as long as I live. All but I am, a dream within a dream, a picture on a screen, a game within a game.

Every aspect of our lives is surveilled, monetized, passively controlled, put through the wringer. We live in a cruel system with no way out, mandatory gameplay. Almost everyone has crippling anxiety, depression, burnout, massively inflated bills, dopamine/phone addiction, and every year it both collectively and individually gets worse. Greed is the core of human suffering and a fuel to those who run this system. It's fueling the environment into nonexistence. It's fueling humanity into existential ruin. Responsibility, empathy, accountability, authenticity, and compassion have largely gone missing.

173 When my boyfriend says I can't have NYQUIL FOR DINNER? MORE LIKE DEADGUYQUIL. Its every god damn day and nyquil with you.

For the dozens of cyber angels who genuinely and authentically make the world a better place, there's hundreds, thousands of digital denizens who make it worse. The way we communicate in the e-realms, distorted as it is, can be in many ways more authentic than in the corporeal world. This sounds like a dystopian fantasy but we're living in it. Even the way that people online respond to my posts about depression and anxiety is haunting in a way I can't really explain. They find my core of authenticity and manage to pierce it, somehow seeing past the layers and layers of bullshit I keep building[174]. There's.. so many of us in absurd amounts of stress and suffering, and the systems we live in don't nurture us at all.

As Mark Fisher points out in *Capitalist Realism*, people aren't exposed to alternatives to capitalism enough to make a concentrated effort to avail themselves of its torturous grasp. The capitalist system is reinforcing itself so well that other economic systems shatter upon trial, like a Lv1 mage against a Lv100 boss. Within the left-wing hierarchy (oh youre not a leninist? you never read trotsky?) it can feel difficult to come together and fight against the oligarchy. Earlier generations had Marx, Lenin as central figures. Who do we have now? Bernie Sanders – where is he? The creator economy pushes new "thought leaders" "woke icons" and "cultural critics" into egoic virality[175]. There is no central figure to unite us and lead the way against capitalist structures. "It's easier to imagine the end of the world, than it is the end of capitalism". And meantime, if we cannot destroy the system, we fuck the system. Jack the system off. Goon the system. Shake ass on the system. Slobber on the massive throbbing cock of capitalism. If you can't beat it, beat it off.

Massive overhauls are needed in healthcare, housing, and education. It hurts my brain to even think about how much effort it really takes to become self-educated in what school doesn't teach, how much effort it takes to become

174 So full of shit the toilets jealous.

175 Just as every pervert has a niche fetish, every political activist has a niche theorist.

rich without money. If we want a way out, yes, we have to learn how we are controlled. How the capitalist system works. We have to study it, marinate in it, forge our own paths through surviving within it.

I've developed a worldview that's like fuck it, everything is in such disarray so do whatever you want, express yourself freely and do harm to none - as fucked up as the world is we should still ideally have things we enjoy that keep us going (and gooning). That's partially why I post so unhinged~ly and so unrestrained~ly and why I've continued to do my OF until it meets its inevitable expiration. The entropic heat death of the horny e-universe. As the world decays to its end, we think of fucking. It's why I keep doing my *Cyberhorny* writing.

This is my place of reactionary porn, a counterpoint to all that has been. In a time where everything is already corrupted and chaotic, where even body and image can be commercialized and gamified, spread out like the body of a centerfold on the altar of lived experience, where subjectivity goes to die, I just do what I can to exist and survive. One bloviating paragraph at a time, all I can give you now is this collection of fourteen chapters on navigating the enchanting and dystopian cyberhorny universe from my prism of subjectivity. Just a story. And I get to choose how it ends. I'm gonna make it.

Sometimes there's no explanation.
No meaningful, helpful, useful navigation tool.
It's just fluff, pedantic and pompous, selfish and silent.
Sometimes I don't have anything to say, lest I overshare brazenly into the void.
Sometimes the day just ends.

Good times create hard men
Weak men create hard times
Hard times create weird porn
Weird porn creates weird fetishes
Weird fetishes create hard times
Hard times create weird men
Weird men create good times
Good times create hard men
This is the way the cyber world ends.
This is the way the cyber world ends.
This is the way the cyber world ends.
Not with going horny but with going missing.

Lonely prostitute at night, sailors delight
Lonely prostitute in morning, sailors take warning

The Goonersburg Undressed:

Four whore and seven hundred simps ago ☝️ 📃 our simulation designers 💻 brought forth on this cuntinent 👅 🌍 , a new presence on the sexualized media platforms 🍑 👀, conceived 🤰 in sperm of the moment existencc, and dedicated 😫 to the sex position that all men 👮 👷 👨‍🌾 👨‍💻 👨‍🔧 👩‍🚀 👨‍✈️ 🙆 are created to goon ✊ 💦

Now she is engaged in a great war 🤼 of inner demons, 👺 👹 😈 😈 testing whether that a cyber whore 👩‍💻 🍆 🏩 🏩 as herself, or any cyber citizen so CUNTceived 💊 💊and so deDICKated, can long endure the great jacking. 🖥️ 👩‍⚕️ 🙆 💧 💧 💦 💦 💦

We are met on a HORNY 😵 interconnected network♾️ 🌐 🌐, a battle-fuck 🤼 💥 of that war: the battle of gooning and edging. 📉 📈 😩 😩
We have CUM (many times.. many, many times) 🤓 🤗 😵 to deDICKate a WHOREtion of that network🌐 🌐, as a final fisting place 👊 ✊ 👏 for those who here gave their holes 🕳️ 👄 so that our gooners 🥒 🍆 🥔 🍆 might jack it. 🆘 🆘 🔞 🔞

It is altogether titilating and pornographic 🔞 💧 that we should do this.🗣️ 🗣️ ✊ 😩 😩

But, ☝️ in a larger sex, 😨 we can not DICKtate 🙅-- we can not CUMsecrate 🙇-- we can not suck dry and swallow 🎯 👅 🎯 -- this ground. The brave men, 🎖️ gooning and perverted, 🪖 🪖 😵 😵 who tugged it here, 🍆 🍆 ✌️ 👌 have conSUCKrated it, far above our power to add or DICKtract. 📐 ➗ ✖️ 💦 The world 🌎 will little note, nor longggggg RIMmember 🧠 👅 ✍️ what we say 💬 here, but it can never 4some 👯 👯 what they jacked here. It is for us the perverts😜 😝 🤪, rather, to be dedicated 🤲 here to the uncircumsized 🚀work which they who fingered 🖐️ here have thus far so nobly pubed. 🙄 🙄 😫 💯 💯

It is rather for us to be here jacking it 🍆 🏅 to the great tASSk 🍑 👏 remaining before us -- that from these horny redditors 💻 📱 😛 😛 😭 😭 we take increased DICKvotion to that cause 🤝 for which they gave the last full measure 📐 😳 😳 📏 of their loads ⛲ -- that we here highly resperm ☝️ that these pervs 😈 😈 🛗 shall not have gooned in vain 👅 👅 💧 🌋 -- that this nation, under COCK 🍆 , shall have a new birth of freeDOM ⛓️ 😫 ⛓️ -- and that government 🏛️ 🗽 💦 💦 of the perverts, by the perverts, for the perverts, 👄 shall not 🙅♂️be backshotted from the earth ⛲ ⛲ ⛲ 🌍 😵

Life brings upon me loads. The loads can never be refused. They are limitless. My clock runs not on a 9-5 but on a 24hr timeline; during the course of that, no loads refused. I would be a fool to. Thus, the project continues, in perpetuity. Shroedingers job: I work but I do absolutely nothing. No one sees me work. I must do this completely alone. Even in my collabs, the girls I'm with each exist in our subterranean sphere though we make content together. This field is an isolating one and it's critical to find community.

Time is of the essence: horniness is very time-specific. If someone is horny NOW, there is no guarantee for a session later. It's not always something I can pencil into my calendar – I need to be ready now, all the time, any time. Always on guard for loads.
~Nastya Valentine

Afterword by the Editor

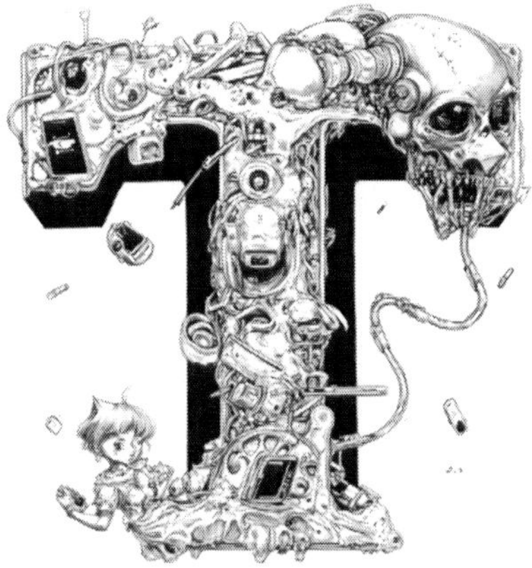

This project has been a sublimation, in one sense. A work demanding to be created, this book propelled itself out of the author. The traumatic elements of the field screamed for expression. Yet it reeks of pathology. An oedipal war rages in Valentine's mind beneath the surface. Valentine can't get her dad to give her any money, so she has to bankrupt every other man in the world. [anal stage]. Her mother partied frequently at the playboy mansion, imparted eminent complexes regarding self-image, self-esteem upon her. Book cannot be separated from author. Auto-theoretical, auto-erotic, autobiographical... at times autophilic. We have arrived here through defying genre- the *book* itself quite in line with the art that Valentine creates.

I I I, ME ME ME... as cognizant and erudite as the author is, you can hear the fragmentation of her psyche in the writing - that perhaps was present before - but certainly exacerbated by her line of work. Many segments of the text begin with a question and end with one too. If you saw any exclamation mark in the text, I will admit that it was added by my own hand. So what does this mean. ? ! A symbolic disposition towards uncertainty - despite 200+ pages. Maybe we do need feminism. Occasionally, while being dragged through the rollercoaster of her reflections, one can't help but fall off the tracks. Final destination.

Often when I sit with my clients, as they trace memory back to the origin of their pain I see glimpses of what they looked like as children. A facial tick, a furtive glance, an aspect of their voice - something becomes childlike. Little Nastya emerges in this project. The emphasis on money is not strictly materialism. It is a demand for love. A little girl wanting to be taken care of. A neglected child reveling in the attention of the day. The burnout refrain: a demand for care. What emptied itself out of her childhood repeats with craven incessence. Both the poverty and neglect that adorned her youth are rectified through the work on only-fans. Her career yields both attention and money. Validation and gifts. And in the same vein she has forged this book in some derivation of the spirit of charity. The aim to provide a resource to others embarking upon or immersed in dynamics of online sex work.

Originally intended as somewhat of a guide, the project shifts, morphs between diaristic scrawlings and emotional-logistical advice. Guardrails, shields, force fields against the psychic damage that SWers can experience are outlined. Additionally, the consequences of not adopting these maneuvers comes to bear in her own personal experience. As we have seen, every rose has its thorns. Quod me nutrit me destruit. Sorry for all the bible quotes, but Jesus was cooking. A key element of WWE wrestling is evident in the spiritual language that emerges. Jesus Christ, friends with faggots and retards and prostitutes, gained his subscriber base through the promise of salvation. Turning strife into sanctity. Internet whores need this too. His teachings bombastically attacked the circumstances of his own culture - exactly the same way Valentine decries hers. OK I am kind of joking but still. Lacan likened Freud to Jesus in his own way, implying that both of their followers were kind of stupid.

With all that being said. The repetition compulsion continues its work in the shadows. The asymptotic line to the point where Valentine no longer has to work is imminently unreachable. Despite the empathy and valorization she gives them, her patrons ultimately will disappoint her. The job is a self-evident hazard to her finding of the charms and baubles of romance in her life. No man who she dates in the furnace of reality will be able to provide a heat strong enough to compare to the million tiny flames of the cyber simps. A sublimation is often simply a repetition. Soloppysistic. Indeed when eroticism and commerce meet the classic field of entropy surrounding the project of love is exploded.

She has become book. The project is a reconsolidation. In life, in art, no loads should be refused. Who are you to think you can refuse a load? The holes in herself, excavations made by the simps, must be filled by *something*. Part after part is doled out throughout the weeks[176]. Time measured not by the ticking of clocks - what Faulkner referred to as the mausoleum of all hope and desire, but by the fiscal dimensions of income and excome.

This sense of mortification is countered by book and rectified by creativity. The constant messaging back and forth to simps, the praxis and utilization of language is reconfigured. The project has been a version

176 Much like the therapist uses and disabuses the self.

of her simping for herself. Writing converted back into her control, her domain. Yet this interplay sets a new standard for the ramifications of time. For myself as a psychoanalyst a similar process unfolds. Hours become not measured by the movement of the clock's hands, but by the progress (or lack thereof) of my patients.

What is there left to say?

> When I was young, she said, I liked walking the garden path at twilight
> and if the path was long enough I would see the moon rise.
> That was for me the great pleasure: not sex, not food, not worldly amusement.
> I preferred the moon's rising, and sometimes I would hear,
> at the same moment, the sublime notes of the final ensemble
> of *The Marriage of Figaro*. Where did the music come from?
> I never knew.
>
> Because it is the nature of garden paths
> to be circular, each night, after my wanderings,
> I would find myself at my front door, staring at it,
> barely able to make out, in darkness, the glittering knob.
>
> It was, she said, a great discovery, albeit my real life.
>
> But certain nights, she said, the moon was barely visible through the clouds
> and the music never started. A night of pure discouragement.
> And still the next night I would begin again, and often all would be well.
>
> I could think of nothing to say. This story, so pointless as I write it out,
> was in fact interrupted at every stage with trance-like pauses
> and prolonged intermissions, so that by this time night had started.
>
> Ah the capacious night, the night
> so eager to accommodate strange perceptions.
>
> I felt that some important secret
> was about to be entrusted to me, as a torch is passed
> from one hand to another in a relay.[177]

---

177 Louise gluck a sharply worded silence

The editor himself has been somewhat of a victim to the subjective destitution of online romance, cyber carnality. Addicted to any app that ends in an R he sought out the validation from men on the internet as well. Working in animal rescue, becoming a psychoanalyst, also mere cries for help. The cold mother and raging father of his childhood transfigured into images on a screen - pixelated individuals to garner attention from - to pacify and be pacified by. Because desire is circuitous. A primrose path. Even the least pathological of us has felt unwanted, has experienced the breast being taken away.

Walking the garden path at midnight a vision becomes clear. A life just beyond reach our reach that forces each step forward. What is the soundtrack where does the music come from. Our unconscious seethes and broiles like an ocean.

Cyberhorny cannot be linear, cannot be contained in the traditional format of book (or am I just BAD at my JOB!?!lol). It is the eruption and the excess - the waste - from the production of desire. Desire is the net we use to try to catch the serpent in the garden of our dreams. Yet all we can capture are our own images, representations, reproductions. We hope in these wonderings you have found a glittering knob[178]. Porn as a journey of self-discovery. A skeleton key that unlocks the secrets of your own desire. Wherever you go, there you are.

Beyond the image is the text.

So we pass our torch to you dear reader. Illuminate. Next time you open the apps, open yourself. What there is being repeated, what pain is crying out for expression. What strange perceptions are you wrestling with? Or perhaps are you just a normal person looking for love, for sex, companionship?[179]

The great discovery is our real life.

---

178 ;)

179 You are not.

Index

In the court of law, she is mother's basketball
I'm gonna start pissing in a urinal (also see: equality)

J
Jigsaw
JOI (jerk off instructions)
Jung, Carl
JURLLLL
Just keep chooching

K
Kinks
Kisa cat
Kubrick, Stanley

L
Lacan, Jacques
Leaked nudes
Leary, Timothy
LFG I just took my cialis and I'm bout to go crazzyy
Libido
Little Cat
Little Nastya
Loads
Loneliness crisis
Love map
LSD
Lurk and jerk

M
MAGA rage
Man brain
Manosphere
McKenna, Terence
Me climbing out the mausoleum postcrypt
Memes
Menstruation
MGTOW
MILFS in YOUR AREA want to CHAT 🤪
Marx, Karl
Mother
Musk, Elon

N
NASTYA
Negging
Neon Genesis Evangelion

NoFap
NyQuil?? More like DEADGUYQUIL

O
Object permanence
Objectification
OK… time to throw down
One must catch the heart off guard and blow it open
Onlyfans porn ban of 2021
Oversaturation distress

P
Pain is not enough
Pandemic
Paraphilia
Pegging
Philosophy
Plath, Sylvia
Porn addiction
Pornhub
Postmodern posse

Q
Quoth the raven, tip the whore

R
Rachael (Blade Runner)
Reddit
Red-pilled pornstar tradwife
Reid, Spencer
Repetition compulsion
Rule34

S
Sex addiction
Sex education
Sexual collective unconscious
Scammers
Shrek
Simps
Simulacra and Simulation
Skinnylicious menu at the cheesecake factory
Sleep, those little slices of death – how I loathe thee
Sniffies
Specular image
Sugar babies, daddies
SWERFs

T
Tesla (Sardine)
Thanatos
That's cool you do cyber security, can u secure a place in ur heart for me? 😳
Thompson, Hunter S
Tis some visitor, I muttered, ass cheeks clapping at my chamber door
Trecartin, Ryan
Tuxedo Tuesday
Twin Peaks
Twink death

U
Usernames
u/PM_ME_BIG_TITS
U really think u had something to say huh

V
Validation disorder
Venmo
Videodrome

W
We must bring water to the village
Westworld
What's walter white's crackhead twink's name? Jesse pinkman
Wolf, Naomi

X
XXX Trauma Oasis

Y[180]
Years of love had been forgot, in the gooning of a minute
YouTube

Z
Zero Illumination
Zizek, Slavoj
Zoom

---

180 WHYYYYYYYYYYY

Acknowledgements

It goes without saying that I am thankful for every sex worker I've encountered. I'm thankful also for the simps subscribed to me, the fans who love me despite, or because of, my unhingedness.

In writing this book, my feline daughters Giga cat and Kisa cat have been instrumental, as have the shoulders of giants whom I've quoted here, mothers and fathers of everything that has been. The cultural canon of critical theory. The women who have paved the way for me to give birth to ideas, and laboriously gestate this book.

This book would not be possible without Evan Dunn and Jason Tarkington, elite soldiers of the Cyberhorny mobilization effort. Literally, literary, these men need a medal. Nobel War Prize for their military efforts. Thank you Jason for the immense amount of help with the administrative structure of Cyberhorny, and for more than anything believing in me and in the importance of this project, legitimizing it as a business. And Evan, the psychoanalytic expertise that lent itself to cooking, cranking, jacking (in and out of the box) this book is a treasure. You guys ARE Cyberhorny.

As the project deepened and interest in my work grew, the creators who have held space for me in various projects, readings, interviews and podcasts: Alison, Pam, Cat, Sinead, Ms. Duffy, Weirdo Music Forever, Car Crash Collective, Coaxial Space, others who have peripherally included me in their work, others still to come.

My ride or die Celeste, close friend and artistic collaborator whose own work and presence inspires me – hours long conversations about online woes, sexuality, humanity, and of course tea, gossip, drama. It was on our trip to Vegas in the beginning of 2021, the first time that I can remember taking real time off from OnlyFans and doing a media detox, that the term "Cyberhorny" hit me. In a space away from the internet, I started to develop and codify my research on being horny online. My closest friends, my coven of mystical baddies and true chosen family.

My therapist, a custodian of my psyche and internal duress who has helped me see that living life as myself is bearable. Eternally thankful for those slices of time every week that have supported my well being.

My OF girlies Sage, Rose, Jen, Kat, Lux, Peach, Ellie, Jasmine and many other hotties who I've worked with, communicated with, felt seen by, looked up to. This project is really for the whores, for the girlies.

My parents, who once upon a time in a sperm of the moment decision had sex, and nine months after Valentine's Day welcomed their only child: a little princess, a monster, a gentle fawn, a bloodthirsty assassin, a horny legend. …

My men: Carl, Russell, Biscuit.

Jigsaw. Without you, there would be no games to play. I would have no framework for my own variations of the game. A player without a game is like eyes without brows, or a gooner without his treasured porn.

The snipers. I'm ready when you are.

Carl Jung once said "life begins at 40; everything before is just rehearsal".
I'm waiting.

Sources Cited

"Desire and its Interpretation" Jacques Lacan

"The Psychedelic Experience" Tim Leary

"Das Kapital" Karl Marx

"The Archaic Revival" Terence McKenna

"Burnout" Emily Nagoski

"In Favor of the Sensitive Man" Anais Nin

"The Bell Jar" Sylvia Plath

"Simulation and its Discontents" Sherry Turkle

"The Body Keeps the Score" Bessel Van Der Kolk

"Catching the Big Fish" David Lynch

"Prometheus Rising" Robert Anton Wilson

"How Sex Changed the Internet" Samantha Cole

"Capitalist Realism" Mark Fisher

"Bringers of the Dawn" Barbara Marciniak

"Eroticism" George Bataille

"Seduction" Jean Baudrillard

"Simulation and Simulacra" Jean Baudrillard

"Anti-Oedipus: Capitalism and Schizophrenia" Gilles Deleuze and Felix Guattari

"Philosophy in the Bedroom" Marquis De Sade

"Civilization and its Discontents" Sigmund Freud

"The Doors of Perception" Aldous Huxley

"The Red Book" Carl Jung

"Black Books" Carl Jung

"The Whore of New York" Liara Roux

"Thriving in Sex Work" Lola Davina

"Techno Doping" Paul Placides

"Cyber Rights" MIT Press

"Meditations for Party Girls" Caitlin Dee

"The Cyberhorny Dream Diaries" Nastya Valentine, Evan Dunn

James Baldwin. The Evidence of Things Not Seen

Mark Z. Danielewski, House of Leaves

"ASH WEDNESDAY" TS ELLIOT

NEON GENESIS EVANGELION

CRIMINAL MINDS

EDGAR ALLAN POE

THE BIBLE

Author Bio + Editor Bio

I'm Nastya Valentine and Cyberhorny is my project.
cyber-horny.com is its home.

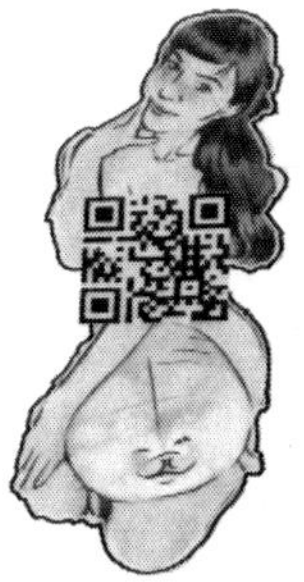

How would I describe myself? Nothing. There is no self.
How would I like to be remembered? Doesn't matter.
What were my dreams as a child? Nightmares.

I want to create a space where any and all people participating in the cyber realms can confront themselves -- deeply, psychologically, HORNILY --
and investigate the philosophical aspects of sex work.
Given that we are all suffering together in this doomed abyss of the internet,
Cyberhorny is for everybody. Maybe with deeper understanding, we can suffer just a little bit less.

(It's giving scorpio sun, leo rising, aquarious moon)...
You think I wrote this book??? Neither of us did??

According to the Lesser Key of Solomon the King (an ancient and cursed grimoire) **Evan Dunn** is a psychoanalyst, writer and a Greater King of Hell - with twenty-two legions of demons in his thrall. He knows of hidden things, can find treasures, and can tell the past, present and future. After being conjured he will appear in an aerial body to answer verily of all secret divine things and dispense knowledge regarding the creation of the world.

According to the latest numbers from the S&P 500: **Nastya Valentine** is, in the girl economy, a product of valuable exchange rate. The fortified crystal 8 ball in her brain, ALSO can see the past, present and dissociative future of our cultural consciousness. Play the tape and you will find I have put an OnlyFans sponsored fish hook in your intestines, that I will only extract for a suitcase filled with $75,000 in unmarked bills. You're nothing to me but customers.

When we are cursed, we bless; when we are persecuted, we endure it; when we are slandered, we answer kindly. We have become the scum of the earth, the garbage of the world—right up to this moment. ~Corinthians 1:4

Made in United States
North Haven, CT
04 November 2026

21771725R00169